DON'T MISS *YOUR* FORTUNE. WITH *MISSED FORTUNE 101*, LEARN HOW TO:

- **Put the lazy, idle dollars trapped in your home to work safely**—and reap as much as an extra million.

- **Discover hidden and perfectly legal tax breaks**—and treat yourself to some surprising windfalls.

- **Play the bankers' favorite game**—borrow at one rate and invest at a higher one.

- **Explore lesser-known retirement vehicles**—and avoid falling into a higher tax bracket when you stop working.

- **Turn your life insurance policy into an investment**—and keep your taxes down and your capital up.

- **Find out which low-return instruments should be in your portfolio today**—and why they'll become high-return stars tomorrow.

- **Reach your "freedom point"**—your financial independence—long before "retirement age"!

MISSED FORTUNE 101

A Starter Kit to Becoming a Millionaire

DOUGLAS R. ANDREW

BUSINESS
PLUS

NEW YORK   BOSTON

For more information on how to optimize your human, intellectual, financial, and civic assets, visit www.missedfortune.com or www.empoweredwealth.com. You may contact Douglas Andrew via email at info@pfs-inc.org or call toll free, 1-888-987-5665.

Business Plus
Hachette Book Group
237 Park Avenue
New York, NY 10017

www.HachetteBookGroup.com

Printed in the United States of America

Originally published in hardcover by Hachette Book Group.

First Trade Edition: April 2010

10 9 8 7 6 5 4 3 2 1

Business Plus is an imprint of Grand Central Publishing.
The Business Plus name and logo are trademarks of Hachette Book Group, Inc.

The Library of Congress has cataloged the hardcover edition as follows:
Andrew, Douglas R.
    Missed fortune 101 : a starter kit to becoming a millionaire / Douglas R. Andrew.
        p. cm.
    Includes index.
    ISBN 978-0-446-57657-4
    1. Finance, Personal, 2. Finance, Personal—United States. 3. Investments. 4. Financial security. I. Title.

HG179.A55993 2005
332.024'01—dc22   2004055469

ISBN 978-0-446-69351-6 (pbk.)

To my family and posterity
Who will be the Successor Trustees of
Our Family Empowered Bank
Where all of our
Human, Intellectual and Financial Assets
Are deposited for the
Enrichment of each Family Member's
Health, Happiness and Well-being
Into Perpetuity

May the principles and insights
Contained in this book
Bring you
Clarity, Balance, Focus and Confidence
To help you accomplish
Your Greatest Dreams

Acknowledgments

An author's work can only be unique in the expression of ideas, which rarely, if ever, claim just one originator. Ideas are the result of countless interactions with people who influence the path one takes.

I wish to express sincere gratitude for the wonderful people who have helped and inspired me to create *Missed Fortune 101*.

To my incredible literary agent, Jillian Manus, I express sincere gratitude for your encouragement and confidence in my communication abilities. You are one of the most well-connected persons I know. You have a wonderful heart. Thank you for your good will.

I offer special thanks to my chief editor at Warner Books, Mr. Rick Wolff, for a great working relationship. And thanks to all of your team, especially Bob Castillo and Bill Betts, for their great contribution to the refinement of the final work.

I also offer thanks and deep appreciation to Lee Brower, founder and president of Empowered Wealth, LC, who has inspired me and co-authored those sections of this work that deal with the Empowered Wealth concepts. Also, I appreciate Marshall Thurber for his insights and encouragement in the development of this book.

I am extremely grateful for Heather Beers, a wonderful friend and talented editor. You are a delight to work with. I sincerely appreciate your special skills and your encouragement.

I wish to extend special thanks to Toni Lock at tmdesigns for the great relationship that has contributed to the layout and design of the illustrations in this work. Thanks also to Kristin Varner for your unique and professional artwork. You both have extraordinary talent and always come through beautifully.

I am especially grateful for the many teachers and mentors in my life: Thank you Dan Sullivan, Lee Brower, Adrienne Duffy, and Leo Weidner, my coaches. Thanks to John Unice, Craig Collins, Jerry Davis, Don Blanton, Todd Ballenger, Jack Tilton, Paul Barton, Marv Neumann, and Philip Bodine for the brainstorming during our careers that

has contributed to this work. I express appreciation to my fellow entrepreneurs in The Strategic Coach program for their encouragement.
Thanks to all of my TEAM members for the sharing of countless ideas
to perfect the way the message of this book is communicated.

I express special appreciation to Mark Victor Hansen and Pat Burns
for your encouragement, inspiration, and advice. Thank you for con-
necting me with some wonderful people.

I express gratitude to my talented and dedicated unique ability
team comprised of Patrese Burke, Geoff Meyers, and my six children
and their spouses for the countless hours of help and assistance you
render in our mutual endeavors: Mailee, Adrea and Scott, Emron and
Harmony, Aaron, Mindy and Brian, and Ashley. Thanks to all of my extended family for your understanding and encouragement while I focused on the completion of this work. May we build a million more
memories together to deposit in our family bank.

Finally, to my wife and sweetheart, Sharee, thank you for thirty
wonderful years of life together. Your support and encouragement have
been incredible. Thanks for the countless hours of help in pursuit of all
our endeavors. I love you!

Contents

Foreword

Have you ever attempted to walk for an extended period of time into a strong wind? To move forward in this environment one has to constantly stay focused and exert continuous effort. Frequently, traditional approaches to wealth creation create this type of experience.

This book asks you to turn around and allow the wind of success to support you. With the wind at your back, wealth creation becomes easier. Doug Andrew provides provocative observations, methods, predictions, and strategies that, when followed, will make you financially wealthy.

I have known and worked with Doug for many years. Most recently he has served as an advisory board member of Empowered Wealth, LLC, an intellectual capital firm that specializes in intergenerational wealth transfer. Doug's mastery of wealth creation and retention tools is extraordinary. Like the sun burning off the early-morning mist, *Missed Fortune 101* dispels many money-making myths.

Empowered Wealth focuses on the Empowered Wealth's Quadrant System®. It teaches that sustainable wealth requires "Quadrant Living," which is the integration of your human, intellectual, civic, and financial assets.

Doug conveys his convictions that peace of mind comes through the optimization of *all* of your assets—not just your financial assets. Financial wealth by itself is not sustainable without integrating the other quadrants. It is like a balloon with many holes in it.

I congratulate Doug for his book, which takes direct aim at the financial asset quadrant. His thorough evaluation explores the secrets utilized by many of the "financially" rich. You must, of course, *use* the tools and concepts provided in this book. The greatest pencil in the world, regardless of its elegance, has never written a single line of poetry by itself.

Many self-made wealth creators have systematically followed Doug's predictable path. I encourage you to do the same.

Lee Brower, President
Empowered Wealth, LLC

Preface

In front of you is an empowering starter kit to becoming a millionaire, stocked with insights and opportunities you may not have known existed. *Missed Fortune 101* contains a collection of common money myths, or what I call money "myth-conceptions," systematically dispelled by wealth-enhancement strategies.

Missed Fortune 101 is a simplified offering of wealth-enhancement principles that are explained in greater detail in my more comprehensive original work, *Missed Fortune*. However, do not be mistaken—"simplified" does not mean "condensed." *Missed Fortune 101* will amply supply you with the knowledge you need to attain financial independence.

You have the ability to use some of the identical strategies self-made millionaires use. You will learn how to be your own banker—I will teach you what banks, credit unions, and insurance companies do to amass wealth. You will discover how to develop a Perpetual Life of Asset Nurturance (P.L.A.N.) in order to create a meaningful transformation in every aspect of your life. Isn't it time *you* became wealthy? Don't miss your fortune!

I'm sure you are familiar with the cliché "You can't see the forest for the trees." I believe there are certain financial opportunities that have always been in front of us, but whose true potential we couldn't see. This book will lift you, like a helicopter, above the trees for a better perspective. Your vision will open up, and you will begin to take in the bigger picture—a point of view that can change your life.

CONTRARY TO POPULAR BELIEF

This book contains strategies that are contrary to traditional approaches for the accumulation of wealth, estate planning, debt management, and retirement planning. But I assure you, as you study the concepts contained herein, you will never view your house, mortgage, retirement plans, savings, investments, and insurance the same way. Either the new insights you gain will spur you to action, or they will leave you wondering how much more your financial net worth could have been had you taken action.

The statement I make in my original work, *Missed Fortune*, bears repeating: The worst form of ignorance is when we judge or reject something we know little or nothing about. So let me suggest a few ground rules before embarking on this experience:

- Be open-minded to new ideas that may even be counterintuitive.
- Be willing to suspend your disbelief.
- Withhold justifying why you may not be doing certain things right now. Remember, different isn't always better, but *better is always different.*

The strategies contained herein are sound and proven, yet not common knowledge. The ideas are not novel, but the approach is. When financial planners or CPAs study and understand these concepts, they cannot refute the numbers. The variable that will assure success or failure is the discipline of the individual implementing the strategies. For those who are financially mature and responsible, a tremendous amount of wealth can be safely created and preserved. But I'll issue the same warning I did in my original work: *This book is not for financial jellyfish.*

LIKE ORANGES AND CHOCOLATE

To fully understand the concepts, the reader will need to be patient on occasion while I explain certain tax laws or financial concepts. To get to the sweet, juicy center of an orange, it is necessary to go through the bitter peel that surrounds the heart of the fruit. Likewise, cocoa powder is almost intolerable to the taste buds until sweetener is added. But without the bitter ingredient, we could not savor the chocolate delicacies. So it is with the financial strategies I will disclose in this work. Sometimes we must get through the bitter, or tedious, portion to enjoy the satisfying portion.

You will learn through interesting examples, case studies, and illustrations. There are some technical details—explained in simple terms—that will educate every reader, from the novice to the expert. If you would rather learn general concepts, skim the numbers and charts. If you want to study the evidence, it's provided for you. If you want further in-depth information, please refer to my original work, *Missed Fortune*.

DEVELOP YOUR LEARNING SYSTEM

Most educational books are information-based. My desire is for you to have an *insight-based experience* while reading this book. My goals will be accomplished if you experience several "ah-ha" moments, because when something becomes *your* insight, you change! Information is not scarce. In fact, the amount of information available to humanity today doubles every eighteen months. Rather, we have a scarcity of *time* and *attention* in this world. In order for you to give adequate time and attention to becoming enlightened, it would be in your interest to have a *system*.

I am grateful to a wonderful friend and associate, Marshall Thurber, who taught me, "You are only going to get what your system will deliver." Mark Victor Hansen, a personal friend and mentor, taught me to think of "system" as an acronym representing:

Save

Your-

Self

Time

Energy

Money

May I suggest you begin by using the following system:

- Clearly define why you are reading this book.

- Determine what you really expect to get out of studying it.
- Clearly establish what would be required for you to have a quality educational experience.
- Identify the barriers, roadblocks, or hindrances that need to be eliminated to have a successful transformation.

May I suggest that after reading each chapter, you write down the three greatest insights gained from reading that chapter. Then write down the first action you are going to take to implement any new concepts that are in harmony with your goals and objectives. Writing these things down will crystallize your thinking. You see, if you are only *interested* in something, you will do it only when it's convenient. When you are *committed* to something, you will complete it at almost any cost—and a meaningful transformation will take place.

WELCOME TO YOUR FUTURE!

The strategies you will learn are not "get rich quick" schemes but safe, methodical systems to dramatically enhance your net worth, substantially increase your retirement income, and empower your wealth.

As you record the actions you are going to take as a result of the insights gained, the most important word that should repeatedly come up is "tomorrow." In other words, my sincere hope is that each day you will rethink what you are going to *do* tomorrow as a result of your new insights, because *tomorrow is the first day of the rest of your life*.

Welcome to your exciting, abundant future!

MISSED
FORTUNE
101

CHAPTER 1

All the Dogs Barking Up the Wrong Tree Doesn't Make It the Right One!

Why socking money away into IRAs and 401(k)s and paying extra principal on your mortgage is counterproductive

HAVE YOU EVER WONDERED if you're on the right path? In my professional travels, I participate in conferences and conventions all over the world. During the past several years, I have traveled to Chicago every three months to meet with a group of fellow entrepreneurs in a program called The Strategic Coach, founded by Dan Sullivan. As anyone who has traveled to the Chicago area knows, O'Hare Airport is one of the busiest airports in the world and can be confusing. On the first few trips, I would retrieve my luggage and walk outside to be picked up at the bus shuttle center. I would follow the crowd from the baggage claim area outside to the ground transportation area, then across eight lanes of traffic to the shuttle center, often in freezing, windy conditions, without a coat.

One blustery cold, wet day, I followed the crowd and arrived at the shuttle center with my hair windblown and my suit sopping wet. To my surprise, I met the gentleman who had sat next to me on my flight.

His hair was in place and his suit was dry. I said, "How did you get here before me and in such great shape?"

He replied, "Oh, didn't you know there's an easier way to get here? And you stay warm and dry!" He told me about a corridor that leads people safely underground to the shuttle center, sheltered from traffic and unpleasant weather.

The next time I flew into O'Hare, I learned that the path leading to the shuttle center had always been there; I just hadn't noticed it. Now it's up to me each trip to choose the path I'm going to take: the way the crowd goes or the safer, more sheltered route.

One day I asked the hotel shuttle service why they didn't instruct people on how to reach the shuttle center by the safer, protected route. They said, "Oh, it's too hard to get people to understand, so we just tell them to follow the crowd."

The ideas presented in this book are not novel; the approaches are. With the insights you are about to gain, I hope you will choose not to always follow the crowd, but to find the *best* path on your journey toward financial independence.

For the first step on that journey, let's take a look at the two places most Americans accumulate the most money: our home and our retirement plan.

THE FIRST STEP

Following accepted wisdom, we set aside money in qualified retirement accounts, such as IRAs and 401(k)s, enjoying tax-deductible funding and/or tax-deferred accumulation. At the same time, we assume it's best to achieve the goal of outright home ownership and save money on mortgage interest expense by sending extra principal payments against our mortgages.

Unaware, like naïve, inexperienced drivers, we proceed down the highway of life, pursuing financial security with one foot on the brake pedal and the other foot on the gas pedal. We may eventually make it to our destination, but only after a pretty jerky ride. We wonder why a few others arrived at the station of financial independence sooner, achieving more, with a much smoother ride.

"BUT I'M DOING EVERYTHING RIGHT!"

We suddenly realize that during all of those years of earning money, we socked a portion away in investment vehicles that gave us a tax deduction on the front end, just to be hammered with taxes on the back end. At the same time, we were killing our partner, Uncle Sam, by eliminating one of the best tax deductions we have as Americans—our home mortgage interest.

During our "golden years" of retirement, we painfully come to the realization that we increased our tax liability by postponing it to a time when we no longer had significant deductions. In frustration, we complain, "But I did everything right! Everyone concerned about their retirement puts money into IRAs and 401(k)s, and I've always been taught that you should pay off your mortgage by sending extra principal payments to the mortgage company!" There is a valuable lesson a friend and mentor, Marshall Thurber, taught me: All the dogs barking up the wrong tree doesn't make it the right one!

If what you thought to be the best way to save for retirement or to pay off your mortgage turned out *not* to be the best way, when would you want to know? Now is the time to discover the best way to safely accumulate more money. The sooner you empower yourself with the knowledge to attain financial independence, the greater your net worth will become.

THE LURE OF IRAS AND 401(K)S

Most Americans are lured into saving for retirement with traditional qualified retirement plans, such as IRAs and 401(k)s. They are convinced by financial advisors to contribute pre-tax dollars to 401(k) plans or place tax-deductible contributions into IRAs because of the tax advantages during the contribution and accumulation phases of their retirement planning. They seem to ignore the two most important phases—when you withdraw your money for retirement income, and when you pass away and transfer any remaining funds to your heirs. This book will help you understand how to receive tax-favored benefits during all four phases of retirement planning: the contribution, accumulation, distribution, and transfer phases.

Most of us don't want to outlive our money, and no one is getting out of here alive. When people die, they usually leave behind some money in their IRAs and 401(k)s that is transferred to their beneficiaries. Unfortunately, non-spousal heirs far too often end up with only about 28 percent of the money that was left in their parents' IRAs and 401(k)s.

Most people and their advisors feel that tax-deductible or pre-tax contributions to qualified plans such as IRAs and 401(k)s will provide the greatest retirement benefits because of tax-deferred growth. But do they?

If you were a farmer, would you rather save tax on the purchase of your seed in the springtime and pay tax on the sale of your harvest in the fall, or would you rather pay tax on the seed and sell your harvest without any tax on the gain? I would rather purchase the seed with after-tax dollars and later sell my harvest tax-free. In this book, I will teach you how to do the latter.

A Roth IRA is one way to accomplish this, but I believe it still has too many strings attached. The maximum yearly contribution that can be made by an individual was $3,000 for tax years 2002 to 2004; from 2005 to 2008 the limit is $4,000. Distributions may not be taken until at least five years after the first contribution is made. In addition, distributions without penalty can only be made after the owner reaches the age of 59½, except in the event of the owner's death or disability, or for "qualified first-time homebuyer expenses."

Fig. 1.1   **IS POSTPONING TAX REALLY THE BEST IDEA?**

**Your IRA, pension, and 401(k) benefits
will probably be taxable at retirement at a higher rate.**

- Did you know there is a means to avoid paying tax on up to 85 percent of your Social Security benefits at retirement?
- Did you know there is a means by which you can draw out your retirement income tax-free?

Are you interested in a strategy that could accomplish this?

THE NOT-SO-ADVANTAGED TAX ADVANTAGES

One of the original IRA tenets held that deferring tax until retirement was advantageous because funds would likely be taxed at a lower rate. That is no longer axiomatic. You may well live out your retirement in the same or a higher tax bracket if you accumulate a respectable retirement nest egg. In fact, effective tax rates will likely be higher in the future. So why postpone the inevitable and increase your tax liability?

As a financial strategist and retirement specialist, when I discover how much money my first-time clients have accumulated in yet-to-be-taxed IRAs and 401(k)s, I often ask them if they are planning *their* retirement or Uncle Sam's.

Is postponing tax and thereby increasing the tax you will owe really the best idea? You should be aware that *your IRA, pension, and 401(k) benefits will probably be taxable at a higher rate at retirement (figure 1.1).*

A BETTER RETIREMENT ALTERNATIVE

In my opinion, there is a better alternative to achieve tax-free retirement income, as well as create indirect tax-favored benefits on the contribution amounts without all of the restrictions and rules.

When I contribute money to my retirement fund, there is no restriction on how much I can put in. During good years, I can contribute generously; during not-so-good years, I don't have to contribute anything. Moreover, I can withdraw money if needed without IRS penalties, and I am not obligated to put it back. As a homeowner, I also structure my retirement plan to get indirect tax deductions on my contribution amounts. Most important, my retirement funds accumulate tax-free, and I can access the funds whenever I want on a tax-free basis (including the interest or gain) without having to wait until I'm 59½. If I don't use up my retirement funds before I pass away, they will blossom in value and transfer free of income tax to my heirs.

There is a means by which you can draw out your retirement free of income tax. Not only that, but there is also a means to avoid paying tax on up to 85 percent of your Social Security benefits at retirement. Are you interested in how you can accomplish this?

Through proper planning, a homeowner can utilize home equity retirement planning that may provide tax advantages during the contribution and accumulation years, and more important, you may enjoy tax-free income during your retirement years and transfer any remaining funds to your heirs tax-free. This strategy can increase your net spendable retirement income by as much as 50 percent! How is this possible? Read on.

THE TRUE COST OF EXTRA PRINCIPAL PAYMENTS

Another common misconception about the path to financial independence is that the best way to pay off a house is to make extra principal payments on your mortgage. There are various methods that people use to do this. Some homeowners use the biweekly payment plan to accelerate their mortgage payoff. Others use fifteen-year mortgages rather than thirty-year mortgages to accomplish their goal of outright home ownership. I will prove in this book that *no method of paying extra principal on your mortgage is the wisest or quickest method of accomplishing financial independence.*

A homeowner can accumulate the amount of cash needed to pay off a home just as soon or sooner by using a conservative, tax-deferred mortgage acceleration plan. The most important elements of home equity management are maintaining liquidity and safety of principal and creating the opportunity for home equity to grow in a separate side fund, where it is accessible in the event of an emergency.

It is essential to maintain control of your home equity to allow it to earn a rate of return. Home equity has no rate of return when it is trapped in the house, as I will explain in chapter 6. I'll also explain why your home may likely sell much more quickly and for a higher price with a high mortgage balance rather than a low mortgage balance.

Learning to manage the equity in your home wisely will allow you to utilize one of the few tax deductions that we Americans have left: our mortgage interest. *You can actually pay off a home using a thirty-year mortgage in thirteen and a half years with the same cash outlay required to pay off a fifteen-year mortgage.* And you can accomplish this by using some of Uncle Sam's money instead of your own! This book will teach you how to dramatically enhance your net worth and generate an extra million dollars or more by safely using lazy, idle dollars that are trapped in the equity of your home.

Let me reiterate and clarify why many Americans are remiss in arriving at the degree of financial independence they could otherwise obtain. While we do everything in our power to get tax deductions on our retirement contributions and investments, we simultaneously eliminate one of the few and best deductions we have: our home mortgage interest.

Hence, most Americans prepare for the future by postponing tax while getting rid of their tax deductions.

P.L.A.N. FOR TRUE WEALTH

To get where you want to go, you have to know how to get there. I've discovered that the secret to wealth accumulation is to use the best P.L.A.N.—an acronym for "Perpetual Life of Asset Nurturance."™ When we learn to nurture all of our assets properly, we create a new life for them that will live on into perpetuity. To understand how, we must first define "true wealth." So let's shift gears in order to view your future from a loftier perspective.*

Wealth is usually associated with the accumulation of assets. When asked what their assets are, most people usually think of their house, cash, stocks, bonds, real estate, and insurance. These *things* constitute our *financial assets* and represent our material possessions.

But, if I were to ask what their most important assets are, most people would list their family, health, relationships, virtues, values, morals, character, unique abilities, heritage, and the future. This category represents *human assets*—that is, *people* rather than things.

Another category of assets represents the *wisdom* we gain in life: our *intellectual assets*. Wisdom is a product of knowledge multiplied by experiences—both good and bad. Intellectual assets also include our formal education, reputation, systems, methods, skills, ideas, alliances, and traditions.

ASSETS THAT MATTER

Imagine these three categories—financial, human, and intellectual assets—on a "family balance sheet." Say you had to leave one category behind, but you could keep and transfer the others to future generations. Which would you choose to lose (figure 1.2)?

*In 2000 I enrolled in The Strategic Coach, an entrepreneurial coaching program in Chicago founded by Dan Sullivan. Lee Brower was my coach, and as a result of working with Lee, I became acquainted with his company, Empowered Wealth, LLC, and was invited to serve as an advisory board member of that firm. The experience expanded my horizon of the meaning of "true wealth" and the optimization of all assets. Asset optimization and wealth empowerment is an integral part of the concepts referenced throughout the book.

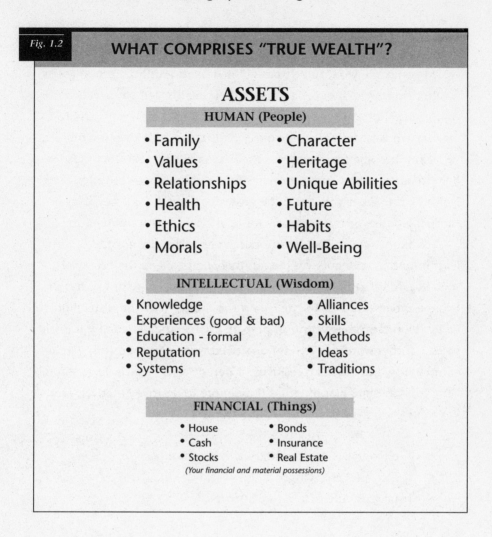

Fig. 1.2

WHAT COMPRISES "TRUE WEALTH"?

ASSETS

HUMAN (People)

- Family
- Values
- Relationships
- Health
- Ethics
- Morals
- Character
- Heritage
- Unique Abilities
- Future
- Habits
- Well-Being

INTELLECTUAL (Wisdom)

- Knowledge
- Experiences (good & bad)
- Education - formal
- Reputation
- Systems
- Alliances
- Skills
- Methods
- Ideas
- Traditions

FINANCIAL (Things)

- House
- Cash
- Stocks
- Bonds
- Insurance
- Real Estate

(Your financial and material possessions)

I have asked this question of a wide variety of individuals who have had financial net worths ranging from $10,000 to $2,500,000,000, and the answer is the same. They would choose to give up their financial assets.

Why? Because we can rebuild the financial assets with our human and intellectual assets. Most religions of the world believe that we come into the world possessing the human and intellectual assets to one degree or another. While we live our life, we enhance these assets.

Then when we leave this mortal existence, we take the enhanced human and intellectual assets with us to the next life.

Most people would not trade their human and intellectual assets for more money. When people spend their health trying to create more financial wealth, they usually end up spending their wealth trying to regain their health. If we trade our morals and ethics for more money, we soon become bankrupt in the human asset category. George Bernard Shaw said, "There are two sources of unhappiness in life. One is not getting what you want; the other is getting it." Money does not cause happiness or misery; but your relationship with money can.

It's unfortunate that traditional estate planning focuses on the least important category on the family balance sheet: the financial assets. Regardless of its complexity, traditional estate planning has become a process of four Ds: *divide* up the estate, *defer* the distribution, *dump* the financial assets on ill-prepared heirs, and eventually it *dissipates*. In other words, wealth is transferred without responsibility or accountability. Lee Brower, president of Empowered Wealth, LLC, states, "Traditional estate planning has done more to destroy American families than the federal estate tax could ever do!" Why?

- It encourages extraordinary consumption.
- It discourages savings.
- It takes families from "we" to "me."

Before I explain possible solutions, let's explore one final category of assets. There is an element of financial assets that is as important as the return on those assets, if not more important. That element is *choice* and *control*. There are certain financial assets over which we give up, for all practical purposes, choice and control. These assets are our *civic,* or social, *assets*. When most people think of civic assets, they usually think of taxes. Throughout the world, most governmental systems require the citizens of their country, state, and municipality to give back to society in the form of taxes. Hence, most people think of taxes as a liability; but, as Lee Brower explains, taxes are actually an asset. For example, a road or highway—paid for by taxes—is a public asset.

In America, the government has provided ways for us to take a certain amount of control over how we allocate our social dollars. However, if we choose not to take control, the government will! One way you can regain choice and control over civic assets is to redirect some of your financial assets that would otherwise be paid in tax to charitable causes, preferably through your own family foundation. Another way is to redirect otherwise payable income tax to investments that stimulate the economy while enhancing your own net worth. This book will teach you how to redirect otherwise payable income tax to causes you support, including your retirement and financial security for your family.

THE NEED FOR THE RIGHT P.L.A.N.

How does one create a Perpetual Life of Asset Nurturance™? I urge everyone to identify the method that best meets individual needs—but beware of relying on traditional wisdom. Marshall Thurber, attorney and internationally renowned systems analyst, states that "94 percent of all failures are a result of the system." The typical system for accumulating wealth and transferring that wealth to future generations almost assures failure.

According to the Family Firm Institute of Brookline, Massachusetts, "only a little more than 3 percent of all family enterprises survive to the fourth generation and beyond." Throughout the world, financial assets have dissipated by the end of the third generation following the wealth creation. Hence the saying "shirtsleeves to shirtsleeves in three generations." Robert Frost said, "Every affluent father wishes he knew how to give his sons the hardships that made him rich."

Cornelius Vanderbilt (1794–1877) was the most powerful and successful American businessman (the Bill Gates) of his time. He made his fortune in steamship lines and railroads. He helped build the nation's transportation system. Vanderbilt did not support charities, but late in life, he gave $1 million to Central University in Nashville, Tennessee, now known as Vanderbilt University. At his death, Vanderbilt left an estate valued at $105 million—the largest in American history up to that time. According to Arthur T. Vanderbilt II, author of *Fortune's Children: The Fall of the House of Vanderbilt*, when 120 of Cornelius Vanderbilt's descendants gathered together in a reunion in 1973, there was not a millionaire among them. The wealth had dissipated. It had been transferred without responsibility or accountability. William K. Vanderbilt, grandson of Cornelius, said, "It has left me with nothing to hope for, with nothing definite to seek or strive for. Inherited wealth is a real handicap to happiness."

In contrast, let's consider the Rothschild family—one of the few families who perpetuated their family wealth for several generations. Mayer Amschel Rothschild (1743–1812) opened a bank in Frankfurt, Germany, where he made profitable investments for the royal families of several European countries and founded a banking dynasty. He taught his five sons conservative money management by making investments that produced reasonable profits rather than aggressive returns. His methods made him a tremendous fortune. Nathan Rothschild, the third son, became a financial agent of the English government. He stated, "It requires a great deal of boldness and a great deal of caution to make a great fortune; and when you have got it, it requires ten times as much wit to keep it."

Basically, the Rothschilds established the following system:

- They loaned their heirs money or entered into joint ventures with them.
- The loans had to be paid back to the "family bank."
- The knowledge and experiences those heirs gained had to be shared with other family members.
- The family gathered at least once a year to reaffirm its virtues and intentions, or they couldn't participate in the family bank.

Subsequently, the Rothschilds' wealth compounded and grew as it passed to future generations.

GETTING YOUR FAMILY INVESTED IN THE P.L.A.N.

Abraham Lincoln once said, "The worst thing you can do for those you love is the things they could do for themselves."

To help your family become invested in your legacy of true wealth, it is important they see the value of capitalizing all four categories of assets.

Lee Brower, president of Empowered Wealth, emphasizes that the best way to capitalize an asset is to give it a new life by sharing it or giving it away. We ought to focus on the four Ps: *preserve* the assets, *protect* true wealth, *perpetuate* it to future generations, and em*power* family members with stewardship and accountability of more than just financial assets.

When we have a reservoir located in the mountains above us, it can be used as a water source and especially comes in handy during times of drought. It can also be used as a recreational resource. If we install some turbines at the base of the dam, tremendous power can be generated that gives new life to an entire city, without giving up the use of water for consumption and recreation. In much the same way, human, intellectual, financial, and civic assets can be capitalized on to give them a new life.

Since discovering this, my passion has been to assist families in identifying their stewardship to true wealth by creating systems, strategies, and structure for family and financial empowerment, with ongoing accountability, while retaining choice and control.

It would be well for families to develop and use some type of a system designed to:

- Enhance the individual health, happiness, and well-being of each family member
- Support and encourage family leadership

- Capture family virtues, memories, and wisdom
- Protect, optimize, and empower the family's intellectual and financial capital

By now, you may be wondering why I am pursuing all these tangents on family empowerment, happiness, and human, intellectual, and civic assets. Isn't this supposed to be a book on maximizing financial assets?

It's simple. It is highly important to get a handle on values before learning how to handle and value assets. And people—including you and your family—will generally pay far more for something they perceive has the greatest value. How is value created? Just one more tangent.

CREATING VALUE—A PERSONAL STORY

Until recently our family had owned and operated a purified drinking water business in northern Utah. Drinking water in the simplest commodity form had a value of about 1 cent per eight ounces. We had approximately $1 million of equipment at our plant that took water through a six-step purification process. When we amortized the cost of equipment through the production process, the cost of water doubled to 2 cents per eight ounces. We packaged water in a unique eight-ounce plastic pouch rather than a bottle, which added 2 cents to the cost.

We then packaged the pouches in convenient ten-pack tote boxes, which increased the per-unit cost to 7 cents. Four tote boxes were shipped in a corrugated box, increasing the unit cost to 8 cents. (Packaging often costs far more than the commodity.) Labor and overhead for our production plant averaged about 4 cents per unit, thus increasing the cost to 12 cents. Shipping a heavy commodity such as water from Salt Lake City to our customers on the East Coast added another 4 cents to our cost. If we marked up our price 25 percent from our cost of 16 cents, our wholesale price became 20 cents. So we sold 2 cents' worth of water for 20 cents, or ten times as much, because we had taken a commodity and converted it into a unique product.

When our unique product was sold at the grocery store, sometimes it retailed for as much as 35 to 40 cents per pouch. When it entered the convenience sector such as a travel/fuel station, it retailed for 60 to 75 cents. When my parents heard this, they exclaimed, "No way—just for a drink of water!" But hold on, I'm not finished.

A few years ago my wife and I joined a group of friends for three wonderful days in Orlando, Florida, attending the various amusement parks. It was one of the hottest months of May on record. One day we stopped three different times at a convenience cart filled with ice and shelled out $2.50 for a twenty-ounce bottle of chilled drinking water. You do the math. There are 6.4 twenty-ounce portions in a gallon—6.4 times $2.50 equals $16 per gallon of water! As we left the park the next day, we stopped to fill our vehicles with gasoline costing us $1.60 per gallon. Twenty-five years ago, if anyone would have told me that someday people would pay as much for a drink of water as they do for a gallon of gas, I would have laughed at them. But ten times as much? And we even discarded a remaining half bottle of warm water at the end of the day without hesitation!

Why are people willing to do this? It's because of the unique experience they are having. Authors B. Joseph Pine II and James H. Gilmore explain this concept in their book *The Experience Economy*. We value a unique product more than just the commodity. We value convenience more than a unique product. We value a unique experience more than we value convenience.

REALIZING VALUE—YOUR FUTURE STORY

There is one level that exceeds them all: a meaningful transformation. *When we can experience a meaningful transformation in our life that will benefit all of our family members, we consider it of greatest value.* My goal is to create a meaningful transformation in your life through the concepts, truths, and strategies contained in this book.

Most educational books are information-based. This book, on the other hand, will provide an insight-based experience for you. When a person experiences personal epiphanies, he or she is motivated to change. As you continue to read, it is my sincere desire that a meaningful transformation will take place as you learn to give new life to your human, intellectual, financial, and civic assets.

CONCEPTS COVERED IN CHAPTER 1

- With the insights gained in this book, choose not to always accept conventional advice on your journey toward financial independence.
- Setting aside money in qualified retirement accounts, such as IRAs and 401(k)s, while paying down our home mortgage is like going down the highway with one foot on the brake pedal and the other on the gas pedal.
- There are two ways to handle new information: ignore it as false or increase your level of understanding to accommodate new ideas.
- The most important phases of retirement planning are the accumulation, distribution, and transfer phases. It is better to enjoy tax-favored benefits during the harvest rather than on the seed of a savings accumulation plan.
- Roth IRAs are a step in the right direction, but there are still too many strings attached.
- *Your IRA, pension, and 401(k) benefits will probably be taxable at a higher rate at retirement,* so don't postpone the inevitable and increase your tax liability.
- *There are ways to receive tax-favored benefits during all four phases of retirement planning*—the contribution, accumulation, distribution, and transfer phases.
- *No method of paying extra principal on your mortgage is the wisest or quickest method of accomplishing financial independence.*

- Dramatically enhance your net worth and generate an extra million dollars or more by safely using lazy, idle dollars trapped in the equity of your home.

- When we learn how to nurture all of our assets properly, we will create a new life for them that will live on into perpetuity.

- "True wealth" on the family balance sheet is comprised of human assets, intellectual assets, financial assets, and civic assets.

- *Traditional estate planning focuses on the least important category on the family balance sheet: the financial assets.* It has become a process of divide, defer, dump, and dissipate, as assets are transferred without responsibility or accountability.

- The government has provided ways for us to take a certain amount of control over how we allocate our social dollars. However, *if we choose not to take control, the government will!*

- The typical system for accumulating wealth and transferring that wealth to future generations almost always assures failure.

- *Focus on the four Ps: preserve assets; protect true wealth; perpetuate it to future generations; and em*power *family members with stewardship and accountability of more than just financial assets.*

- Families should develop and use a system designed to enhance the individual health, happiness, and well-being of each family member; support and encourage family leadership; capture family virtues, memories, and wisdom; and protect, optimize, and empower the family's intellectual and financial capital.

- *It's more important that values are understood before assets are valued.*

- We value a unique product more than just the commodity. We value convenience more than a unique product. We value a unique experience more than we value convenience. When we experience a meaningful transformation in our life, we value it most.

CHAPTER 2

Taxes Are Actually an Asset!

Leverage your tax dollars to support your retirement and
financial security

MOST OF US ARE CONDITIONED to view taxes as a liability. But are they really? It's true that when we owe the government tax, it represents a liability to us. However, tax revenues are often
expended on public assets—roads, schools, parks, airports—education,
and protection.

As explained in chapter 1, most governmental systems throughout
the world have some method whereby the public is required to give
back to society in the form of taxes. Most people don't object to paying their fair share of tax as long as the government exercises prudence
and proper stewardship over public funds. It's when we feel we are paying more than our fair share, or we feel the government is wasting or
mismanaging public funds, that we get riled.

What many Americans don't realize is the government has given
us the opportunity to take a certain amount of control over the management of our civic assets. If we don't exercise choice and control,
they will! When we take responsibility for our own financial well-
being, our future retirement security, insuring our own health care,
or supporting charitable organizations that care for the poor and
needy, the government's need to intervene becomes less. Generally,

government-funded programs of social services are expensive and in-efficient. The Internal Revenue Code contains provisions whereby tax-payers can redirect otherwise payable taxes to causes they are passionate about that will also benefit their own families.

WHY ALL THE TAX BREAKS?

Why do tax laws allow a taxpayer to deduct money contributed to an IRA from gross income and accumulate a retirement account on a tax-deferred basis?

When was the last time you washed a rental car or changed its oil? People don't wash rental cars; they wash and take care of the cars they *own*. The secret to American wealth lies within the freedom to own as-sets with deeds, titles, and articles of incorporation.

The government understands this premise, so similarly, they en-courage you to take financial responsibility for your own retirement so you won't be a drain on public funds. The government also encourages you to postpone taxes to a future date so your funds will grow to a larger amount and likely be taxed at a higher rate, as I will explain in chapter 3.

Why do tax laws allow a taxpayer to deduct mortgage interest ex-pense from their gross income? It's because home buyers stimulate the economy, which creates more tax revenue than the revenue they are giving up. The government would rather have its citizens owning their own home than living in subsidized housing or renting. People take care of assets when they have personal ownership of them. Why do tax laws allow a taxpayer to deduct money contributed to charitable causes? Because those civic dollars benefit society. Therefore, govern-ment welfare programs will have less demand on them.

Why do tax laws allow exemptions on a tax return for each de-pendent in the household? It's better for parents to care for the needs of their own children than to have government collecting additional tax and allocating it back for human services. It stands to reason, then, that *the more choice and control we exercise over our civic assets, the less government will need to tax us to provide services we can provide for ourselves.*

What if a 30-year-old couple could redirect $500 a month of otherwise payable income taxes to their retirement account? If they accumulated $500 per month for thirty-five years (to age 65) in a non-taxable environment at 7.5 percent interest compounded annually, it would grow to $1,021,727. They could withdraw $6,385 per month in interest thereafter ($1,021,727 x 7.5% = $76,630 ÷ 12 months) and never deplete their principal. This book will teach you how to do this.

Remember that sweet, juicy orange encased in the bitter peel that I mentioned in the preface? Here's one of those moments when we'll need to "get through the peel" to arrive at a delightful principle. So bear with me in this chapter as I educate you on some basic tax laws and strategies that are necessary ingredients for making a dramatic difference in optimizing all of our assets.

HOW TAXES, INTEREST RATES, AND UNFORESEEN EVENTS IMPACT YOU

There is nothing more constant than ever-changing income tax laws. As of the date of publication of this book, the most recent changes in tax law occurred with the Economic Growth and Tax Relief Reconciliation Act of 2001 and the Jobs and Growth Tax Relief Reconciliation Act of 2003. Both of these acts, passed by Congress under the Bush administration, were intended to help stimulate a sluggish economy amid the economic storm caused by post-Y2K monetary and fiscal policy. With all the fears of computers' Y2K incompatibility, the Federal Reserve did not want anyone to go to the bank or credit union and be unable to get their money during the turn of the century. Through a series of interest rate reductions, the money supply was increased. Shortly after January 1, 2000, the Federal Reserve felt there was too much money in the economy and began to perform an enormous liposuction of money out of the market through a series of interest rate increases.

The terrorist attacks of September 11, 2001, reversed that process, and the Federal Reserve again started a second pattern of lowering interest rates and continued until they reached the lowest rate in forty years.

Beyond the immediate and tragic loss of lives, the grim "success" of a terrorist attack is measured by the resulting change in the psyche of those who feel their freedoms are infringed. Widespread, long-term damage occurs when the consuming public stops consuming, investing, traveling, eating out, building, and living normally.

When two aircraft fly into two skyscrapers in New York and immediately people begin to lose their jobs 2,700 miles away in California, it reminds us of the importance of preparing financially against external forces over which we have no control. So let's understand the fiscal and monetary basics so you can use them to your advantage in creating financial security.

UNDERSTANDING TAX BRACKETS

Prior to the 2001 and 2003 tax acts, the two lowest federal income tax brackets held consistent at 15 and 28 percent from 1986 until 2001. The income thresholds at which these tax rates applied gradually increased about an average of 3 percent annually during these years. The 2001 act provided for the implementation of a 10 percent rate bracket that benefited all taxpayers with a tax liability. Under the 2003 act, the taxable income at which the 10 percent bracket ends was adjusted from $6,000 to $7,000 for single individuals and married individuals filing separately; and from $12,000 to $14,000 for married taxpayers filing jointly. The 2003 act accelerated the reductions in the regular income tax rates above the 15 percent rate. The former 28 percent bracket, which had been the second bracket, is now the third bracket and was reduced to 25 percent.

Under the 2003 act, there was a temporary expansion of the 15 percent rate bracket for married couples for 2003 and 2004 tax years only. For 2003, the 15 percent bracket for joint filers applied to taxable income above $14,000 but not above $56,800. The threshold in 2002 was $46,700. Therefore, the temporary increase was 21.6 percent rather than the typical 3 percent increase. (This was done in an effort to pump more money back into the economy.) Many provisions of the 2003 act are scheduled to expire between 2005 and 2008, but Congress might extend these changes or make them permanent. There is nothing certain about future tax law, especially with sunset provisions that will restore previous laws and with various challenges facing Congress, such as financing the war on terrorism.

Inasmuch as the tax threshold endpoint for the 15 percent rate bracket would have been about $50,000 for tax year 2005, and may revert to that approximate amount according to the 2003 act, for the sake of simplicity, the examples in this book will assume all taxable income above $50,000 for a married couple filing jointly and above $30,000 for single taxpayers will be the beginning of the 25 percent federal tax rate. The next threshold is the 28 percent rate, which started at $117,250 for married couples filing jointly and $70,350 for single taxpayers for tax year 2004. There are two more thresholds above this level: the 33 and 35 percent brackets (figure 2.1). The 35 percent bracket applied to incomes in excess of $319,100 in 2004 and will likely be indexed to a higher income threshold for the tax year 2005.

OUR SAMPLE TAX BRACKET

Because the principles taught in this book remain the same regardless of changes that determine precise tax brackets, all figures and examples will be calculated using a combined federal and state income marginal tax bracket of 33.3 percent. You can interpolate any illustrations for your personal income tax bracket. *To illustrate concepts, it is very simple mathematically to assume that exactly one-third is allocated for taxes.* This would be the approximate tax rate on all income in excess of $50,000 under the above assumptions for a married couple living in

Fig. 2.1	FEDERAL TAX RATES		
YEARS	2000	2001 - 2002	2003 - 2010*
1st Bracket	10%	10%	10%
2nd Bracket	15%	15%	15%
3rd Bracket	28%	27%	25%
4th Bracket	31%	30%	28%
5th Bracket	36%	35%	33%
6th Bracket	39.6%	38.6%	35%

*After 2010 tax rates are scheduled to revert to the levels that applied before the Economic Growth and Tax Relief Reconciliation Act of 2001.

2004 FEDERAL INCOME TAX THRESHOLDS Taxable Income Endpoints					
FILING STATUS	10%	15%	25%	28%	33%
Single	$7,150	$29,050	$70,350	$146,750	$319,100*
Married Filing Jointly	$14,300	$58,100	$117,250	$178,650	$319,100*

*Income in excess of these amounts is taxed at 35.0%.

a state that had an 8.3 percent state income tax rate (25 percent federal rate plus an 8.3 percent state rate). It would also apply to all income in excess of $117,250 (for tax year 2004) for a married couple living in a state that had a 5.3 percent state income tax rate (28 percent federal rate plus a 5.3 percent state rate). By the way, these assumptions do not include FICA (Social Security taxes) or Medicare. Those taxes are added on top of federal and state income tax in the amount of 7.65 percent, matched by the employer for another 7.65 percent.

UNDERSTANDING DEDUCTIONS

Fortunately, federal and state income taxes are calculated only on "taxable" income. Taxable income is calculated as gross personal income less personal deductions and exemptions. Deductions are usually allowed for expenses or investments that directly or indirectly contribute to various civic assets or otherwise stimulate the economy. Exemptions are allowed for dependents living in the household of the taxpayer. These deductions and exemptions are subtracted from the last, not the first, dollars you earn each year.

Hence, assuming a married couple filing jointly has a $70,000 combined gross income and has $20,000 in personal deductions and exemptions, their taxable income (the amount eligible for taxation by the federal and state governments) would be $50,000. If they were not able to claim $20,000 in deductions and exemptions, they would have paid a combined federal and state tax of $6,666—one-third of the last $20,000. That's money they would owe Uncle Sam and their state government if they didn't use those deductions. If the tax withheld from their paychecks during the year exceeded the amount they owe in taxes, this money would be refunded to them after they filed their joint tax return. Otherwise, if they owe taxes after completing their tax return, they would simply pay $6,666 less in taxes.

Under current tax law, there are three primary categories that American taxpayers most commonly deduct if they itemize deductions on Schedule A of their 1040 federal tax return:

- State income and sales taxes, as well as local taxes such as property tax
- Cash and non-cash charitable contributions
- Qualified mortgage interest expense

Under hardship circumstances, excessive medical care costs and casualty and theft losses can also qualify for deductibility.

MARGINAL VS. EFFECTIVE TAX BRACKETS

The tax bracket that your last dollars earned put you in is called your "marginal" tax bracket. Your marginal tax bracket is different from your "effective" tax bracket. Your *effective tax bracket* is the tax percentage rate you pay when compared to your total income. For example, a married couple with a combined income of $100,000 might be in a marginal federal tax bracket of 25 percent and a state tax bracket of 8 percent—a combined bracket of 33 percent.

But if you have deductions and exemptions of $30,000, perhaps comprised of mortgage interest, charitable contributions, and dependents in the home who qualify as exemptions, your taxable income might be $70,000. You might pay income tax of only 18 percent on the first $12,000 (which equals $2,160), 23 percent from $12,000 to $50,000 (which equals $8,740), and 33 percent on the remaining $20,000 (which equals $6,600) for a total of $17,500. This is only 17.5 percent of your $100,000 gross income—your *effective tax bracket*. Your *marginal bracket* is still 33 percent. Again, keep in mind this simple example does not include FICA or Medicare.

When analyzing the actual benefit of a tax deduction, you should calculate it using your marginal tax rate rather than your effective tax rate. For example, if you deduct $10,000 of mortgage interest, it reduces your taxable income because the $10,000 comes off the last dollars you earn. In this example, you would actually save 33 percent of $10,000, or $3,300 of otherwise payable income tax you wouldn't have saved without the deduction. Here's the simple rule: *If you want to calculate the true tax savings achieved by virtue of deduction, you should always use the marginal tax rate times the amount of the deduction.* This is always true unless other deductions and exemptions have already taken your gross income below the threshold. In that event, you may want to use the next lower tax rate to calculate the value of a new deduction.

When taxpayers have their tax returns completed by a tax preparer, they are often informed that they are on the verge of moving into the next higher tax bracket. In other words, their taxable income is about to cross the threshold from 15 to 25 percent or from 25 to 28 percent on federal tax. This alarms the taxpayer because of the misconception that all income up to that threshold, as well as any over that threshold, will be taxed at the higher rate. This is not true! *You pay the higher rate only on dollars earned in excess of each tax threshold.*

WHY LET THE IRS MAKE INTEREST OFF *YOUR* MONEY?

Throughout thirty years of financial consulting, I have reviewed many tax returns. I have found that a lot of people get consistent tax refunds of about $2,000, $3,000, or $4,000. I can't help asking them, "Why do you continue to overpay the IRS thousands of dollars each year just to get it refunded?" They say, "Well, this is our forced savings account!" or "We save this way every year and then in the spring we splurge—buy something or go on a vacation with our tax refund." If you are of the same frame of mind, I implore you *not* to use the IRS as your savings vehicle. In case you haven't noticed, if *you* owe the IRS money, there are interest charges and penalties accruing from the time you should have sent them the taxes owed. However, if the IRS owes *you* money, *they do not pay you at all for the use of your money!*

Many wage-earning taxpayers don't understand how to adjust their withholding. The purpose of the form W-4, Employee's Withholding Allowance Certificate, is so your employer can withhold the correct federal income tax from your pay. The form is a personal allowances work sheet. Some people are of the impression that you can claim only as many withholding exemptions as there are dependents in your household, plus yourself. Not true! It is simply a guide. Sometimes, wage earners may want to claim fewer exemptions because if they don't, they may have to cough up more tax on April 15. The actual exemptions you can claim for withholding purposes can be totally different from the actual exemptions you claim on your 1040 tax return. If you are sure you will not owe a certain amount in federal tax in any year because of deductions and exemptions, you can claim as many exemptions as necessary to avoid unnecessary tax being collected that would be refunded to you upon filing your tax return. (For more information, refer to your company's human resources department.)

Since the Tax Reform Act of 1986, there have been only three types of income subject to taxation:

- Earned income—This is money you physically earn as a result of providing goods and services.
- Passive income—This is money realized from passive financial activities, such as rental income from property or lease income.
- Portfolio income—This is money usually realized through the receipt of interest and dividend income on savings and investments.

Earned, passive, and portfolio income are all classified as "ordinary income" and are taxed as such. Passive and portfolio income are not subject to FICA or Medicare tax, but earned income is.

A capital gain is not subject to tax until it is realized, which isn't until an asset is sold. At that point, the difference between the original purchase price and the net sales price of that asset is considered the capital gain. In 1997, the maximum tax rate on capital gains was reduced from 28 to 20 percent (10 percent for taxpayers in the 15 percent tax bracket). Long-term capital gains tax rates apply only to assets held for more than twelve months. The gain on a sale that results purely from depreciation from capital assets is "recaptured" and taxed at 25 percent. The 2003 tax act lowered the maximum rate on long-term capital gains from 20 to 15 percent for capital assets sold after May 6, 2003. The 10 percent rate for taxpayers whose regular income tax rate is less than 25 percent was reduced to 5 percent for 2003 through 2007 and then to zero for 2008. In 2009, the former 20 percent and 10 percent rates are scheduled to return unless Congress acts to extend the temporary rate cut. The 2003 act did not change the treatment of gains from unrecaptured depreciation taken on real property. That tax rate remains at 25 percent.

EARN MORE IN A TAX-FREE ENVIRONMENT

Throughout the remainder of this book, I will be teaching strategies that can substantially increase your financial net worth. These strategies are dramatically enhanced if the accumulation of money is accomplished in a tax-free environment. Money that accumulates tax-deferred is advantageous, but under those circumstances, taxes are simply postponed, and most often the tax liability increases in the process. Taxable investments may require the investor to incur greater risks in order to achieve the same net after-tax rate of return as non-taxable investments.

Are you still wondering whether there is much of a difference between tax-free and taxed-as-earned growth? Consider this illustration of a dollar doubling every period during a time frame of twenty periods tax-free, versus a dollar doubling every period for twenty periods and taxed as earned (assuming just a 25 percent tax bracket).

At the beginning, you have $1 invested in a tax-free account that doubles every period for the twenty periods. One dollar grows to $2 during period 1, then to $4 during period 2, $8 during period 3, $16 during period 4, and so on (figure 2.2). At the end of twenty periods, the account would be worth $1,048,576.

On the other hand, in a taxable environment, assuming a 25 percent tax rate, your money would be taxed as earned. Therefore, at the end of the first period, instead of having $2, you would have only $1.75, because $1 profit less 25 percent tax equals $.75. The next period, you would double $1.75 and pay 25 percent on that profit and so on, until the twentieth period. At the end of the twenty periods, your investment would be worth only $72,401.17, not $1,048,576! There is a tremendous advantage in using investments that are tax-free, not just tax-deferred, as I will illustrate in chapters 4 and 11. (For now, let us just note that under a tax-deferred scenario, the account also accumulates to $1,048,576. Later, however, when taxes are paid on the back end—during the so-called harvest years—the actual amount comes to 33.33 percent less, or about $699,085.)

Fig. 2.2	A DOLLAR DOUBLING EVERY PERIOD FOR 20 PERIODS TAX-FREE VERSUS A DOLLAR DOUBLING EVERY PERIOD FOR 20 PERIODS TAXED AS EARNED*		
Periods		**Tax-Free**	**Taxed as Earned**
		$1	$1.00
1		$2	$1.75
2		$4	$3.06
3		$8	$5.35
4		$16	$9.36
5		$32	$16.38
6		$64	$28.66
7		$128	$50.15
8		$256	$87.76
9		$512	$153.58
10		$1,024	$268.76
11		$2,048	$470.33
12		$4,096	$823.08
13		$8,192	$1,440.39
14		$16,384	$2,520.68
15		$32,768	$4,411.19
16		$65,536	$7,719.58
17		$131,072	$13,509.26
18		$262,144	$23,641.20
19		$524,288	$41.372.10
20		**$1,048,576**	**$72,401.17**

assuming a 25 percent tax bracket

IN WHICH ENVIRONMENT WOULD YOU PREFER TO ACCUMULATE YOUR WEALTH?

PAY THE TOLL OR FIND AN ALTERNATE ROUTE

There are many legitimate tax deductions and tax-favorable strategies that purposely exist in the tax code for the taxpayer's benefit. If these laws are understood, used, and leveraged properly, they can generate thousands of extra dollars in your personal net worth, which may create different taxable events for the government to ultimately reap its fair share. Tax planning strategies are not "loopholes," a term that connotes a taxpayer is getting away with something until the IRS and

Congress discover and eliminate it. The difference between income tax avoidance and income tax evasion is usually about ten years (in jail!).

Seriously, if a person were to travel to work every day and had the choice of taking a toll road or an alternate route toll-free, the choice would be clear: either pay the toll or legally avoid paying the toll by taking an alternate route. However, if the commuter were to break through the tollgate, he would be guilty of evading the payment of the toll. I recommend that, whenever feasible, taxpayers legally avoid the payment of unnecessary tax or redirect it along the legitimate avenues provided to us.

In chapters 6 through 8, I will be teaching you the dynamics of successfully managing equity in your home to increase liquidity, safety, rate of return, and tax deductions. *It is important to understand that whenever a taxpayer borrows money, such as a home mortgage, the borrowed funds are not subject to tax.* This is also a critical factor when using the tax-free, retirement planning alternatives to IRAs and 401(k)s explained later. In other words, retirement income that comes in the form of loan proceeds is not deemed earned, passive, or portfolio income and therefore is not subject to income tax. I'll explain more about this in chapters 9, 10, and 11.

Before moving ahead, it is imperative to understand two more tax-related concepts: (1) the difference between preferred and non-preferred interest expense and (2) the tax-free gain allowed on the sale of a personal residence.

PREFERRED AND NON-PREFERRED INTEREST

In this book, I refer to two types of interest. *Preferred interest* is tax-deductible interest expense. To illustrate, if a married couple with a combined annual income of $70,000 has $10,000 of deductible interest by virtue of interest paid on a mortgage or equity line on their personal residence, their taxable income is reduced to $60,000. In a 33.3 percent combined federal and state tax bracket, this couple would actually save $3,333 they would otherwise pay in tax.

Non-preferred interest is non-deductible interest expense. If the same couple did not have a mortgage, but had $10,000 of interest they paid during a tax year on automobile loans or credit card debt, this would represent non-deductible interest, and their taxable income would remain at $70,000.

If we borrow money that qualifies as preferred debt, because the interest is deductible, the true cost of borrowing the money is calculated after tax. For example, in a 33.3 percent tax bracket, borrowing money at 9 percent deductible interest really only costs us 6 percent (one-third less). This is because of the 3 percent we save in tax by getting it back from Uncle Sam either in a refund or in owing less in tax than we otherwise would. Likewise, if we borrow at 6 percent preferred interest, our true cost is only 4 percent. (It is essential to understand this when I address the importance of positive leverage using arbitrage to accumulate wealth using the same method banks and credit unions do. See chapters 7 and 8.)

UNDERSTANDING DEDUCTIBILITY

The deductibility of home mortgage interest is often misunderstood. A homeowner can deduct mortgage interest expense on Schedule A of an itemized tax return on loans up to $100,000, over and above acquisition indebtedness on a qualified residence. This is true unless the loan proceeds are used to increase the acquisition indebtedness by doing home improvements. Internal Revenue Code Section 163 defines a qualified residence, acquisition indebtedness, and home equity indebtedness.

A *qualified residence* is the principal residence of the taxpayer and one other residence belonging to the taxpayer, selected by the taxpayer and used by the taxpayer as a residence. This secondary residence can be a condo, cabin, motor home, camp trailer, or even a boat as long as it meets certain requirements, such as having bathroom facilities.

Acquisition indebtedness is any debt that is incurred in acquiring, constructing, or substantially improving any qualified residence of the taxpayer and is secured by the residence. There is a $1-million limitation. The most common misunderstanding about acquisition indebtedness is that even though it may begin as the amount you borrowed when you bought, built, or fixed up your house, it reduces as you pay down your mortgage. For example, if you purchased a home for $250,000 and financed 80 percent of the purchase price, your original acquisition indebtedness would be $200,000. However, if you paid down the mortgage to a balance of $100,000, your acquisition indebtedness is now only $100,000.

Home equity indebtedness is any indebtedness (other than acquisition indebtedness) secured by a qualified residence to the extent that the total amount of that indebtedness does not exceed the fair market value of the qualified residence, less the acquisition indebtedness. This is usually money you borrow out of your house for purposes other than improving the house. There is a limitation for deducting interest on home equity indebtedness. The total amount of home equity indebtedness that would qualify for deductible interest cannot exceed $100,000 ($50,000 in the case of a separate tax return by a married individual).

Let's say your home appreciated in value to $400,000 since its original purchase, and your original $200,000 mortgage was paid down to $100,000. If you refinanced the home with a new mortgage of $300,000 and used the equity for purposes other than home improvements, you could deduct interest on only $200,000 ($100,000 above the acquisition indebtedness that you reduced to $100,000).

A key element of Section 163(h)(3) is that according to Temporary Regulation 1.163-8T(m)(3), qualified residence interest is allowable as a deduction *without regard to* the manner in which such interest expense is allocated under the rules of this section. It is important to understand these tax implications when applying the strategies contained in this book. *A taxpayer should always seek advice and confirmation as to the deductibility of interest from a competent tax advisor regarding any particular set of circumstances.*

To maintain the highest amount of deductible interest on a qualified residence, it may be in a homeowner's best interest to use an interest-only mortgage and accumulate the excess that would have gone to reducing the principal of the loan in a separate side fund. As I will show in chapters 6 to 8, this may prove to be the best strategy to get your home "paid off," while increasing liquidity, safety, rate of return, and tax deductions. *When you sell a home and purchase a new residence, it would behoove you to establish the highest amount of acquisition indebtedness possible, by paying little or no cash down payment.* This strategy not only establishes greater deductibility of interest but also allows you to manage the equity in your home to dramatically enhance your net worth over time. Keep reading and you'll discover why.

UNDERSTANDING CAPITAL GAINS ON THE SALE OF A PERSONAL RESIDENCE

The Taxpayer Relief Act of 1997 changed the rules for the recognition of gain on the sale of a principal residence. It repealed the rules allowing a homeowner to sell a home and roll over the gain into a new home. Under this law, a married taxpayer may exclude up to $500,000 ($250,000 if unmarried) of gain on the sale of a principal residence. This exclusion can generally be used only once every two years. In the case of a sale of a principal residence due to a change in employment, health, or other unforeseen circumstances, a homeowner is eligible for a reduced exclusion even if the two years have not passed. Because of the 1997 law, homeowners no longer need to worry about keeping records of rollover gains from one home to the next. Of course, a homeowner still needs to keep track of the basis in the current home. Here are the main points to remember:

- The *basis* is the purchase price, plus home improvement costs, minus any depreciation taken on the home.
- When the home is sold, the capital gain is calculated as the difference between its basis and the net sales price.

- The $500,000 exclusion ($250,000 if unmarried) is then applied.

A common misconception among homeowners is that to avoid capital gains tax, you have to use as much as possible of the cash proceeds from the sale of a previous residence in purchasing a new home. The fact is, no equity from a former residence needs to be paid into the acquisition of a new home. The pre-1997 law required only that a house of equal or greater value had to be purchased to avoid a capital gain. I have never taken any equity from the sale of my former homes and invested it into my newer homes—not even for a cash down payment. *In fact, I have never paid a cash down payment for any home I have ever purchased.* I will teach you why in the ensuing chapters. All the equity I have realized when selling previous homes was kept separate from new properties. Not only did this establish the highest acquisition indebtedness possible for tax deduction purposes, but also it allowed me to generate thousands of dollars through the prudent and wise management of my home equity, thereby increasing liquidity, safety, and rate of return.

It is the taxpayer's responsibility to research and understand all legitimate deductions that may be taken or to hire someone who will. For those who lack the expertise or time to do their own research, perhaps the assistance of a professional CPA is the answer. I think an aggressive, thorough certified public accountant can be well worth the investment. A good CPA will meet with you a few times a year to assess your situation and discuss strategies to alleviate unnecessary tax.

CONCEPTS COVERED IN CHAPTER 2

- The government has given us the opportunity to take a certain amount of control over the management of our civic assets.
- The secret to American wealth lies within the freedom to own assets with deeds, titles, and articles of incorporation.

- *The more choice and control we exercise over civic assets, the less government will need to tax us for social services.*
- The principles taught in this book remain the same regardless of changes that determine the precise tax bracket.
- Taxable income is calculated as gross income less personal deductions and exemptions.
- The tax bracket that your "last dollars earned" put you in is called your marginal tax bracket. To calculate the true tax savings achieved by virtue of a deduction, use the marginal tax rate.
- You pay higher tax rates only on dollars earned in excess of each tax threshold.
- Do not use the IRS as your forced savings vehicle.
- If you are sure you will not owe federal tax in any year because of deductions and exemptions, you can claim as many withholding exemptions as necessary to avoid unnecessary tax being collected.
- There are only three types of income subject to taxation: earned income, passive income, and portfolio income.
- A capital gain is not subject to tax until it is realized.
- Money that accumulates in a non-taxed environment grows to a substantially greater sum than money taxed—even at 25 percent.
- There are many legitimate tax deductions and tax-favorable strategies allowed in the tax code for the taxpayer's benefit.
- When borrowing money, loan proceeds are not taxable.
- Tax-deductible interest is a preferred interest expense.
- A homeowner can deduct mortgage interest expense on Schedule A of an itemized tax return on loans up to $100,000, over and above acquisition indebtedness on a qualified residence.
- Acquisition indebtedness is any debt incurred in acquiring, constructing, or substantially improving a qualified residence and is secured by the residence. There is a $1-million limitation.

- Qualified residence interest is allowable as a deduction, without regard to the manner in which such interest expense is allocated.
- A taxpayer should always seek advice and confirmation as to the deductibility of interest from a competent tax advisor.
- A married taxpayer may exclude up to $500,000 ($250,000 if unmarried) of gain on the sale of a principal residence. This exclusion can generally be used only once every two years.

CHAPTER 3

Plan Your Retirement—Not Uncle Sam's

If you think deferred taxes will save retirement dollars, think again

IF YOU'RE READING THIS BOOK, it's probably safe to assume you're planning for retirement using some type of tax-advantaged fund. Chances are, it's a tax-deferred fund. And why not? Everybody assumes it's better to defer payment of taxes until you retire; you'll be in a lower tax bracket by then, right?

Not necessarily. A common myth-conception among retirement-minded Americans is that they will be in a lower tax bracket when they retire than when they were employed. The reality is that most Americans who have saved for retirement will find themselves in a tax bracket at least as high as—if not higher than—they were in during their earning years. That's because *retirees usually have fewer deductions and exemptions.*

From a financial standpoint, there are often three phases in an adult's life:

1. The learning years, when we receive our basic education
2. The earning years, when we are compensated for our unique abilities in the marketplace

3. The yearning years, when too many people suffer from lack of proper saving and investing to prepare for retirement

What may be surprising, however, is that those who do save in traditional qualified retirement accounts, such as IRAs and 401(k)s, almost curse the day they started their plan because of the amount of tax they pay on the back end, versus the tax they saved on the front end.

THE PROS AND CONS OF QUALIFIED PLANS

First, let's define a *qualified retirement plan*. It's qualified with whom? The IRS. A qualified retirement plan is qualified with the IRS under the rules established by Congress as outlined in the Internal Revenue Code. Traditional qualified plans allow the individual to either contribute money with pre-tax dollars or receive a tax deduction for the amount contributed. The account is generally allowed to grow tax-deferred. Qualified plans include, but are not limited to, IRAs, 401(k)s, TSAs, 403(b)s, 457s, pension plans, and profit-sharing plans.

Traditional qualified plans have the following advantages:

- Tax-deductible funding
- Tax-deferred growth
- Possible matching by the employer

Traditional qualified plans also carry the following disadvantages:

- They are fully taxable as the funds are used.
- Distributions must be taken after age 70½ in minimum annual amounts determined by the government's life expectancy formula.
- The remainder is potentially taxed twice upon passing to non-spousal heirs.

All qualified plans come with strings attached. There are restrictions and rules for each type of qualified plan. Let me paraphrase a few of the most prominent rules for traditional plans:

- You can only contribute up to a certain dollar amount and/or a certain percentage of your income each year.
- If you withdraw money from your qualified retirement account before age 59½ (except under special circumstances), you will incur a 10 percent penalty, in addition to the normal tax due.
- If you borrow money out of your qualified plan (or use it as collateral) and don't repay the loan, the loan proceeds become a taxable distribution, with any applicable penalties.
- If you don't start taking at least minimum distributions (based on the IRS's life expectancy formula) beginning at age 70½, you will be assessed a 50 percent penalty tax, in addition to the normal tax on the amount you should have withdrawn and taken as income.
- If you are an employer, most qualified plans require that you provide plans for your employees under similar rules to your own plan.

When we elect to contribute money into traditional qualified retirement accounts, we defer, or postpone, the tax. People usually do this because they think they will be in a lower tax bracket when they retire, or they think that pre-tax dollars will grow to a larger sum, thereby generating greater income later. *The simple fact is, deferred taxes equal increased taxes.* When taxes are postponed and money is allowed to compound tax-deferred, the tax liability continues to increase too. Wouldn't it be wonderful to accumulate money with no tax, then use it during retirement with no tax, and still get tax-favored benefits on the seed money? This book will teach you how.

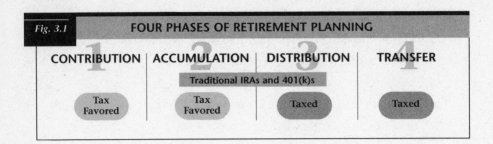

THE FOUR PHASES OF RETIREMENT PLANNING

People tend to get their money trapped in IRAs and 401(k)s because no one ever explained to them what happens during the harvest years. But first, let's fully understand the four phases of retirement planning (figure 3.1).

Phase I—Contribution

The first phase of retirement planning is the contribution phase. During this phase, we make contributions or deposits into investments or savings vehicles. If the account is a qualified plan, we are allowed to deduct those contributions from our gross income on our tax return or contribute money with pre-taxed dollars. (Otherwise, the contribution would be done with after-tax dollars.)

Phase II—Accumulation

The second phase of our retirement planning overlaps the first phase. In this phase, we can accumulate money through compound interest, asset appreciation, or the reinvestment of dividends and capital gains. The accumulation takes place free of tax under qualified plans because any dividends, capital gains, or credited interest stays and compounds with the account and is not reportable as a taxable event on your annual tax return. Therefore, the compounding that takes place in a tax-deferred environment allows greater growth because the "children" of the investments (the interest) also help your account to blossom without being taxed during the accumulation phase.

This arrangement may seem ideal—to be able to contribute dollars before being taxed and have them continue to compound and grow without being taxed on the gain during the growth process. Most retirement account advisors focus only on the contribution and accumulation phases. I ask, however, "What about the most important phase: the time when you will use your accumulated money during retirement?"

Phase III—Distribution

The distribution phase is when we withdraw money for retirement income. Under traditional IRAs and 401(k)s, we must now report 100 percent of our distribution on our annual tax return to be taxed. All too often, when we thought we would be in a lower bracket, we find ourselves in a bracket as high—or higher. We are no longer contributing money to IRAs; we have no mortgage interest deductions because our mortgage is paid off; we no longer have children at home (who qualify as dependents); and so on.

Phase IV—Transfer

What if you do not use all of the money before you pass away? What happens to your qualified retirement funds during the transfer of that money to a spouse or non-spousal heir? The transfer phase is often overlooked until it is too late.

People don't want to outlive their money, so they try to keep enough saved in case they need long-term health care. (The fastest-growing age group in American society is the group over age 100.) But we are not getting out of here alive, so when people do die, they usually end up leaving behind some money. If that money is in a qualified retirement plan, the beneficiaries will be subject to income tax when they use the money, and might even be subject to an additional estate tax. Estate tax may be due (based on the size of the estate and the tax laws at the time of death) upon the second of two spouses' deaths, as the remaining money passes down to non-spousal heirs. Therefore, *retirement plan assets may be taxed twice.*

To avoid this, many financial advisors recommend the heirs use a "stretch IRA," which means that either the IRA continues to grow tax-deferred or the distributions are stretched out over a long period of time. Under such arrangements, the taxes might be less in each given year than if the entire account were distributed in one year; but stringing out the tax liability may end up increasing the overall tax that is paid. It may be better to bite the bullet, pay the tax in today's brackets, and reposition the net after-tax amount into vehicles that will grow from that point forward tax-free. We'll discuss this strategy in chapter 5.

CASE STUDY—A TEACHER'S LESSON

Let me give you a typical example of why people find themselves at retirement in a tax bracket as high as or higher than they were in during their earning years. A schoolteacher came to me for retirement planning after she had worked under the state retirement system for thirty years. Her defined benefit pension allowed her to receive 2 percent for every year of service, calculated on the average of her best three years' salaries (out of the previous five years of employment). Her average best salary was $60,000, and she had thirty years of service. So her monthly retirement income would be $3,000, or $36,000 per year (2% x 30 years = 60% x $60,000 = $36,000). Knowing that she would receive only about 60 percent of her earned income, she prepared for thirty years to make up the shortfall by putting money in TSAs, 403(b)s, and the state's 401(k), where she received matching contributions. She socked away about $3,000 per year in these vehicles at an average 8 percent return, which resulted in a balance of $375,000 by her retirement date. Based on interest-only withdrawals from her qualified accounts, she will have $30,000 a year (8 percent of $375,000) of taxable income in addition to the $36,000 defined benefit pension. Her total income in retirement ended up being $66,000 per year plus $16,000 in Social Security income, for a gross income of $82,000.

Sounds pretty good, right? What didn't sound so good were the looming taxes she would be clobbered with because she had no mortgage on her home and no dependents. She was shocked her retirement tax bracket was greater than during her earning years. Fortunately, we were able to substantially reduce her taxes through strategies explained in chapter 5.

TAXES—SAVE NOW, PAY MORE LATER?

It's sad but true: Traditional qualified plans are the best savings bond Uncle Sam ever came up with *for himself*. Let's look at a simple example to see why (figure 3.2). Jim and Mary Followthecrowd represent a husband and wife who each started setting aside $3,000 per year into IRAs or 401(k)s when they were age 30. They thought this was a good idea because, together, they were saving $6,000 before tax. It really only required them to give up $4,000 in a 33.3 percent tax bracket because Uncle Sam was contributing the other $2,000 in tax savings. Jim and Mary were excited every year because they were saving $2,000 in otherwise payable income taxes—$2,000 per year over thirty-five years means they saved $70,000 in tax on their contributions. Let's assume they earned the equivalent of 7.5 percent interest on their qualified accounts—$6,000 invested per year for a total of thirty-five years (to age 65) equals total contributions of $210,000. They are thrilled because their $6,000 per year investment grew to the $1-million mark in thirty-five years and one month. Now they're ready to retire and enjoy the harvest of the fruit they've nurtured.

If Jim and Mary were to make interest-only withdrawals (to not deplete their $1-million nest egg), their annual interest income would be $75,000, assuming they continued to average a 7.5 percent return. Lo and behold, they find that this income, on top of their Social Security and other income (plus the fact they have very few tax deductions in retirement), keeps them in a 33.3 percent tax bracket. So on the $75,000 annual income coming from their IRAs and 401(k)s, they end up paying at least $25,000 in tax, and they get to keep and spend only $50,000.

Within the first three years of retirement, they will pay back to

---

Fig. 3.2 | **WHY DIDN'T SOMEONE TELL ME "THE REST OF THE STORY"?**

Annual IRA/401(k) Contribution = $6,000 X 35 Years = $210,000 Total Contributions
Tax Bracket = 33.3%
Tax Savings: $6,000 X 33.3% = $2,000 X 35 Years = $70,000 Total Tax Savings

---

$6,000 Per Year at 7.5% for 35 Years, 1 month = $1,000,000+

$1,000,000		
X 7.5%		
$75,000	Interest Income	
X 33.3%	Tax Bracket	
$25,000	**Annual Tax**	

Therefore:	$75,000	Supplemental Retirement Income
Creates:	[25,000]	Potential Annual Tax
RESULTS:	**$50,000**	**Net Spendable Income**

Uncle Sam every dollar they saved in taxes over thirty-five years on contributions. They wonder, "Were we planning *our* retirement or Uncle Sam's?" Not only that, but if Jim lives twenty years to age 85 (life expectancy for a 65-year-old male), they will have paid $500,000 in taxes on their IRA and 401(k) distributions, versus the $70,000 they saved over thirty-five years on contributions!

A GLIMPSE OF SOMETHING BETTER

How much difference would it make if Jim and Mary were able to enjoy the harvest with no tax? Imagine if they had $75,000 per year of tax-free income, instead of netting $50,000 per year!

To see the significant difference between taxable and tax-free harvests, let's assume Jim and Mary need to net $75,000 per year to meet medical expenses and live the lifestyle they would like during retirement (such as visiting their children and grandchildren, golfing, and taking a trip or two each year). If the $1-million nest egg were earning 7.5 percent per year of non-taxable income, they would be withdrawing only interest each year. Their principal would be preserved, and the income would go into perpetuity.

However, if their investments were taxable, in a 33.3 percent tax bracket, Jim and Mary would need to withdraw $112,500 each year, paying $37,500 in tax (33.3 percent of $112,500), to net the $75,000 they need to live on. If they withdraw $112,500 per year out of their account, with a beginning balance of $1 million earning 7.5 percent, the account would be totally depleted in fifteen years! This is because they have to pull out some of their principal each year to cover the tax liability. Thus, Jim and Mary would run out of money in their IRAs and 401(k)s at age 80—probably several years (at least) before their lives ran out.

What if instead they had used an investment that yielded tax-free harvests—an investment that would generate another $1,500,000 of retirement income if one or both of them lived to age 100 ($75,000 a year times twenty years)?

Chapters 9 to 11 will teach you how to establish a non-qualified retirement planning alternative that can be funded with after-tax dollars—with the seed money (contributions)—and accumulate money tax-free. Then later, during the harvest years, you can access it for retirement free of income tax. What's more, if there is any money remaining when you finally pass away, it will transfer tax-free to your heirs.

Would you like to have your cake and eat it too? I will also show you how to get indirect tax breaks on the front end equivalent to IRA and 401(k) tax breaks, without giving up tax-free access to your money during retirement. This can increase your net spendable retirement income by as much as 50 percent, as you will see in the next chapter.

WHAT ABOUT ROTH IRAS?

Many Americans have recognized the advantage of tax-free harvests and have begun to deposit money or convert traditional IRAs into so-called Roth IRAs, which were introduced under the Taxpayer Relief

Act of 1997. (Of course, Uncle Sam loves it when people convert traditional IRAs to Roth IRAs because it creates immediate tax revenue for the country's coffers.)

I will admit, a Roth IRA contains a critical feature of which I am a proponent. As a rule, it is usually better to pay taxes on the seed money contributed to a retirement fund and enjoy a tax-free harvest later than to contribute tax-favored seed money and pay taxes during the harvest years. So Roth IRAs are a step in the right direction. However, a Roth IRA still has too many strings attached in the form of government restrictions.

The Roth IRA is sometimes referred to as a back-loaded IRA. Contributions to a Roth IRA are not deductible. *But all earnings are tax-free, provided withdrawals meet certain requirements*. One requirement is that a distribution may not be made until at least five years after the first contribution is made. In addition, a distribution without penalty can only be made under one of the following conditions:

- On or after the owner attains the age of 59½
- In the case of the owner's death
- For the purchase of a first home, with a limit of $10,000
- In the case of the owner's disability

When Roth IRAs were first introduced, the maximum yearly contribution an individual could make to a Roth IRA was $2,000, which remained the limit until the 2001 tax act. Then the annual contribution limit became $3,000 for the years 2002 to 2004 and $4,000 for the years 2005 to 2007. (This also applies to annual contribution limits for traditional IRAs.) Under the provisions of the 1997 act, Roth IRA limits are reduced for couples whose income exceeds $150,000 ($95,000 for single filers). The eligibility to contribute the full annual limit is phased out between $150,000 and $160,000 for married taxpayers filing jointly and between $95,000 and $110,000 for single filers. After those limits, a person is not eligible for a Roth IRA. The annual contribution limit is also reduced by the amount of contributions made to any other IRAs. There is a 6 percent tax on excess contributions to a Roth IRA.

Roth IRAs can be rolled over tax-free to other Roth IRAs. The rollover is subject to the rollover rules for an ordinary IRA. An ordinary IRA can also be rolled over to a Roth IRA, but only if the taxpayer meets the following conditions: The taxpayer's adjusted gross income for the tax year cannot exceed $100,000, and the taxpayer cannot be married and filing separately. Roth IRAs are not subject to the age 70½ required distribution rules that apply to traditional IRAs.

A BETTER RETIREMENT PLAN

I strongly feel there is a better approach to achieve tax-free income for retirement or other purposes, as well as to create indirect tax-favored benefits on the cash contributions—without all of the restrictions and rules attached to qualified plans.

When I contribute money to my non-qualified retirement fund, there is virtually no restriction on how much I can invest each year. During prosperous years, I can contribute generously; during the lean years, I don't have to contribute anything. In fact, I can withdraw money if needed, without IRS penalties, and I am not obligated to put the money back. As a homeowner, I also structure my retirement planning to get indirect tax deductions on my contribution amounts. Most important, my retirement funds accumulate tax-free, and I can access the funds whenever I want on a tax-free basis (including the interest or gain) without having to wait until I am 59½. If I don't use up my retirement funds before I pass away, they blossom in value and transfer free of income tax to my heirs. To understand how to receive tax-favored benefits during all four phases of retirement planning—contribution, accumulation, distribution, and transfer—please read every chapter of this book!

WHAT GOES UP . . . WILL KEEP GOING UP

I have taught financial strategy seminars for more than thirty years. Often I ask my audience, "How many of you think that future tax rates are going to be lower?" Nobody raises a hand. I then ask if anyone thinks rates will remain the same. Again, no hands go up. Finally, I ask, "How many think that future tax rates are going to be higher?" The entire audience raises their hands in unison.

Why do we, as Americans, believe this to be so? It's because of the congressional track record over the past several decades. But wait a minute, I thought Congress, under the 2001 and 2003 tax acts, just lowered taxes. Yes, it did. But you and I know that these were temporary measures designed to stimulate the economy so tax revenue could be generated to finance new expenditures, such as prescription drugs for seniors and the war on terrorism. The government giveth, and it taketh away.

TAX LAWS THAT IMPACT YOU

When the 1986 Tax Reform Act was passed to simplify our taxing structure, the books containing the tax code ended up being twice as thick. Several tax brackets prior to 1986 were reduced and simplified to two brackets: a 15 and a 28 percent bracket. Since 1986, we have migrated back to seven different tax brackets. The effective tax the average American paid prior to 1986 was 13 percent of income. Today it approximates 20 percent, due to fewer allowable deductions.

The 2001 act made substantial modifications to estate taxes, retirement arrangements, and individual taxes. Estate tax, often referred to as the inheritance tax, is the tax liability owing on assets when they are transferred to non-spousal heirs. Prior to the 2001 act, federal estate and gift transfer taxes had a death-time transfer exemption of $675,000. For estates valued in excess of $675,000, the estate tax basically started at 37 percent and topped out at 55 percent for estates in excess of $3 million. The applicable exemption was scheduled to increase gradually until it reached $1 million in 2006.

The most important thing to understand under the 2001 act is that all the tax changes in the act will "sunset," or end, on December 31, 2010. In other words, the "sunset" restores the law in 2011 to the law as it existed before the act was signed. That is why it is important for us to understand the laws as they existed in 2001.

Under the 2001 act, the unified credit exemption amount (that part of an estate that is exempt from estate tax) is increased to $1 million for years 2002 and 2003, $1,500,000 million for years 2004 and 2005, $2 million for years 2006 through 2008, and $3,500,000 million in 2009. The estate tax is then repealed in year 2010, and the old 2000 tax law is reinstated on January 1, 2011!

We call this the big tease. If Congress doesn't do anything about the sunset provision, a lot of elderly wealthy may conveniently plan their demise (or have it planned by their heirs) in 2010! The point I want to make is that when it comes to estate planning, everybody seems to focus on tax savings as billions of dollars are transferred from wealthy individuals to the next generation. However, there is a trade-off that most people do not realize.

After repeal of the estate transfer taxes, the current law providing a step-up in basis to fair market value will also be repealed. This means that inherited appreciated assets may be subject to increased capital gains taxes when sold. For example, assume your parents bought some stock or a piece of real estate for $10,000, held on to it for several years, and when they passed away, it was worth $100,000. A step-up in basis means that when you inherited the asset, you didn't have to pay tax on the gain from $10,000 to $100,000. You would only have to pay tax on any gain above $100,000 if you sold it later. Your new basis for tax purposes is stepped up to the fair market value at the time it was inherited.

It is estimated that only about 1 percent of American taxpayers will directly benefit from the repeal of the estate tax. However, the repeal of the current law providing a step-up in basis to fair market value is estimated to generate far more tax revenue than will be given up with the repeal of the estate tax. This would come at the expense of a much broader base of taxpayers than just the top 1 percent comprised of the wealthiest individuals. Hence, again, the government giveth, and it taketh away!

If we are convinced, then, that future tax rates will likely be higher than today's, does it make sense to defer or postpone paying tax to the future?

WHAT ABOUT EMPLOYER MATCHING BENEFITS?

Employers often match contribution amounts on qualified plans to create "golden handcuffs"—ties designed to help keep employees loyal to the company by preparing for their future retirement. Matching benefits may be useful for employees, but people need to examine the opportunity carefully, as these benefits have their limits.

Often people contribute the maximum amount allowed under law on their 401(k)s or other qualified plans, while their employer matches between 50 and 100 cents on the dollar—but only on the first 4, 5, or 6 percent of their income. Sometimes an employer will contribute a percentage of an employee's income to a company-sponsored 401(k) regardless of whether the employee is contributing anything. True matching is where an employer agrees to match dollar for dollar on a certain percentage of an employee's contributions. To take advantage of matching, it is usually in the best interest of the employee to contribute at the least the amount or percentage required to qualify for the full matching benefit. However, I have found many employees contribute beyond that, thinking it is the best way to save for retirement.

As an employee, should you contribute not only up to but over the amount being matched by your employer? This is really a function of yield and performance on the particular portfolio in which the 401(k) (or other qualified plan) is invested. If the same yield can be achieved in a non-qualified personal retirement account that is tax-free during the harvest, *I* would generally advise an employee to contribute to a qualified plan only up to the amount matched by the employer. It is most advantageous when the employer offers at least a 50 percent matching benefit. This is only my general rule of thumb and does not apply in all circumstances.

Simply speaking, if you contribute a dollar and it is matched 50 cents on that dollar, you now have $1.50 earning interest. The illusion is that you are receiving a 50 percent return on your money. It's true that the principal is increased 50 percent, but the interest rate from that point forward is whatever the portfolio earns. As the account continues to compound and grow, you do not receive an annual 50 percent increase on the account. The 50 percent increase is only on the seed money deposited into the account. If you could withdraw your money without incurring a 10 percent penalty immediately after it was contributed, and the matching was immediately vested in a 33.3 percent tax bracket, you would pay out in taxes the 50 cents the employer contributed. In this example, your employer is more or less paying the portion you will end up having to pay in tax. Assuming the account continues to grow, the tax liability will also grow. Still, employer matching can be an attractive part of a retirement plan if used properly and understood.

I generally recommend that, *all other things being equal, an employee should not contribute any funds to a qualified plan beyond the amount required to receive matching contributions by the employer.* If you contribute to a qualified plan, you should understand all strings attached and know that any distributions on the back end, or harvest years, will be fully subject to federal and state income tax.

EMPLOYER AND EMPLOYEE EDUCATION IS CRITICAL

From the industrial age up until the information age, the responsibility for an individual's retirement was thought to be the employer's. As more entrepreneurs have entered the marketplace, this responsibility is resting more with the individual. I have always believed that security is found in the individual and his unique abilities—not in the job and benefits offered by an employer.

Employers who want to offer benefits should be willing to match retire-

ment savings whether the employee contributes to a qualified or a non-qualified plan. But first, employers need to be educated on the options, understanding that their contributions can be deductible for both qualified and non-qualified plans.

Employers should then help educate employees through retirement planning seminars where employees can learn the difference between qualified and non-qualified plans. Until this education takes place, the predominant approach will continue to be matching funds on only qualified plans.

QUALIFIED PLANS AND SOCIAL SECURITY BENEFITS

In chapter 2, we discussed the three types of income the IRS taxes: earned income, passive income, and portfolio income. Under current law, having portfolio or passive income does not directly reduce the amount of your Social Security benefits. Currently, retiree Social Security recipients between the ages of 62 and 65 have limits on what they can earn before experiencing a reduction in benefits. After age 65, Social Security recipients can have unlimited earned, passive, or portfolio income without experiencing a direct reduction in benefits. However, up to 85 percent of Social Security benefits may be subject to income taxation depending on a beneficiary's tax filing status and "provisional income." For most people, provisional income is adjusted gross income, plus tax-exempt income, plus one-half of Social Security income benefits.

All of this could change in the future (and likely will). If it does, I don't believe it will be for the better. I would not be surprised to see the return of something similar to the "success tax" that existed before the 1997 Taxpayer Relief Act. The success tax was a special 15 percent excise tax assessed when people were deemed too successful in accumulating money for their retirement. In other words, directly or indirectly, we could be penalized in extra tax or reduced Social Security benefits if we have saved money prudently and have excessive earned, passive, or portfolio income during our retirement.

The federal government's plight is that when Social Security was first established, there were approximately sixty workers to every one recipient of Social Security benefits. Not many years later, when benefits were expanded, there were about fifteen workers to every recipient of Social Security. In the 1980s, that ratio reduced to six workers to every recipient. Currently, there are approximately three workers to every recipient. *As baby boomers begin to retire in 2006, America will shortly arrive at the point of two people pulling the wagon for every one person riding in it!* In other words, two-thirds of American citizens will be providing for the other third—many of whom contributed faithfully for years—because there is not sufficient cash on hand to pay the benefits without new contributions from current workers. The younger generation replacing baby boomers consists of a smaller workforce. They will have to earn the income taxed for Social Security so it can provide benefits for an expanding group of retired individuals who are living longer. We may witness the Social Security system in serious trouble.

YOUR FINANCIAL CRYSTAL BALL

How would you define financial independence? The most common response I get is, "when I have enough money tucked away in a stable environment that would indefinitely produce the monthly income I'm accustomed to." So let's use that definition as a minimum standard to figure out how much of a retirement nest egg you might need to accumulate.

You can calculate what the cost of living may be at your retirement age by using the Rule of 72. The Rule of 72 is generally used to calculate the number of years it takes to double invested money. Applied that way, you take the interest rate, divide it into 72, and the result is the number of years it will take to double your money. This formula, requiring only simple arithmetic, assumes that no additional principal is added to the investment over the years it is held. For example, the result of 72 divided by 8 indicates that at an 8 percent interest rate, you will double your money every nine years. If you can earn 10 percent interest, your money will double about every seven years.

Let's assume you are retiring today and could make ends meet with a $3,000-a-month income. If you want to know how much you would need thirty years from now to buy the same loaves of bread or gallons of gasoline at a 2 percent average inflation rate, you divide 72 by 2. That tells you the cost of living will double approximately every thirty-six years. So, assuming a 2 percent average annual inflation rate, you would need $6,000 a month thirty-six years from now to buy the same amount of goods and services you can get today for $3,000 a month. If I had a $1-million nest egg accumulated, a 7.2 percent return on it would generate $72,000 a year, or $6,000 per month indefinitely.

Fortunately, during the 1990s up to the publication of this book, inflation has been very low. But during the 1970s and early 1980s, we experienced a high rate of inflation into the double digits. So to be safe, let's assume an average inflation rate of 5 percent for the next thirty years—72 divided by 5 tells us that the cost of living at 5 percent inflation will double approximately every fifteen years. So you would need $6,000 a month fifteen years from now and $12,000 a month thirty years from now to buy the same amount of goods and services you can get today for $3,000 a month.

So how much would you need to accumulate in a retirement nest egg to generate $12,000 a month in tomorrow's dollars? Simply take $12,000 per month times twelve months, which equals $144,000 in annual income. Assuming you could earn an average of 8 percent return on your retirement accounts, you would need $1,800,000 ($144,000 ÷ 8%) to generate $12,000 a month. This is an interest-only solution, where you would not deplete your principal of $1,800,000, which might be helpful to hedge against cost-of-living increases.

How much would you need to set aside each year if you were earning an average of 8 percent interest to accumulate $1,800,000 in thirty years? A financial calculator comes in handy here. Enter $1,800,000 as the future value, 8 percent as the interest rate, and 30 as the number of years, and then solve for the annual payment. The answer is

$14,712. That is how much you would need to invest earning 8 percent per year to accumulate $1,800,000 by year 30. Assuming you could earn 10 percent interest, you would need to set aside only $9,948 a year. And at 12 percent interest, you would need to set aside only $6,660 per year.

As a general rule of thumb, I usually counsel my younger clients, who have at least thirty-five years in which to contribute to retirement plans, to set aside a minimum of 10 percent of their income annually. If they manage their investments and savings wisely, 10 percent of their income set aside annually at a moderate rate of return (8 to 10 percent) should produce a retirement income thirty-five years down the road that would be comparable to the standard of living enjoyed during their earning years. If they want to enjoy a higher standard of living than their earning years or if they want to retire earlier, it would behoove them to set aside 15 or 20 percent of their income.

The most important factor is to choose investments that will give you tax-favored benefits during the accumulation, distribution, and transfer phases of retirement planning. It's better to pay tax on the price of the seed and then later to enjoy the harvest tax-free. If you are convinced future tax rates will likely be higher, don't delay the inevitable—postponing taxes will usually increase taxes. Optimally, you should structure your investments to receive tax-favored treatment during all four phases of retirement planning. To understand how, read on!

CONCEPTS COVERED IN CHAPTER 3

- Most Americans who have saved for retirement will find themselves in a tax bracket at least as high as—if not higher than—during their earning years.
- Traditional qualified plans allow the taxpayer to contribute money with pre-tax dollars or receive a tax deduction for the amount contributed.

- Traditional qualified plans include IRAs, 401(k)s, TSAs, 403(b)s, 457s, pension plans, and profit-sharing plans.
- *Qualified plans defer taxes, which results in increasing tax liability.*
- The four phases of retirement planning are the contribution, accumulation, distribution, and transfer phases.
- You can establish a non-qualified retirement planning alternative (funded with after-tax dollars) with tax-favored treatment during the accumulation, distribution, and transfer phases.
- *If future tax rates will likely be higher, why delay the inevitable?*
- All tax changes in the 2001 tax act will end on December 31, 2010.
- If estate transfer taxes are repealed, the current law providing a step-up in basis to fair market value will likely also be repealed.
- *Matching benefits may be useful for employees, but people need to examine the opportunity carefully—benefits have their limits.*
- Employers who want to offer benefits should be willing to match retirement savings in either a qualified or a non-qualified plan.
- The younger generation will have to earn the income taxed for Social Security so it can provide benefits for retiring baby boomers.
- The Rule of 72 is used to calculate the number of years it takes to double invested money.
- At a 5 percent inflation rate, the cost of living will double every fifteen years, so it would require a $12,000 monthly income thirty years from now to have the same purchasing power that $3,000 has today.
- Depending on the lifestyle you desire in retirement, *you should put 10 to 20 percent of your income in long-term investments.*

CHAPTER 4

Solve Your IRA/401(k) Dilemma

Qualified plans, such as IRAs and 401(k)s, do *not* provide the most attractive retirement benefits

BEFORE WE GO ANY FURTHER, stop and play a game with me for a moment:

1. Pick any number between 1 and 10.
2. Now double that number.
3. Next, add 8 to that number.
4. Now divide that number by 2.
5. Subtract the number you started with from that number.
6. Now take your resulting number from this exercise and select the corresponding letter of the alphabet that matches this number. For example, if the resulting number was 1, the corresponding letter would be A; if it was 2, the corresponding letter would be B; if it was 3, the corresponding letter would be C; and so on.
7. Now pick a country in the world that starts with that letter.
8. Take the next letter of the alphabet that comes after that letter and choose a typical zoo animal that starts with that letter.

9.   Finally, pick a logical color for that animal.

When I have an audience do this exercise, I know exactly what about 80 percent of them will come up with for their answers. Let's see if you are among the majority. Decipher the following three words that are spelled backward: *kramneD, tnahpele, yarg*. Are those the three words you thought of? How did I do that? I simply created predictability.

Retirement planning strategies are no different. Predictably, qualified retirement plans motivate the majority of people to invest in order to get tax-favored treatment during the contribution and accumulation phases of retirement planning. Later, when traditional qualified plans are liquidated and used for retirement, they produce the taxable results that the government predicted—and intended. It always sounds better to us when we are shown the tax breaks we can get immediately. But *I maintain it doesn't make sense to postpone tax for some perceived advantage in the future.*

A MATHEMATICAL RIDDLE

Let's try another exercise. Follow closely as I unfold a story problem. Three men went on a fishing trip. After a wonderful first day of fishing, they stopped at a small lodge to stay for the night. When they checked in, the clerk quoted them $30 for the room. So each of the three men shelled out $10 for a total of $30. So far so good? As they were getting settled in their room, the clerk discovered that he had overcharged the men. The room was only $25 per night, not $30. He promptly gave five one-dollar bills to the bellboy and sent him to the men's room to refund the overcharge. The bellboy wasn't honest and started wondering how the three men would split up the $5 evenly. He ended up telling the men they were overcharged $3 and gave a dollar back to each of the men, keeping $2 for himself. Got it? Okay. Let's do an accounting. Each man paid $10 originally and each got back a dollar, meaning that each man actually paid $9 for the room, right? So three men times $9 equals $27, plus the $2 the bellboy kept, equals $29. Where is the extra dollar to equal $30? Think about it for a while. I'll disclose the answer later.

WHY DELAY THE INEVITABLE?

In chapter 3, you learned that retirement affects the amount of income taxes you pay. I dispelled the myth-conception that you are likely to be in a lower tax bracket when you retire than when employed. Let's continue to destroy the myth that qualified plans such as IRAs and 401(k)s provide the most attractive retirement benefits. The reality is that other, *non-qualified* retirement vehicles may provide greater net spendable retirement income. In chapters 6 to 8, you will learn that proper equity management can provide indirect deductions that may be comparable to qualified retirement plan contributions. Chapters 10 and 11 will illustrate how this strategy can allow you to have tax-free retirement income. So I ask, "Why delay the inevitable?" Deferred taxes usually result in an increase in taxes. I'll reemphasize this by using another illustration.

Assume you calculate that you need an extra $30,000 per year of net spendable income at retirement to meet your objectives. Let's also assume you will retire about twenty-five years from now. In a 33.3 percent tax bracket, you will need additional gross earnings of $45,000 per year to net $30,000 ($45,000 – 33.3% = $30,000). In other words, with $45,000 of supplemental retirement income, you would incur an annual tax liability of $15,000 and end up with only $30,000 to spend. You meet with a financial planner. Your planner feels you can average about 7.5 percent annual return on your retirement plan contributions. For tax years 2005 through 2007, the maximum contribution limit to a traditional IRA is $4,000. If both you and your spouse contribute $4,000 each for a total of $8,000 per year that earns 7.5 percent for twenty-five years and four months, your account balance at the end of that period will be approximately $600,000.

If you continued to earn 7.5 percent interest throughout your retirement, and you took out all of your interest earnings each year, $600,000 would generate $45,000 per year of annual income ($600,000 x 7.5% = $45,000). But each year, in a 33.3 percent tax bracket, you pay $15,000 in combined federal and state tax. This supplemental income forces you to pay income tax on up to 85 percent of your Social Security benefits. You suddenly realize you saved $2,666 in tax for each of the twenty-five years you contributed $8,000 ($8,000 x 33.3%), for a total of $66,650 (25 x $2,666). However, you will pay back every dollar you saved in tax on twenty-five years of contributions during the first four and a half years of retirement (4.5 x $15,000 = $67,500). If you live twenty-two years after retiring, you'll potentially pay back five times more in taxes during the distribution phase than you saved in taxes during the contribution phase.

So what are better options? First, we must understand the various sources we have to obtain money. Then we can explore the various savings and investment options that will generate the greatest results.

HOW DO WE GET MONEY?

Human beings basically have four sources of money:

- People at work
- Money at work
- Other people's money (OPM)
- Charity

As much as we think we're in control of our ability to earn money by working, there are times due to disability or incapacity that earning money may be difficult, if not impossible. Money at work is far more dependable, especially when invested wisely. Money can grow with interest, without requiring rest, 365 days a year. Self-made millionaires usually master the art of putting money to work. Most wealthy people with a substantial financial net worth also employ the use of OPM (other people's money). I suppose there are two ways to use other people's money: You can borrow it and pay yearly, or steal it and pay dearly. I recommend the former. Obviously, the legitimate use of OPM, maintaining utmost honesty and integrity, is a far better path.

In chapters 6 to 8, I'll show you how to use OPM to amass a fortune by simply doing what banks and credit unions do. As far as charity is concerned, it is usually more rewarding to be on the giving end than on the receiving end. It doesn't require much to be charitable. Your overall harvests in life will be greater when your time and talents are shared with others, in addition to any financial contributions. Giving at least 10 percent of your human, intellectual, and financial assets for charitable purposes will create the most enduring true wealth. I'll discuss this in more detail in chapter 12. For now, let's focus on different alternatives for saving and investing money from a tax standpoint.

TAXES AND THE FIVE SAVINGS OPTIONS

There are five basic options American taxpayers have with regard to tax treatment on savings. The differences in long-term results are dramatic, so it's important to understand them thoroughly. Generally, whenever people work to earn money, it is subject to income taxation. When money is put to work, it can be structured to be subject to taxation or not subject to taxation. When borrowing money, there are tax advantages that can make money at work perform better through safe leverage. Let's study each of the five options carefully.

Before doing so, let's make sure you thoroughly understand the difference between using 66.66-cent (after tax) dollars and 100-cent (before tax) dollars when saving, investing, or consuming. If you, as a taxpayer in a 33.3 percent tax bracket, want to buy an automobile that costs $20,000, you have to allocate $30,000 of gross income, then pay $10,000 (33.3 percent) in taxes, to net $20,000 to purchase the vehicle. In other words, you are forced to use 66.66-cent after-tax dollars much of the time in order to spend your money. The same is true when you want to save or invest money in traditional savings accounts and investments. When you can deposit money in investments that allow you to use pre-tax dollars or you get to deduct the contribution from your gross income on your tax return, you are in essence using 100-cent dollars.

Option 1

You can save or invest after-tax dollars that you earned by working (66.66-cent dollars in a 33.3 percent tax bracket) in financial instruments that are taxed as interest is earned, dividends are paid, or capital gains are realized. Traditional savings accounts that are non-qualified, such as passbook savings, money market accounts, and certificates of deposit, usually fall into this category of taxation. Non-qualified mutual fund accounts may also fall into this category. If you invest in stocks and bonds or even real estate under a non-qualified situation, it is usually done with after-tax dollars, and the dividends, interest, capital gains, or rental income is taxed as earned or realized.

The tax liability due on the increase is either on income categorized as portfolio income (interest and dividends) or passive income (rents and leases). As explained earlier, under recent tax reform, capital gains tax is calculated at a lower rate than income tax and is not payable until the gain is realized by selling the asset with a profit over the cost or basis.

Depending on the rate of return, it may take fifteen years before we break even with what we have to earn or allocate when using 66.66-cent after-tax dollars on the front end and paying tax on the increase as we go. In other words, we may have to work to earn an additional gross of $6,000, paying income tax of 33.3 percent ($2,000), to net $4,000 to invest. What's more, $4,000 invested every year at a 9 percent taxable interest rate will result in a net after-tax yield of only 6 percent. Similarly, $4,000 invested each year at a net return of 6 percent will grow to $98,690 in fifteen years. Compare that result to the fact that you had to work to earn $6,000 of annual taxable income for fifteen years, totaling $90,000 ($6,000 x 15), to come out ahead by only $8,690!

When we look at it that way, we earned the equivalent of only 1.16 percent interest compounded annually, the whole time we thought we were earning 9 percent—because we were investing after-tax seed money and paying tax on interest as we went. In this example, if you could earn only 6 percent return (a net of 4 percent after-tax), it would be twenty years before a net after-tax investment of $4,000 breaks even with what you had to earn by working twenty years ($6,000/yr x 20 yrs) to accumulate a nest egg of approximately $124,000.

Therefore, option 1 can be a very discouraging approach. In my opinion, it is the worst way to save and invest, yet it is the most common method used in America.

To make a comparison among all five options, let's use a uniform example. Let's assume we have a cumulative total of $150,000 of our gross income over a certain number of years to allocate to long-term savings. For the sake of simplicity, I'm going to assume we have all $150,000 at the very start as a onetime lump sum. We have the choice on the front end of our investments to use either 66.66-cent after-tax dollars or 100-cent before-tax dollars, depending upon which of the five savings options we choose. We'll assume a 7.2 percent return on all investments.

Under option 1 (figure 4.1), our total of $150,000 came from gross income we received by working, so we had to pay tax on the front end in the amount of $50,000 (33.3 percent) in order to have $100,000 to save or invest. We know by the Rule of 72 that if we earn 7.2 percent interest, our account will double in ten years. However, if we have to pay tax on our yearly increase, we will end up with a net of only $159,816 (column 4, year 10, in figure 4.1). After ten years, assume we want to begin taking out our annual interest earnings to supplement our other income. If we keep earning 7.2 percent taxable interest, we would have $11,507 of annual interest income. However, we would have to pay 33.3 percent tax on that interest income each year, or $3,835. So we would realize a net of only $7,672 in spendable annual income.

Fig. 4.1	$150,000 OF CUMULATIVE GROSS INCOME ALLOCATED TO LONG-TERM SAVINGS

OPTION 1:

Invest After-Tax Dollars (66.66 Cents in a 33.33% Tax Bracket) in Financial Instruments Earning 7.2% that are Taxed as Earned

Gross: $150,000
- [$50,000]   Less: 33.3% Tax
$100,000   Net to Invest

Year	Gross Interest Earned [1]	Tax Liability at 33.33% [2]	Net Interest Earned [3]	Year End Balance [4]
1	$7,200	$2,400	$4,800	$104,800
2	$7,546	$2,515	$5,031	$109,831
3	$7,908	$2,636	$5,272	$115,103
4	$8,287	$2,762	$5,525	$120,628
5	$8,685	$2,895	$5,790	$126,418
6	$9,102	$3,034	$6,068	$132,486
7	$9,540	$3,180	$6,360	$138,846
8	$9,997	$3,332	$6,665	$145,511
9	$10,477	$3,492	$6,985	$152,496
10	$10,980	$3,660	$7,320	$159,816

Convert to Annual Income:

$159,816   10 Year Total Account Value
x   7.2%   Annual Interest Income

$11,507   Annual Taxable Income
[$3,835]   Less: Annual Tax Liability at 33.3%

$7,672   **Net Spendable Annual Income**

Option 2

You can save or invest after-tax dollars in investments that accumulate tax-deferred and pay taxes on the gain when later realized.

Typical investments in this category include real estate that is not leveraged and perhaps some stock or mutual funds for which there are no dividends but grow only through unrealized capital gains until the asset is sold. Non-qualified deferred annuities also fall into this category.

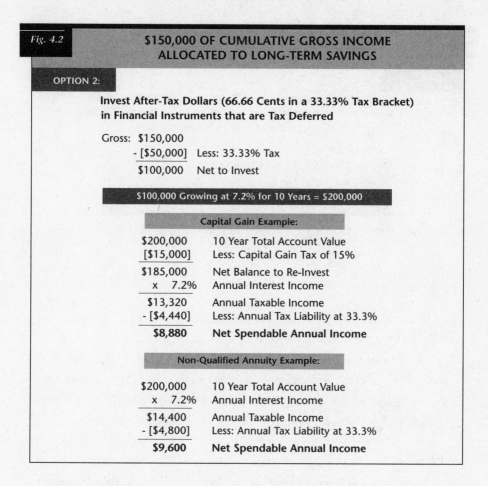

Fig. 4.2

$150,000 OF CUMULATIVE GROSS INCOME ALLOCATED TO LONG-TERM SAVINGS

OPTION 2:

Invest After-Tax Dollars (66.66 Cents in a 33.33% Tax Bracket) in Financial Instruments that are Tax Deferred

Gross: $150,000
       - [$50,000]   Less: 33.33% Tax
         $100,000   Net to Invest

$100,000 Growing at 7.2% for 10 Years = $200,000

Capital Gain Example:

$200,000	10 Year Total Account Value
[$15,000]	Less: Capital Gain Tax of 15%
$185,000	Net Balance to Re-Invest
x 7.2%	Annual Interest Income
$13,320	Annual Taxable Income
- [$4,440]	Less: Annual Tax Liability at 33.3%
$8,880	**Net Spendable Annual Income**

Non-Qualified Annuity Example:

$200,000	10 Year Total Account Value
x 7.2%	Annual Interest Income
$14,400	Annual Taxable Income
- [$4,800]	Less: Annual Tax Liability at 33.3%
$9,600	**Net Spendable Annual Income**

Under option 2 (figure 4.2), we invest the net $100,000 (66.66-cent after-tax dollars) in an investment that is tax-deferred. So the $100,000 doubles to $200,000 at 7.2 percent in ten years. If we now realize our profits, we may owe $15,000 in capital gains tax on the $100,000 gain we made. This would leave us a net of $185,000 assuming a 15 percent capital gains tax rate. If this were now invested in an account earning 7.2 percent taxable interest, it would generate an interest income of $13,320 each year indefinitely. With a tax liability each year on that interest in the amount of $4,440, we would realize a net spendable income of $8,880.

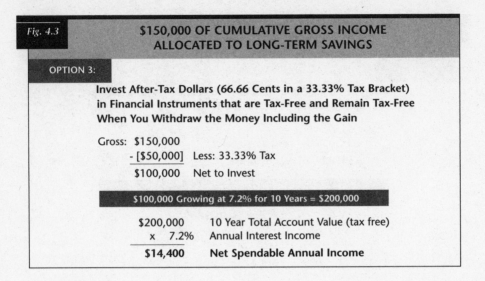

Fig. 4.3

$150,000 OF CUMULATIVE GROSS INCOME ALLOCATED TO LONG-TERM SAVINGS

OPTION 3:

Invest After-Tax Dollars (66.66 Cents in a 33.33% Tax Bracket) in Financial Instruments that are Tax-Free and Remain Tax-Free When You Withdraw the Money Including the Gain

Gross: $150,000
          - [$50,000]   Less: 33.33% Tax
          $100,000   Net to Invest

$100,000 Growing at 7.2% for 10 Years = $200,000

$200,000   10 Year Total Account Value (tax free)
x   7.2%   Annual Interest Income
$14,400   **Net Spendable Annual Income**

If the $100,000 grew to $200,000 in a non-qualified deferred annuity and it generated 7.2 percent of annual interest income, the gross annual interest would be $14,400 ($200,000 x 7.2%). This income would be fully taxable because annuities receive LIFO (last in, first out) tax treatment, as I will explain in chapter 9. After paying a 33.3 percent tax of $4,800 each year, the net income would be $9,600.

Option 3

You can save or invest after-tax dollars in investments that accumulate tax-free and also use the money tax-free later, including the gain you made. These types of investments include Roth IRAs and insurance contracts that are properly structured and used (chapters 10 and 11).

Under option 3 (figure 4.3), we invest the net $100,000 (66.66-cent after-tax dollars) in an investment that is tax-free during the accumulation phase. So the $100,000 doubles to $200,000 at 7.2 percent interest in ten years. However, now we also get to enjoy the gain and income it can generate tax-free. Therefore, $200,000 earning 7.2 percent annually gives us a tax-free, net spendable income of $14,400 per year indefinitely!

Fig. 4.4	$150,000 OF CUMULATIVE GROSS INCOME ALLOCATED TO LONG-TERM SAVINGS

OPTION 4:

Invest Pre-Tax or Tax-Deductible Dollars in Financial Instruments that are Tax-Deferred and then Later are Fully Taxable

Gross: $150,000

[$0]	No Tax
$150,000	Net to Invest

$150,000 Growing at 7.2% for 10 Years = $300,000

Lump Sum Distribution Example:

$300,000	10 Year Total Account Value
- [100,000]	Less: Tax of 33.33%
$200,000	**Net After-Tax Value**

Interest Only Example:

$300,000	10 Year Total Account Value
x 7.2%	Annual Interest Income
21,600	Annual Taxable Income
- [7,200]	Less: Annual Tax Liability at 33.33%
$14,400	**Net Spendable Annual Income**

Option 4

You can save or invest 100-cent pre-tax or tax-deductible dollars in investments that accumulate tax-deferred, then later when you use the money, it is fully taxable, including the basis you invested. Investments such as traditional IRAs, 401(k)s, and other qualified plans fall into this category.

Under option 4 (figure 4.4), we get to use 100-cent dollars. So the full $150,000 can be invested on the front end. At 7.2 percent interest, this investment doubles to $300,000 in ten years. However, if we withdraw that money, we now have to pay tax on the full $300,000. If we were still in a 33.3 percent tax bracket, we would net only $200,000 ($300,000 – $100,000 = $200,000). Instead, if we decide to take 7.2 percent (our annual interest earnings) of income each year thereafter from our IRA account worth $300,000, it would generate $21,600 of taxable income, leaving us a net of $14,400 after tax ($21,600 less 33.3 percent).

Hold on! Did you notice that all things being equal, there is *no difference* between the net results of options 3 and 4? Because I am not confident that in real life all things will be equal—in fact, I think tax rates will be higher later, especially if I accumulate a respectable nest egg—I would choose option 3 over option 4. Let me have my money tax-free during the harvest years of my life.

But let's see if we can have our cake and eat it too.

Option 5

You can use 100-cent dollars because of indirect tax deductions that can be created using the strategies contained in chapters 6 to 8. You can also enjoy tax-free accumulation and tax-free use of the money using the investment vehicles explained in chapters 9 to 11. Not only that, but you can transfer any remaining funds to your heirs tax-free if you use properly structured insurance contracts.

Under option 5 (figure 4.5), we can use up to 100-cent dollars if we are able to get indirect tax deductions due to mortgage interest offsets. If we succeed in offsetting all our contributions with this strategy, the full $150,000 would be available to save or invest on the front end. By using tax-advantaged capital accumulation vehicles as in option 3, we can have tax-favored treatment for all four phases (contribution, accumulation, distribution, and transfer) of our non-qualified retirement plan (figure 4.6). Thus, $150,000 would double to $300,000 at 7.2 percent interest for ten years. If we can now take tax-free income at 7.2 percent on $300,000, it generates $21,600 of net spendable income.

As we review each of the five options, note that option 5 almost tripled the net spendable income that option 1 generated. It more than doubled the net spendable income option 2 generated. Option 5 also generated 50 percent greater net spendable retirement income than options 3 and 4.

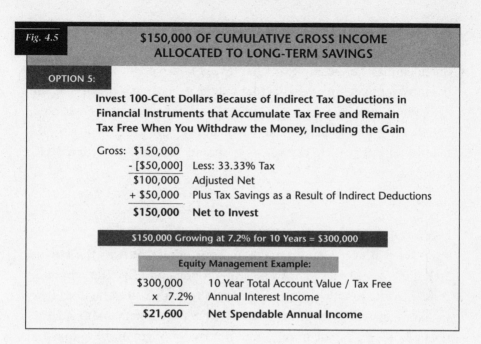

Fig. 4.5

**$150,000 OF CUMULATIVE GROSS INCOME
ALLOCATED TO LONG-TERM SAVINGS**

OPTION 5:

**Invest 100-Cent Dollars Because of Indirect Tax Deductions in
Financial Instruments that Accumulate Tax Free and Remain
Tax Free When You Withdraw the Money, Including the Gain**

Gross: $150,000
- [$50,000]   Less: 33.33% Tax
$100,000   Adjusted Net
+ $50,000   Plus Tax Savings as a Result of Indirect Deductions
$150,000   Net to Invest

$150,000 Growing at 7.2% for 10 Years = $300,000

Equity Management Example:

$300,000   10 Year Total Account Value / Tax Free
x   7.2%   Annual Interest Income
$21,600   Net Spendable Annual Income

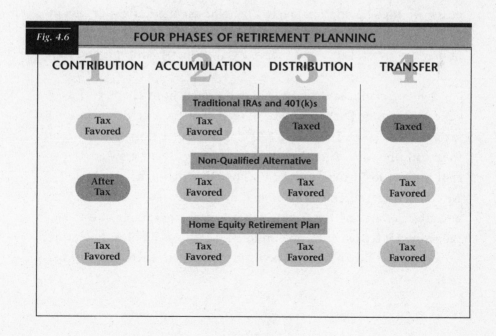

Fig. 4.6   **FOUR PHASES OF RETIREMENT PLANNING**

CONTRIBUTION	ACCUMULATION	DISTRIBUTION	TRANSFER
1	2	3	4

Traditional IRAs and 401(k)s

| Tax Favored | Tax Favored | Taxed | Taxed |

Non-Qualified Alternative

| After Tax | Tax Favored | Tax Favored | Tax Favored |

Home Equity Retirement Plan

| Tax Favored | Tax Favored | Tax Favored | Tax Favored |

After illustrating these dramatic differences, let me emphasize that there are several factors related to each of these options that create real-life dilemmas. For example, in chapter 3, I talked about the advantage of employer matching benefits that may make option 4 perform equal to option 5. It's important to conduct a careful analysis to determine whether it is wise to participate in a qualified plan. There is no simple, blanket rule that dictates "yes, you should" or "no, you shouldn't" participate.

HAVE YOUR CAKE AND EAT IT TOO

"Did you ever have to make up your mind?" Just as the Lovin' Spoonful's song lyrics say, "to pick up on one and leave the other behind"? In the song, a young man couldn't decide whom he liked better between two girls he was dating who were sisters. With a little poetic license, I might surmise he's not the only guy to have loved a "Kate" and "Edith." It's not so rare for the love-struck to want to marry both and have their Kate and Edith too.

Okay, I'll admit some puns are better left unintended, but seriously; we love having tax-favored benefits on the harvest of our investments, but we still would love tax-favored benefits on the seed money we invest. Let's see if there's a way to marry concepts and have it all.

Remember Jim and Mary Followthecrowd from chapter 3? They were setting aside $6,000 per year in IRAs or 401(k)s, getting an annual tax break of $2,000. They saved $70,000 in tax over thirty-five years on their contributions. Their $6,000-per-year investment grew at 7.5 percent interest to $1 million over that period. But when they started to withdraw their retirement income, they pulled out $75,000 each year, and after tax they netted only $50,000. This is an example of someone preparing for retirement using option 4. Let's take a look at how using option 5 would increase net spendable retirement income by 50 percent.

AN ENLIGHTENED APPROACH

Bob and Martha Enlightened represent an atypical couple that broke away from the crowd at age 30. Let's assume Bob and Martha have a home valued at $200,000 with a mortgage balance owing of $80,000. The remaining $120,000 represents the equity in their property. Most mortgage lenders will loan at least 80 percent of the value of a home on a first-mortgage basis with cash coming out to the homeowners. An 80 percent loan-to-value ratio would be $160,000. Bob and Martha could refinance their home or use a second-mortgage equity line of credit to obtain the remaining $80,000 of borrowable equity. If they refinance with a first mortgage in the amount of $160,000, they will replace the $80,000 existing mortgage and end up with an additional $80,000 of excess cash or equity separated from the property.

In chapters 6 to 8, you'll learn that the primary reasons for refinancing or taking out a second mortgage are to increase liquidity, to increase safety, and to increase the rate of return on a home's equity. For the sake of simplicity, let's say Bob and Martha obtain the additional $80,000 of equity with an interest-only loan at 7.5 percent interest. If so, their annualized interest payment would be $6,000.

Bob and Martha would likely set aside a percent of their income for retirement objectives, which would increase their contributions each year over the thirty-five years. To avoid complexity in this illustration, let's just assume they were going to set aside no more than $6,000 a year, all the way to age 65. Let's also keep the original loan of $80,000 at 7.5 percent for the entire thirty-five years.

If Bob and Martha were incurring $6,000 of annual interest expense on an $80,000 loan, this would be equivalent to the same amount they were paying in annual IRA or 401(k) contributions. A $6,000 interest expense deduction on an itemized tax return has the same impact as a $6,000 qualified plan contribution. They are simply reflected in different sections of the return.

If Bob and Martha have a combined income of $70,000 with $6,000 of IRA/401(k) contributions, their taxable income is reduced to $64,000. In a 33.3 percent tax bracket, they effectively save 33.3 percent on the $6,000 they didn't have to report as income. That equals $2,000 in tax savings.

If they have a $6,000 interest deduction because of a mortgage, they will receive the same benefits on their taxes. Their income of $70,000 will be reduced to a taxable income of $64,000 by virtue of having the $6,000 deduction on Schedule A of their tax return. In essence, they save $2,000 of tax, and the mortgage really costs them only $4,000. A mortgage interest expense of $6,000 has the same effect for Bob and Martha as a $6,000 IRA or 401(k) retirement plan contribution. However, instead of a $6,000 contribution, they simply take $80,000 of dormant equity from their home and use it to pre-fund a retirement account in one fell swoop, via a lump sum contribution of $80,000.

At 7.5 percent interest (the same interest rate at which they borrowed), $80,000 will grow to $1,005,510 in the thirty-five years to their retirement age of 65. If they use an investment-grade life insurance contract (explained in chapters 10 and 11) generating an internal rate of return of 7.5 percent, they would have several advantages over an IRA or 401(k):

- They would be able to tap into their fund, if needed, at any time before age 59½ with no income tax penalty.
- They would be able to leave the funds in the policy as long as they wanted without being forced to begin withdrawals at age 70½.
- There would be no restrictions regarding the contribution percentage of their income they could put into the fund, because it is a non-qualified account.
- More important than any of these features is the ability to access income or cash flow on the back end during the harvest years of their retirement account without incurring any taxes on those distributions. (Money can be withdrawn tax-free under Sections 72(e) and 7702 of the Internal Revenue Code,

provided that all tax code and insurance company guidelines are met, as illustrated in chapter 11.)

Bob and Martha's retirement fund in the amount of $1,005,510 would allow them to make interest-only withdrawals at 7.5 percent in the amount of $75,413 per year. They would be able to use the entire $75,413 for spending and consumption during their retirement if they wanted. It would not be reportable anywhere on their federal tax return as earned income, passive income, or portfolio income. Therefore, it would not be subject to any type of tax under current tax law. In case you haven't noticed, $75,413 is 50 percent greater than the $50,000 of net after-tax income Jim and Mary Followthecrowd realized on their IRA/401(k) account! What's more, $75,413 of non-taxable income would be the same as receiving $113,120 of gross taxable income and having taxes reduce it by a third due. Finally, this source of Bob and Martha's retirement income would not affect or disqualify them from receiving their fair share of Social Security or Medicare benefits, and it wouldn't affect the taxability of Social Security income.

BUT DO I WANT A MORTGAGE DURING RETIREMENT?
Critics may say, "But Bob and Martha still have a mortgage on their home when they retire!" As you keep reading this book, you'll see why that will be a significant advantage. First, they could continue to enjoy the tax deductibility of $6,000-per-year interest payments because the net cost in a 33.3 percent tax bracket would still be only $4,000. Assuming they were still earning 7.5 percent tax-free interest on the $80,000 that would be required to pay off their mortgage, their annual earnings would be $6,000, resulting in a $2,000 annual profit. But suppose Bob and Martha arrive at a point where they don't care about maximizing their return; they could withdraw $80,000 tax-free from their $1,005,510 nest egg (created by managing the equity in their home) and pay off their mortgage.

However, it would behoove Bob and Martha to continue the

interest-only mortgage and deduct the true net cost of annual interest expense in the amount of $4,000 from their annual retirement income of $75,413. In that event, Bob and Martha Enlightened would net $71,413 in spendable income, versus the $50,000 Jim and Mary Followthecrowd get to spend annually.

The most powerful illustration is to compare a taxable IRA/401(k) distribution (net after tax) to a $71,413 spendable income. An IRA or a 401(k) with an account value of $1 million would require a $107,120-per-year distribution to net, after tax, a $71,413 spendable income in a 33.3 percent tax bracket. The IRA/401(k) earning interest at 7.5 percent would run totally out of money within seventeen years, based on annual withdrawals of $107,120! In other words, if either Jim or Mary Followthecrowd lived beyond age 82 (which is highly likely), he or she could be totally out of money if they had been trying to live on a net spendable income of $71,413 a year! On the other hand, through using equity management, Bob and Martha Enlightened, at age 82, still have their $1,005,510 generating interest-only income in the amount of $71,413—into perpetuity!

In this example, Bob and Martha's equity retirement planning didn't provide just a 45 to 50 percent greater retirement income—it provided the income for as long as they lived, and it passed down the balance to their heirs tax-free. Thus at age 82, equity management planning would be $1 million better than an IRA or 401(k). If they lived to be 92 years old, equity management would have generated the equivalent of $107,120 of annual income for ten more years without depleting the $1 million of corpus. So by age 92, the equity management plan would be effectively $2 million better than the IRA or 401(k)!

This superior retirement planning strategy was accomplished in this example by separating $80,000 of home equity (borrowing, by using OPM) at 7.5 percent and putting it to work at the same 7.5 percent rate. Can you imagine how this example could be enhanced if Bob and Martha were to borrow at 6 percent and then put the equity to work at 8 percent compounded over thirty-five years to age 65, and

Fig. 4.7	$80,000 GROWING AT VARIOUS INTEREST RATES OVER 35 YEARS			
End of Year	6.50% Compounding	7.50% Compounding	8.00% Compounding	8.50% Compounding
1	$85,200	$86,000	$86,400	$86,800
5	$109,607	$114,850	$117,546	$120,293
10	$150,171	$164,883	$172,714	$180,879
15	$205,747	$236,710	$253,774	$271,979
20	$281,892	$339,828	$372,877	$408,964
25	$386,216	$487,867	$547,878	$614,941
30	$529,149	$700,396	$805,013	$924,660
35	$724,980	$1,005,510	$1,182,828	$1,390,371

then during twenty or thirty more years during retirement? Figure 4.7 illustrates what a 6.5, 7.5, 8, and 8.5 percent internal rate of return would grow to from a onetime $80,000 investment. Can you imagine what fortune you could create if you separated the additional equity in your home every time it appreciated in value? Keep reading and you'll get a glimpse of the potential of the wealth that can be created simply by doing what banks and credit unions do: borrow OPM at one rate and invest it to earn a slightly higher rate.

HOLDING OUT FOR RETIREMENT OR HOLDING OUT ON LIFE?

As a financial strategist and retirement specialist, I often ask my clients, "If you were retiring today, what would you immediately begin doing?" Most of the time I get responses such as, "Oh, we would build the mountain cabin we've talked about building for years," or "We would buy a condo in some resort area." The next question I ask is, "Why don't you start enjoying these things right now?" They usually respond with, "Well, we would like to, but we can't afford it. We're socking away everything we can for the next twenty years into our 401(k)s and IRAs so we'll have the extra money to buy these things when we retire."

For the next twenty years, John and Susie Wannacabin sock away $500 per month into qualified retirement plans to accumulate a nest egg to buy their dream cabin. Let's assume John and Susie do pretty well with their 401(k)s and IRAs and earn an average of 11.25 percent for twenty years—$500 per month invested for twenty years earning 11.25 percent grows to $450,000. They're all ready to retire and buy their cabin when two facts hit them between the eyes: (1) Their $450,000 supplemental retirement account is fully taxable and they are in the same 33.3 percent tax bracket they were in during their earning years, so they will net only $300,000; and (2) the cabin they could have built twenty years earlier for $100,000 will now cost them $400,000! They are really dismayed.

Imagine with me for a moment (in jest) John's conversations with Susie, their children, and their grandchildren over the twenty years they were accumulating money in their 401(k)s. It's a typical Friday evening and John says to Susie, "Honey, how about we spend a romantic weekend going over our 401(k) and IRA statements? It will be exciting trying to figure out where we can reposition our money to time the market." I don't think John is going to score any points with Susie that weekend.

Can you imagine John taking his teenage son aside and saying, "Hey, Jason, stay home with me this Saturday and I'll show you how well our 401(k)s are doing—our dividends and capital gains this year gave us the equivalent of 11.25 percent interest compounded annually."

"No thanks, Dad. Can I borrow the keys?"

Imagine young Grandpa John, taking his little granddaughter in his arms and proudly showing her the diversified portfolio he has created that fifty years down the road may transfer any leftovers at 28 cents on the dollar to her.

Don't you think Susie Wannacabin would rather spend weekends in a cabin than reviewing 401(k)s at home? Building memories with their children and grandchildren at the family cabin will result in more valuable deposits into their family bank than their IRAs and 401(k)s.

MY 401 CABIN/INDIVIDUAL RETIREMENT ABODE (IRA)

Let me tell you about my family's 401 Cabin/Individual Retirement Abode (IRA).

We purchased a cabin for our family to begin enjoying time now with our children and grandchildren, rather than waiting until "retirement." Our cozy cabin sits on twenty acres in an extremely peaceful, serene mountain setting. It originally cost us $100,000, water rights and all. Conservatively, it is appreciating at least 7.2 percent per year. Based on the Rule of 72, our cabin will double in value every ten years ($72 \div 7.2 = 10$). At that rate, our cabin will easily be worth $200,000 ten years after we purchased it, $400,000 in twenty years, and $800,000 in thirty years.

During the same twenty-year period that John and Susie Wannacabin are socking away $500 per month (which equals $6,000 per year) into IRAs and 401(k)s, we are paying 6 percent interest-only mortgage payments on a cabin worth $100,000. Our cabin mortgage is costing us $500 per month, or $6,000 per year. We are getting the same tax benefits that John and Susie are getting because our interest is deductible, since the cabin qualifies as a secondary residence. *In other words, it doesn't matter whether you deposit $6,000 a year in a qualified retirement plan or make $6,000 in interest payments; both are deductible.* Either way, you save $2,000 in tax (33.3 percent of $6,000), and your net outlay is only $4,000 a year.

Compare the two scenarios. John and Susie Wannacabin need to earn 10.36 percent on their $500-per-month investment for it to grow to $400,000 in twenty years. But after tax, they will net only $266,666. They had better earn at least 11.25 percent on their 401(k)s so it will grow to $450,000, pay tax, and net the same $300,000 we will realize. Our cabin mortgage is interest-only, so we will still owe $100,000 at the end of twenty years. (You'll learn why we want to do it that way in chapters 6 to 8.) In year 20, our cabin should be worth at least $400,000, less the mortgage of $100,000, which results in the same net gain John and Susie hope to achieve.

But who is "richer" at the end of twenty years? We have an abundance of memories deposited in our family bank and have cultivated relationships through the process. We have photo albums full of memories at our cabin, compared to John and Susie's file cabinet full of quarterly account statements. Get the picture?

Let's look at a full thirty-year scenario. At a 7.2 percent appreciation rate, our cabin should be worth $800,000 in thirty years. John and Susie would need to have earned 8.35 percent on their $500-per-month investment to accumulate $800,000 in thirty years. However, after tax, they would net only $533,333. John and Susie would have to set aside $600 per month at 9.43 percent interest to accumulate the $1,200,000 needed to net $800,000 after tax. If we pay $600 per month against our $100,000 cabin mortgage, the extra $100 each month will pay off the cabin in thirty years. (Later, I will teach you a better alternative for paying off the cabin. In short, it would be better to deposit $66.65 a month into a conservative side fund and let it grow tax-free to $100,000—enough to pay off the mortgage in thirty years if we wanted.) Most important, we can arrange to enjoy the $800,000 gain on our cabin totally tax-free.

Don Blanton, a good friend and business associate, shared with me that he has a "401 Condo" for his family. A family-empowered bank (see chapter 12) can be structured to provide a "401 Cabin" or "401 Condo"—in the names of your children if necessary to get the tax break. Why wait until retirement to do the things you really enjoy doing? You can probably start enjoying much of what you are striving to achieve without giving up anything. In fact, you may end up a lot better off.

Oh, I almost forgot, you may still be wondering where the extra dollar is in the riddle about the three fishermen I told at the beginning of this chapter. My purpose in using the riddle is to illustrate there are dollars lost all the time through improper accounting. Herein lies the answer to the riddle: If you are accounting for the $30 the three men originally paid, you take 3 times the $9 they ended up paying, which equals $27, *plus* the $3 they got back, which balances out to $30. If you are accounting for the true room cost of $25, you take 3 times the $9 each man ended up paying, which equals $27, *minus* the $2 the bellboy kept, which equals $25. The point is, don't always add up the gain on your retirement accounts without subtracting the taxes you'll owe.

CONCEPTS COVERED IN CHAPTER 4

- Predictably, most people are motivated to invest in qualified plans for tax-favored treatment during the contribution and accumulation phases of retirement planning.
- When traditional qualified plans are liquidated in retirement, they produce the taxable results the government predicted and intended.
- *It doesn't make sense to postpone tax for some perceived advantage in the future.*
- *Non-qualified retirement vehicles can provide greater net spendable retirement income.*
- If you live twenty or more years after retiring, you'll potentially pay back at least five times more in taxes during the distribution phase than the taxes saved during the contribution phase.
- There are basically four sources of money: people at work, money at work, other people's money (OPM), and charity.
- *Most wealthy people employ the use of other people's money.*
- There are basically five different savings or investment options:
    1. You can invest after-tax dollars in instruments that are taxed as interest is earned, dividends are paid, or gains are realized.
    2. You can invest after-tax dollars in investments that accumulate tax-deferred, and pay taxes on the gain when realized.
    3. You can invest after-tax dollars in investments that accumulate tax-free, and also use the money tax-free later.
    4. You can invest 100-cent pre-tax or tax-deductible dollars

in investments that accumulate tax-deferred, then later
pay tax.

5. You can use 100-cent dollars because of indirect tax de-
    ductions and enjoy tax-free accumulation, tax-free use of
    the money, and transfer any remaining funds to your heirs
    tax-free.

- Option 5 far outperforms options 1 and 2 and can generate 50
  percent more net spendable retirement income than options 3
  and 4.

- *Having money that is tax-favored during the harvest years has the
  potential to generate a set amount of income into perpetuity,* while
  taxable investments may require retirees to withdraw 50 percent more (in a 33.3 percent tax bracket) to achieve the same
  amount of net spendable income. Hence, a taxable account
  may become depleted, which can result in retirees outliving
  their money.

- *Tremendous wealth can be created by doing what banks and credit
  unions do: borrow at one rate and invest to earn a higher rate.*

- Building memories at a 401 Cabin/Individual Retirement
  Abode (IRA) can result in more valuable deposits in a family
  bank than IRAs and 401(k)s, while enjoying the same tax benefits and growth.

CHAPTER 5

Free Yourself from the IRA and 401(k) Trap

How to do a strategic roll-out of your IRA or 401(k) with the least tax impact

IF YOU HAVE COME TO THE REALIZATION that you are getting trapped in an IRA or 401(k) that someday will be taxed, don't delay the inevitable! Begin now to develop a plan to strategically convert your qualified funds to non-qualified accounts. Continuing to postpone the tax that will be due may dramatically increase the amount of tax you will ultimately pay.

BENEFITS OF A STRATEGIC ROLL-OUT

Many people preparing for retirement postpone the transfer of qualified funds to a non-qualified status until age 59½ to alleviate the 10 percent penalty. They don't realize that the only thing they may be saving by postponing a transfer *is* the 10 percent penalty. The normal income tax owed will still be due no matter when they withdraw the money.

As you've learned, people usually find themselves in the same tax bracket as in their earning years—even though they have less income—because they have fewer deductions during retirement. Sometimes by procrastinating on the tax and penalty, people will find themselves in a higher tax bracket after age 59½, due to Congress raising tax rates over the interim period or an increase in their personal income. All too often, retirees will not save taxes by postponing them or stretching out the liability to future generations—they are simply avoiding Uncle Sam's unavoidable "payday."

LEVERAGE TAX-YEAR FLUCTUATIONS

What's the best way to begin converting your qualified funds to non-qualified accounts? One strategy is to make your move during tax-advantaged years.

Sometimes taxpayers experience a year in which they have less taxable income. For example, perhaps through a job change their taxable income drops $25,000 below the third tax bracket (the federal rate jumps from 15 to 25 percent at the third tax bracket). These taxpayers should seize the opportunity to convert some of their qualified funds to non-qualified accounts.

If they took advantage of the low taxable income year, they could possibly withdraw and reposition $25,000 of IRA or 401(k) funds and pay the tax they would pay later at a higher rate. Even with a 10 percent penalty, their total tax might be 25 percent: 15 percent plus the penalty. That is the same as the next bracket they might be in if they postponed paying taxes now and compounded their money in a yet-to-be-taxed environment. It may behoove them to get the tax over with and reposition the balance in a vehicle that will be tax-free from that point forward. Remember, you can either pay the IRS now or pay them later (on a much larger sum).

Many couples over the age of 59½ fail to take advantage of a low tax bracket to reposition qualified funds. For example, they may be in a 15 percent bracket with their taxable income $10,000 below the 25 percent income tax threshold. This means they can add $10,000 of income (without having to spend it) through a withdrawal of retirement funds, while still remaining in the lower bracket. In this case, they could reposition $10,000 of qualified funds at the low 15 percent tax rate. Their tax rate may be higher in the future; if they don't reposition now, that opportunity may be lost forever. It is usually advisable to get qualified money out, taxed, and repositioned into a tax-free environment rather than to leave it in qualified plans, compounding the problem.

UNDERSTAND THE RISK OF MINIMUM DISTRIBUTIONS

What if a retired couple does not need the funds from their IRAs and 401(k)s to meet expenses during retirement? It is usually not best to continue postponing the tax until age 70½, when they must begin taking out minimum distributions based on the Internal Revenue Code's minimum distribution formula.

If an individual does not begin withdrawing money by the age of 70½, in accordance with the Internal Revenue Code's minimum distribution formula, the IRS will penalize that individual for not withdrawing those funds. (The IRS would like to have some of the money out and taxed each year before retirees pass away so it can receive revenue during their lifetime. If not consumed, it may be taxed a second time when it transfers to non-spousal heirs.) If a taxpayer, after the age of 70½, leaves money in a qualified plan and does not make the minimum withdrawal based upon the minimum distribution formula, a 50 percent penalty is assessed to the taxpayer on the amount that should have been withdrawn.

Let's study a simple example, illustrated in figure 5.1. For a married couple in which the husband is age 70½ and the wife is younger, within ten years of his age (or any age older), the divisor is shown for a period of twenty-one years. Thus, he must take the total of all his qualified accounts and divide by 25.3 to arrive at the minimum distribution required to avoid a 50 percent penalty during the first year after reaching age 70½. If his qualified accounts totaled $100,000, he would have to withdraw $3,952.57 ($100,000 ÷ 25.3). If his qualified accounts totaled

Fig. 5.1	MINIMUM DISTRIBUTION CALCULATOR				
[1] AGE	[2] DATE	[3] DIVISOR	[1] AGE	[2] DATE	[3] DIVISOR
71½	Apr. 2005	25.3	82	Dec. 2015	16.0
72	Dec. 2005	24.4	83	Dec. 2016	15.3
73	Dec. 2006	23.5	84	Dec. 2017	14.5
74	Dec. 2007	22.7	85	Dec. 2018	13.8
75	Dec. 2008	21.8	86	Dec. 2019	13.1
76	Dec. 2009	20.9	87	Dec. 2020	12.4
77	Dec. 2010	20.1	88	Dec. 2021	11.8
78	Dec. 2011	19.2	89	Dec. 2022	11.1
79	Dec. 2012	18.4	90	Dec. 2023	10.5
80	Dec. 2013	17.6	91	Dec. 2024	9.9
81	Dec. 2014	16.8			

$1 million, he would have to withdraw $39,525.70, whether he needs the money or not. The next year, he would have to recalculate the total value of all his qualified accounts and divide by 24.4 to arrive at the minimum distribution. As seen from figure 5.1, the divisor changes each year as he gets older until by age 90, he must be withdrawing a minimum of approximately 10 percent of the value of his qualified accounts to avoid a penalty.

The best Web site I have found to help you calculate this is found at www.tiaacref.org. Search under the calculators for the minimum distribution calculator. You may be required to register before using the minimum distribution calculator, but all that you will need in order to calculate minimum distributions are birth dates for you and your beneficiaries, the value of your accounts, and the growth rate you feel you'll earn during your retirement years.

I have discovered that more often than not, retired couples pay more than twice the amount of taxes on their retirement plans if they string them out using the government's minimum distribution formula. They may pay 60 percent less in taxes if they pay the tax on a systematic withdrawal plan or strategic transfer over five to seven years. This is true provided they reposition their after-tax distributions into a tax-free environment from that point on. (I'll illustrate this later in this chapter.)

TRANSFERRING RETIREMENT FUNDS TO HEIRS

Upon the death of the first spouse, the surviving spouse may inherit or be the beneficiary of qualified funds. At that point, there are certain rules that allow a beneficiary under the age of 59½ to receive those funds without being subject to a 10 percent penalty. The funds could also be converted to an IRA under the beneficiary's name, but the distribution and subsequent tax would then be postponed. This option is often the temptation for survivors or beneficiaries after inheriting a qualified account. In many instances, it may be better for them to take out the money, pay the tax at today's rates, and be done with the tax liability. They could then reposition those after-tax funds into non-qualified accounts, possibly accumulating tax-free from that point forward (I explain how in chapters 10 and 11).

For a retired couple, if there are still funds remaining in a qualified retirement plan such as an IRA or 401(k) upon the death of the second spouse, the value of the account is included in the estate of the deceased and must be calculated into the total value of the estate assets. If the estate is valued over the unified credit exemption (figure 5.2), the estate tax rate starts at 37 percent and eventually tops out at 45 to 55 percent, depending on the year. (If the 2001 tax act is not changed, the unified credit exemption amount is increased to $3,500,000 by 2009, then repealed in 2010, being replaced on January 1, 2011, by the tax law in effect in the year 2001!)

In addition to possible estate tax liability, the income tax will have to be paid on those qualified funds at the tax rate of the beneficiary if the funds are not rolled over to another IRA. Such a transfer will generally move the beneficiary to a higher federal tax bracket. Assuming the beneficiary is in a 33.3 percent tax bracket, income tax will likely need to be paid on top of any estate tax due. Many people are not

Fig. 5.2	THE ESTATE AND GIFT TAX RATES UNIFIED CREDIT EXEMPTION AMOUNT FOR ESTATE TAX PURPOSES*	
Calendar Year (January 1)	Estate Tax Deathtime Transfer Exemption	Highest Estate and Gift Tax Rates
2000	$675,000	55% + 5% Surtax
2001	$675,000	55% + 5% Surtax
2002	$1 Million	50%
2003	$1 Million	49%
2004	$1.5 Million	48%
2005	$1.5 Million	47%
2006	$2 Million	46%
2007	$2 Million	45%
2008	$2 Million	45%
2009	$3.5 Million	45%
2010	Repealed	Top Individual Tax Rate Under the Act (Gift Tax Only)
2011	2000 Tax Law Reinstated on 1/1/2011	2000 Tax Law Reinstated on 1/1/2011

*as set forth in the Economic Growth and Tax Relief Reconciliation Act of 2001

aware of the tax impact on qualified plans during the distribution and transfer phases. Sometimes, between the estate tax and income tax, surviving heirs realize only about 22 cents on the dollar out of their deceased parents' IRAs, after paying 45 percent in estate tax and 33 percent in income tax.

Often a person's retirement nest egg may look like an adequate resource to sustain income benefits even beyond the death of the account holders, but after the death of the nest builders, predators have drained the egg.

WHEN TO MAKE STRATEGIC CONVERSIONS

In my financial planning practice, I often illustrate the possible benefits of a strategic conversion of qualified accounts to non-qualified retirement planning alternatives for retirees. We begin a strategic conversion out of their qualified accounts by making annual withdrawals and subjecting those withdrawals to taxes each year, perhaps even incurring a penalty if they are under age 59½. (Remember, by doing that, we plan to withdraw that money and keep them in an equal or lower tax bracket than if they postponed—and increased—the tax liability.) If we wait until age 59½ to begin a strategic, qualified plan roll-out (*not* rollover), we save the 10 percent penalty.

Sometimes it behooves people under age 50 to roll out their money under a strategic plan, despite the 10 percent penalty, because the amount of the penalty could be recouped with better interest during a ten- to fifteen-year period before retirement. There are no hard and fast rules. It is generally best for people between the ages of 55 and 59½ to wait until after age 59½ to start their roll-outs. Some people aged 50 to 54 should also wait; others shouldn't. There are several variables to consider, and it is more a function of the investment yield they are earning than the tax bracket they are in. I have witnessed many people who postponed doing a strategic conversion and found themselves only a few years later in more damaging taxable circumstances than if they had not waited—even considering the 10 percent penalty.

Again, you can either pay the IRS now or pay them later. Thus, if you can get the same rate of return in a non-qualified account as you can in a qualified account, and enjoy tax-free growth and access to your account thereafter, I would recommend discontinuing new contributions to any type of qualified plans (unless an attractive matching percentage is available and you understand the consequences of tax postponement). As explained in chapter 4, you should strongly consider redirecting your contributions to non-qualified retirement vehicles funded with after-tax dollars on the front end (seed money) that are tax-free on the back end (harvest years).

USE IT OR LOSE IT

As I just explained, I have witnessed people who postponed and waited, trying to "save" inevitable tax on their qualified money. Unwittingly, for example, many people were avoiding moving from the 28 percent bracket into the 31 percent bracket before the year 2000 stock market crash. They were motivated to save just 3 percent on $59,100 (the available room in the next threshold), which would have been $1,773. By postponing a withdrawal, they lost 30 percent of $59,100, which equals $17,730, or ten times as much, because they left it in the market during a downturn! To add insult to injury, many were forced, because of lack of liquidity, to pull their money out and still pay tax. If they could have done it over again, they would have gladly traded paying $1,773 in extra tax to have an extra $17,730 in retirement funds. If you do not use the available room between your current taxable income and the next tax bracket threshold for possible withdrawals, you will lose it for that tax year. You cannot go back and amend a return to retroactively withdraw qualified funds.

You may already be heavily into a qualified plan. If you are, it may be in your best interest to analyze what a strategic conversion from your qualified plan to a non-qualified situation could achieve during your long-term retirement years, even though it may hurt taxwise in the short term. I prepare many of my clients so that as early as age 59½ they can begin the strategic conversion process, even if they are not ready to retire or don't need the money yet. The idea is to create a plan where they can begin to withdraw money strategically out of their retirement plan over a five-, six-, or seven-year period and get the money taxed at today's rates rather than tomorrow's probable higher rates. They may want to take advantage of any room they have in their current tax bracket before crossing the next threshold.

For example, for a married couple filing a joint tax return (under the tax brackets that existed in 2004), there was $43,800 of room for taxable incomes between $14,300 and $58,100. (Taxable income is the net income after all deductions and exemptions.) So if you had $70,000 in gross income but had itemized deductions of $12,000 in mortgage interest, $7,000 in charitable contributions, $4,000 in state and local taxes, plus two exemptions (a husband and wife) totaling $6,200, your taxable income would be only $40,800, not $70,000. Therefore, you could withdraw $17,300 from a qualified account ($58,100 threshold less a taxable income of $40,800) and probably pay no higher income tax rate on that money than you would if you withdrew the money later.

Hopefully, between the ages of 59½ and 64½—and no later than 70½—couples can have most or all of their qualified plans repositioned and the taxes paid. They can then reposition their retirement funds in a tax-free environment from that point forward and enjoy tax-free income the remainder of their lives, provided they also reposition their after-tax distributions into the appropriate investment vehicles. When retirees do this, they generally save as much as 60 percent of the tax they would have paid had they strung out the tax liability over the remainder of their lives. In addition, they can enhance the value of those funds when they are transferred down to beneficiaries and replenish some or all of the money they gave up in taxes during the roll-out or conversion process. I'll explain how in chapters 9 to 11.

ACCESSING YOUR RETIREMENT FUNDS TAX-FREE

Let's assume a couple has arrived at age 60 and is preparing for full retirement at age 65. We'll name this couple Ben and Shirley Liberated. Ben has worked for a large corporation that provides a defined benefit pension based on the years of service worked for the company. Shirley has been a schoolteacher for thirty years and will also receive a retirement pension based on her years of service. With these two sources of income, in addition to Social Security, they feel they won't need to draw any money from their IRAs or 401(k)s yet, because they are still working, or they can receive early-retirement incentives if they decide to retire sooner. They also have other investment income sources.

Let's assume they have at least $100,000 in IRAs and 401(k)s. If they do what most people do—what most advisors tell them to do—

they continue to defer making any withdrawals from their IRAs, thinking they are saving taxes.

Ben and Shirley have been realizing a 7.75 percent return on their IRAs and 401(k)s. If they leave the funds alone, their $100,000 of qualified funds will grow tax-deferred to $210,947 in ten years (to age 70). To avoid a 50 percent penalty, they must begin taking annual withdrawals at age 70½. If they begin taking annual withdrawals equivalent to their interest earnings of 7.75 percent, the annual income from their IRA and 401(k) accounts will be about $16,350 ($210,947 x 7.75%). However, they will have to report this each year as taxable income, so assuming they are fortunate to still be in a 33.3 percent tax bracket, their annual tax liability on their IRA/401(k) income will be $5,450 ($16,350 x 33.3). This leaves them a net of $10,900 spendable income after tax. Let's assume that at least one of them lives to the age of 90 (twenty more years). Their annual tax liability of $5,450 for twenty years will total $109,000 in taxes paid during their harvest years. Let's see what Ben and Shirley Liberated could do better.

Ben and Shirley have been living in the same home for the past thirty years. They purchased it for $125,000. It has appreciated at an average rate of about 5 percent per year. Based on the Rule of 72, this means their home would have doubled in value twice during that period (72 divided by 5 means the home would double every 14.4 years). It is now worth $500,000, and it is free and clear of any mortgages. This is the home Ben and Shirley raised their four children in, and they no longer need a home this large. They would like to sell it and buy a small summer retirement home, as well as a winter retirement condo in a warm, southern climate—together costing $500,000. At first, they think they will sell their existing home for $500,000 and pay cash for both retirement dwellings, but they are concerned they might incur a large capital gains tax like their parents did when they sold their home during retirement. However, Ben and Shirley have discovered alternatives by reading this book—before making any such mistakes.

Because of the Taxpayer Relief Act of 1997, Ben and Shirley are reminded they can avoid up to $500,000 of capital gain on the sale of a principal residence once every two years. And by paying only 20 percent down on the acquisition of the two retirement dwellings, they tie up only $100,000 of their $500,000 home equity. Ben and Shirley take out new mortgages on both properties totaling $400,000 (80 percent loan-to-value). After studying chapters 6 to 8, they realize how important it is to establish the highest amount of acquisition indebtedness when purchasing a primary or secondary residence. They also learn why it is wise to use interest-only mortgages rather than amortized loans. So let's assume their interest-only mortgages totaling $400,000 are at 6 percent interest requiring monthly payments of $2,000 per month, or $24,000 per year. Inasmuch as 100 percent of the payment is interest, 100 percent is deductible. So in a 33.3 percent tax bracket, Ben and Shirley get back $8,000 each year in tax savings that they were not receiving before. Their net after-tax house payments therefore total $16,000 per year (because Uncle Sam is paying the difference of $8,000, up to the surface payment of $24,000).

By doing what banks and credit unions do—borrow money at a lower rate and put it to work at a little higher rate—Ben and Shirley put their $400,000 of home equity safely to work earning 6, 7, or 8 percent return in a tax-favored environment. Even if they earned only 6 percent net, they could easily make their gross mortgage payment in the amount of $2,000 per month. I'll show you how to do better than that later in this book.

Ben and Shirley decide not to delay the inevitable by postponing taxes on their IRAs and 401(k)s. Instead, they decide to get all of their qualified money out over five years (from age 60 to 65) and reposition it to a non-qualified account that will grow tax-free from that point forward. Assuming they still earn 7.75 percent while they are strategically rolling out their retirement funds, they can withdraw $23,091 each year and it will be completely converted within five years. Because Ben and Shirley have $24,000 of mortgage interest deductions that they didn't have before, this allows them to have $24,000 of additional income without tax because the interest deductions and the retirement fund withdrawals offset each other on their 1040 tax return.

In other words, $23,091 of taxable IRA/401(k) income is washed away (offset) by $24,000 of mortgage interest (Schedule A) deductions—meaning the IRA/401(k) distribution was in essence tax-free.

Assuming they can get the same 7.75 percent return in a non-qualified, tax-favored retirement planning alternative, $23,091 per year for five years grows to $145,240, which in turn grows to $210,947 by the end of the tenth year. That is exactly the same amount that would have accumulated had Ben and Shirley left it in the IRAs and 401(k)s. *The significant difference is that now Ben and Shirley can draw out the entire annual interest earnings of $16,350 tax-free, which is 50 percent greater than the net after-tax income of $10,900 they would realize if it stayed in the IRAs.* Another advantage is that if they don't need the money, they don't have to withdraw anything at age 70½ because the money is no longer in a qualified plan—it's already been subject to tax.

If Ben and Shirley want, they can pay off their $400,000 mortgage balance anytime by taking the money they conserved in one pocket (a safe investment) and transferring it into another pocket (their homes). However, by not paying off the mortgages, they can continue to earn a return greater than the net cost of the interest they are paying each year, which is only $16,000, or 4 percent ($24,000 less 33.3 percent = $8,000 in tax savings). So on top of $16,350 of tax-free income, Ben and Shirley may benefit from an additional $8,000 in taxes saved from continuing to deduct $24,000 of interest from their other taxable income.

When we add up the benefits, Ben and Shirley can be receiving $24,000 per year in tax-favored interest earnings from the $400,000 of home equity they invested, in addition to the $16,350 of tax-favored earnings on their repositioned IRA/401(k) funds. These two amounts equal $40,350. If we subtract the net after-tax cost of the annual mortgage interest in the amount of $16,000, they can realize net spendable income of $24,350, versus the $10,900 they would have netted by leaving the money in their IRAs and 401(k)s and paying cash for their retirement homes! If they live twenty more years, Ben and Shirley would realize $269,000 more in retirement income using this strategy ($24,350 − $10,900 = $13,450 x 20 yrs = $269,000).

Ben and Shirley Liberated's situation represents a simple example. The truth is, I have helped numerous couples preparing for retirement, or couples already in retirement, alleviate or totally eliminate unnecessary income tax on some or all of their qualified retirement accounts, such as IRAs and 401(k)s. In chapter 19 of my original comprehensive work, *Missed Fortune,* I outline in detail three different scenarios involving a 30-year-old couple, a 45-year-old couple, and a 60-year-old couple. (Studying those examples will give you a greater understanding of this strategy.)

THE ULTIMATE LEVERAGE OF IRA/401(K) FUNDS

Let's dive a bit deeper into these principles by comparing three different approaches to leveraging qualified funds.

First, let's assume you are over age 59½, have money residing (trapped) in qualified accounts, such as IRAs and 401(k)s, and you don't need that money—at least for the time being. There are many retired Americans in this category. Let's also assume you have $100,000 of borrowable equity in your home, and you can access it in increments using an equity line of credit that requires interest-only payments (meaning we only have to pay the interest each year—no principal). The equity line of credit has an interest rate of 7.5 percent.

Because it is deductible interest on home equity indebtedness, the net cost of the mortgage interest is really only 5 percent in a 33.3 percent tax bracket (7.5 minus one-third). In order to comply with the Technical and Miscellaneous Revenue Act (TAMRA) of 1988 to make our investment qualify for both tax-favored growth and access (this is explained in chapters 10 and 11), we borrow $20,000 a year for five years before we have used our full $100,000 equity line. Please study figure 5.3. The first year we need to pay $1,500 in interest payments (7.5 percent of the $20,000 loan balance). The next year we need to pay $3,000 in interest payments because our new loan balance is now

Fig. 5.3   A STRATEGIC ROLL-OUT FROM AN IRA OR 401(k)

Annual Investment   Versus   Equity Management Roll-Out

Year	Gross IRA/401(k) Roll-out	Invest Net After-tax	Year-end Balance at 8% Interest	Borrow Home Equity	Gross Payment at 7.5%	Net After-tax Payment at 5.0%	Home Equity Investment Balance at 8%
1	$1,500	$1,000	$ 1,080	$20,000	$1,500	$1,000	$ 21,600
2	$3,000	$2,000	$ 3,326	$20,000	$3,000	$2,000	$ 44,928
3	$4,500	$3,000	$ 6,833	$20,000	$4,500	$3,000	$ 70,122
4	$6,000	$4,000	$11,699	$20,000	$6,000	$4,000	$ 97,332
5	$7,500	$5,000	$18,035	$20,000	$7,500	$5,000	$126,719
6	$7,500	$5,000	$24,878	$100,000	$7,500	$5,000	$136,856
7	$7,500	$5,000	$32,268		$7,500	$5,000	$147,805
8	$7,500	$5,000	$40,250		$7,500	$5,000	$159,629
9	$7,500	$5,000	$48,869		$7,500	$5,000	$172,399
10	$7,500	$5,000	$58,179		$7,500	$5,000	$186,191
		$40,000			$60,000	$40,000	

↑   **Identical Investment Outlay**   ↑

Approach #1

Total after-tax roll-out for ten years:	$40,000
Account Balance after ten years:	$58,179
Annual Interest Percentage Rate:	8%
Annual Interest Earnings:	$ 4,654
LESS Annual Tax at 33.33% :	$ 1,551
Net Spendable Annual Income:	$ 3,103

Approach #2

Beginning balance in IRA/401(k):	$40,000
Balance after ten years at 8%:	$86,357
Annual Interest Percentage Rate:	8%
Annual Interest Earnings:	$ 6,909
LESS Annual Tax at 33.33%:	$ 2,303
Net Spendable Annual Income:	$ 4,606

Approach #3

Beginning balance in IRA/401(k):	$40,000
Total strategic roll-out over a ten-year period:	$60,000
Total of gross payments on equity line of credit:	$60,000
Total of net after-tax payments on equity line:	$40,000
Total of invested home equity at 8% after 10 years:	$186,191
Total balance approximately one month later:	$187,500
Annual Interest Percentage Rate:	8%
Annual Interest Earnings:	$ 15,000
LESS net after-tax interest payment on equity line:	$ 5,000
Net Spendable Annual Income (non-taxable):	**$ 10,000**

$40,000. The third year we pay $4,500 in interest on a new balance of $60,000. The fourth year we pay $6,000 in interest on a new balance of $80,000. Finally, in the fifth year and each year thereafter, we pay $7,500 in annual interest payments on an ongoing loan balance of $100,000.

As illustrated, ten years of interest payments total $60,000. However, these interest payments are 100 percent deductible inasmuch as the interest is paid on home equity indebtedness. So we really don't have to pay $60,000, but only $40,000, because Uncle Sam pays one-third of the interest in a 33.3 percent tax bracket. In other words, during this ten-year period, we can experience $60,000 of income totally tax-free because of the mortgage interest offsets. So let's take advantage of that by rolling out some of our IRA/401(k) funds. If we paid the interest each year with IRA/401(k) withdrawals, we would, in essence, be getting $60,000 out of our IRAs and 401(k)s tax-free. Let's see how much better off you would be by using this strategy.

Approach 1

Let's say you took out the same annual withdrawals from your IRAs and 401(k)s illustrated above, paid the tax due in a 33.3 percent bracket, and invested the remainder each year. You would net $1,000 in year 1, $2,000 in year 2, $3,000 in year 3, $4,000 in year 4, and $5,000 in years 5 through 10 for a total of $40,000 ($60,000 of withdrawals less 33.3 percent, or $20,000, in taxes paid over the ten years). Assuming you invested the net after-tax money in a tax-deferred annuity earning 8 percent, your investment would have a value of $58,179 at the end of ten years. It has not even grown back to the before-tax value of $60,000 you started with! If you started taking annual interest income at that point, $58,179 generates $4,654 of annual interest income at 8 percent. But you will likely need to pay tax on that income in the amount of $1,551 per year (33.3 percent of $4,654), which nets you only $3,103 to spend.

Approach 2

Approach 1 doesn't look like a very good alternative, so you decide to continue to postpone distributions as long as the IRS will allow. It's important to understand here that if your IRAs and 401(k)s were realizing the same 8 percent return, it would require only about $40,000 at the beginning of the ten-year period illustrated to generate the annual interest payments shown in figure 5.3, which end up totaling $60,000 over the ten years. So let's carve out $40,000 and let it reside in the IRAs. At 8 percent return, it would grow to $86,357 in ten years. That looks better to you than the previous scenario. But if you started withdrawing your annual earnings at 8 percent interest on $86,357 in the amount of $6,909, you are faced with a tax of $2,303 (33.3 percent of $6,909), netting only $4,606.

Approach 3

Let's revisit the strategy shown earlier. You would have $20,000 per year from your home equity loan proceeds to invest for the first five years. Assuming you can achieve the same 8 percent return, $20,000 per year grows to $126,719 by the end of five years. Then that amount will continue to grow with no new deposits (because the basis of $100,000 from the home equity line has all been invested at that point) for five more years, at 8 percent, to a total of $186,191. If the proper investment vehicles are selected, this can happen in a non-taxable environment, as I teach later. About one month after the end of the tenth year, you could begin taking non-taxable interest-only income that would total $15,000 per year. You would still have annual interest payments on your equity line in the amount of $5,000 (net after tax). This would net you $10,000 of income to spend!

So let's take a look again at the three scenarios. If you take annual withdrawals, pay the tax, and invest the difference in a tax-deferred annuity, after ten years your net spendable annual income would be $3,103. If you postpone taking withdrawals out of your IRAs and 401(k)s for ten years, your net spendable annual income would be $4,606. However, using the equity management strategy, you have

$186,191 at the end of ten years, which can generate a net income of $10,000.

What if after getting $60,000 of your retirement funds repositioned tax-free by virtue of the $100,000 equity line of credit, you simply want to pay it off? You can take $100,000 from your investment if you choose and pay off the equity line. You would be left with a balance of $86,191, which would give you an annual income of $6,895 (still better than the other two alternatives), assuming the same 8 percent return. Again, to achieve this, I would recommend the nontaxable investments explained later in this book. However, to experience the greatest net spendable income, it would be better to *not* pay off the equity line. By doing what banks and credit unions do—by being your own banker—you can safely use the principal of arbitrage to generate even greater income, as shown. By borrowing money with an equity line at a net cost of 5 percent and using the loan proceeds to earn 8 percent, you are making 3 percent more than the cost of the funds. In this example, that equates to $3,000 more, or nearly $10,000 per year of total income. You make the choice. Which supplemental retirement income would you prefer: $3,103, $4,604, $6,895, or $9,895 per year?

In this example, we increased retirement income on IRAs and 401(k)s first by nearly 50 percent. Then we more than doubled it and even tripled it by using this strategy on just $40,000 of IRA money as it was growing to $60,000. What if you have as much as $400,000 trapped in IRAs or 401(k)s? (If those funds are left to grow to $600,000 before you begin to strategically access them, you will increase your future tax liability.) If so, chances are, you also have a home valued at $500,000 to $1 million or have the capacity to buy a new home (or two homes) of that value. Remember, you can deduct interest up to $1 million of acquisition indebtedness, as explained in chapter 2. I know all you retirees out there are looking for a good solid reason to replace your current home with a new retirement home. Herein lies your best reason and opportunity! Using this strategy, someone with $400,000 trapped in IRA or 401(k) accounts could transfer some or all of those

funds over a ten-year period and substantially reduce or totally eliminate the income tax liability if they created new interest deductions by
taking out mortgages totaling $1 million on newly acquired primary
and secondary residences.

To understand how to manage equity in your home to increase liquidity, safety, and rate of return and maximize tax benefits as alluded
to here, put on your seat belt and get ready for an incredible ride
through the next three chapters. They will provide the opportunity for
even more powerful wealth-enhancement insights.

CONCEPTS COVERED IN CHAPTER 5

- *Develop a plan to strategically convert your qualified funds to non-qualified accounts at the most opportune time taxwise.*
- When they retire, people will usually find themselves in a tax bracket as high as or higher than they were in during their earning years.
- After age 59½, it is usually advisable to get qualified money out, taxed, and repositioned into a tax-free environment, rather than to leave it in qualified plans, compounding the problem.
- Postponing tax until age 70½ and then taking minimum distributions may result in paying substantially more in tax in the long run.
- A strategic conversion of your qualified accounts to a non-qualified status—over a five- to seven-year period—may result in up to 60 percent less tax than stringing the tax liability out over a lifetime.
- *Sometimes between the estate tax and income tax, surviving heirs realize only about 22 cents on the dollar from their parents' IRAs.*
- *You can pay the IRS now, or you can pay the IRS on a larger amount later.* If you can get the same rate of return in a non-qualified account as you can in a qualified account—and enjoy tax-free

growth and tax-free access to your account thereafter—*you should consider discontinuing new contributions to any type of qualified plan.*

- If you do not use the available room between your current taxable income and the next tax bracket threshold for possible qualified plan withdrawals, you will lose it for that tax year.

- Qualified plan roll-outs may hurt taxwise in the short term but can dramatically enhance retirement income in the long term.

- Retirees between the ages of 59½ and 70½ can arrange to have their qualified plans strategically taxed and repositioned in a tax-free environment to enjoy greater net spendable income.

- *People preparing for retirement, or already in retirement, can alleviate or totally eliminate unnecessary income tax on some or all of their qualified retirement accounts,* such as IRAs and 401(k)s.

- *By successfully managing the equity in your home, you can reduce or eliminate the tax (through mortgage interest offsets) on qualified money as it is accessed.* This strategy can substantially increase your net spendable retirement income.

CHAPTER 6

Learn to Manage Home Equity Successfully

Home equity is not liquid or safe and has no rate of return. It is not a prudent investment!

CONSIDER HOW MUCH YOU WOULD DEPOSIT in an investment account with the following features:

- The customer can determine the amount of monthly contributions and length of time for each of the contributions to continue.
- The customer can pay more than the minimum monthly contribution, but not less.
- If the customer attempts to pay less, the financial institution keeps *all* of the previous contributions.
- The money in the account is not liquid.
- The money deposited in the account is not safe from loss of principal.
- Each contribution made to the account results in less safety of principal.
- The money deposited in the account earns a zero percent rate of return.

- The customer's income tax liability increases with each new contribution.
- When the plan is fully funded, there is no income paid out to the customer.

When I present this investment to potential investors, the features make it extremely unappealing. Would you invest serious cash in such an investment account? The fact is, you probably *are* investing in the investment described above: If you have a traditional mortgage, then it's your house!

The dream for many Americans is outright home ownership—a worthwhile goal. Unfortunately, most people go about buying their home the wrong way—costing themselves thousands of dollars unnecessarily all while thinking they are saving money and investing wisely.

As stated in chapter 1, there are two places most people accumulate the most money: their home and their retirement plan. Thus far we have dispelled myths about traditional retirement savings vehicles, such as IRAs and 401(k)s. Since a home is the single largest investment that most Americans make during their lifetime, let's now explore why home equity is not a prudent investment. Let's also define how you can learn to manage your equity better to increase liquidity, safety, and rate of return.

TAKE ADVANTAGE OF YOUR INTEREST

Mortgage interest is your friend, not your foe. Mortgage interest is one of the few deductions we can take advantage of on our tax returns. Although you do not want to incur interest expense just for the sake of a tax deduction, there are situations where it is wise to pay interest in order to earn more interest.

What is the difference between preferred and non-preferred interest expense? Let's say that you're paying credit card interest at the rate of 12 percent that is non-deductible. Therefore, you are paying $120 per year in interest for every $1,000 of credit card debt. Instead, if you were to exchange that debt for home equity debt at 9 percent interest

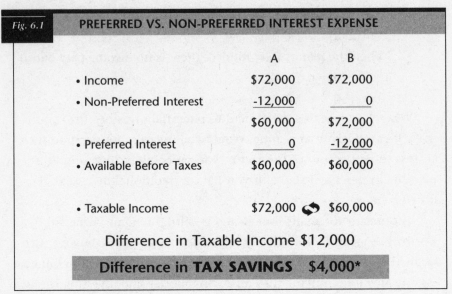

Fig. 6.1	PREFERRED VS. NON-PREFERRED INTEREST EXPENSE		
		A	B
• Income		$72,000	$72,000
• Non-Preferred Interest		-12,000	0
		$60,000	$72,000
• Preferred Interest		0	-12,000
• Available Before Taxes		$60,000	$60,000
• Taxable Income		$72,000	$60,000

Difference in Taxable Income $12,000

Difference in **TAX SAVINGS** $4,000*

*assuming a 33.3% marginal tax bracket

that *is* deductible, as you learned from chapter 2, the real net cost in a 33.3 percent tax bracket is one-third less, or 6 percent. A net of 6 percent interest equals only $60 per year for every $1,000 of debt, thus saving $60 in interest compared to $120 of non-deductible interest. The interest savings could be applied to the principal of the loan to pay it off sooner.

Likewise, if a homeowner has $12,000 of deductible home mortgage interest, that interest comes off the top of his or her income, thereby reducing the taxable income by $12,000. In a 33.3 percent marginal tax bracket, the actual savings is $4,000 in otherwise payable income tax. (That is money that would have been paid in tax if there were no deduction.) If a married couple filing a joint tax return has a combined gross income of $72,000 for the year, $12,000 of deductible interest would save them $4,000, in contrast to no tax savings with $12,000 of non-deductible interest (figure 6.1). (This is because the taxable income would be $60,000 after the deduction, rather than the full $72,000 of taxable income.) *So I refer to deductible interest as preferred interest and non-deductible interest as non-preferred interest.*

WHAT IS YOUR BANK UP TO?

The fact is, bankers and lenders sell money. They "borrow" money from us when we deposit savings in their institutions. What do they want us to do? They want us to keep it there. But do *they* keep it there? No. They lend that money at higher rates of return.

When we borrow money from them, we tend to focus on the interest that we are paying, and we usually accelerate the payoff of the loan by sending extra principal to the lender. Think about it: What do banks do when we pay off, let's say, a car loan? Do they hurry and give us back the money in our savings account and tell us they don't want to hold it anymore? No, they gladly pay us our interest and give us all kinds of incentives to keep our money in a loaned position with them in a savings or similar type of account. The longer they can keep our money in their institution—both the principal and the accruing interest—the more money they make. We could stand to gain a lot by following their example.

Please don't misinterpret what I am saying. It is wise to get out of debt. This book will teach you the smartest, fastest way to become debt-free. But an institution can consider itself debt-free and still have millions of dollars of liabilities. If the institution has adequate assets in a liquid, safe environment earning a return greater than the net cost of those borrowed funds, then it is justified in its claim to be debt-free. In reality, if a bank has money deposited in it, all of that money is a liability to the bank. Why are they willing to carry this liability? The liability of using other people's money (OPM) is the bank's greatest asset to be more profitable. Why can't *you* be your *own* banker? You can!

BE YOUR OWN BANKER

The prevalent myth-conception is that there are only two kinds of people in the world: those who earn interest and those who pay interest. There is really a third kind of person: those who do exactly what banks and credit unions do—borrow money at a lower interest rate and invest it to earn a higher interest rate. These people accumulate a much greater degree of wealth than most people, because they have learned to be their own banker. I maintain that you do not need to pay off your house to be considered "out of debt." If you have a greater amount of assets in a liquid, safe environment than is needed to wash out liabilities, the net result is positive.

It is understandable that a thirty-year mortgage amortization schedule may look discouraging because fifteen years into the mortgage, a home buyer may still owe 75 percent of the original loan amount (figure 6.2). Why? The interest. The principal and interest payment on a $100,000 thirty-year amortized mortgage at 7.5 percent interest is approximately $700 per month. During the thirty-year period, $700 per month will amount to a loan repayment of $252,000, or two and a half times the amount originally borrowed. This interest seems overwhelming and often motivates the home buyer to send extra principal to the mortgage company whenever possible to eliminate that monster interest. What they don't realize is, they are killing their partner, Uncle Sam, in the process.

Every time you send an extra $100 to the mortgage company, you are in effect saying, "Here, Mr. Banker, is an extra $100. Don't pay me any interest on this. If I need it back, I will borrow it on your terms and prove there's a need why I should have it." Sounds ridiculous, doesn't it?

WHAT MAKES A PRUDENT INVESTMENT?

What constitutes a prudent investment? There are three elements a prudent investor should look for: liquidity, safety, and rate of return. If an investment also possesses a tax advantage, it is icing on the cake. When considering a particular investment, you would probably seek the answers to at least three questions:

1. Can I get my money back when I want it back—is my money going to remain liquid?
2. How safe is my money—is it guaranteed or insured?
3. What rate of return can I expect to receive?

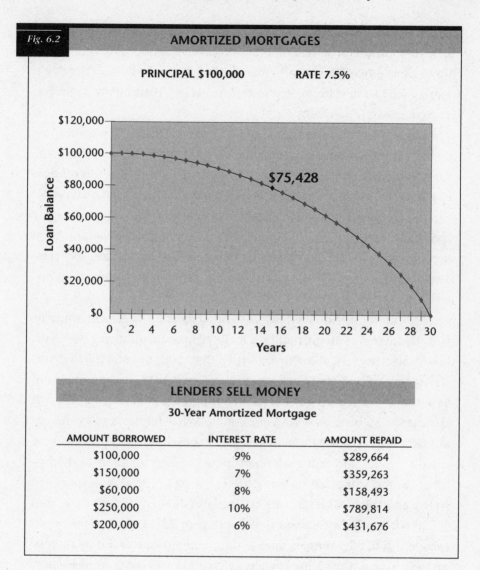

Fig. 6.2

AMORTIZED MORTGAGES

PRINCIPAL $100,000   **RATE 7.5%**

$75,428

(Loan Balance vs. Years chart, x-axis: Years 0 to 30, y-axis: Loan Balance $0 to $120,000)

LENDERS SELL MONEY

30-Year Amortized Mortgage

AMOUNT BORROWED	INTEREST RATE	AMOUNT REPAID
$100,000	9%	$289,664
$150,000	7%	$359,263
$60,000	8%	$158,493
$250,000	10%	$789,814
$200,000	6%	$431,676

How does home equity fare against these questions? Not well. As you are about to see, home equity does not pass the liquidity, safety, or rate of return tests.

HOW LIQUID IS YOUR EQUITY?

How important is it for investors to have liquidity during down times caused by external influences? What happened when the stock market took its dive in the year 2000? It was two years before a glimpse of recovery was manifest.

Those who lack liquidity when times get tough have no choice but to liquidate their assets at low prices and survive the best they can. Americans who possess liquidity during tough times can peel off dollars and keep their credit worthy and meet critical expenses. Likewise, those investors who can ride out low markets because they have liquid funds available can avoid selling their investments at a loss, and they usually come out fine as the market completes its cycle and recovers. The first reason why home equity should be separated from the property is to maintain liquidity.

As you know, home equity is defined as the fair market value of your home minus all outstanding loans against the property. So if you have a home valued at $200,000 with a first mortgage of $100,000 and an equity line of credit with a balance of $20,000, the remaining $80,000 is your equity. Of course, if your home is paid for, then the full fair market value represents your equity. What happens to home equity when the real estate market gets soft? (A soft market means that there are more homes for sale than there are buyers.) In that environment, home values go down. Different geographic areas experience strong and soft markets in various cycles at different times.

In chapter 3, I explained that the Rule of 72 is handy to use when calculating the amount of time a given interest rate will double your money. It can also be used when calculating the compound interest equivalent you realized by dividing the number of years it took to double your money into 72. For example, during a real estate boom, if home values double during a five-year period, as some did in Salt Lake City, Utah, in the mid-1990s, the compound interest equivalent represents about 15 percent appreciation per year (72 ÷ 5).

In the 1990s, during the same time that metropolitan, central Utah real estate was booming, the market in southern California was soft. In contrast, after September 11, 2001, the real estate market in Utah went rather soft for two years, while the market in southern California remained strong. In 2003, many people building a home in Las Vegas, Nevada, could sell their home, after it was built, for 20 percent more than the cost. Homes costing $200,000 to build were sold four months later for $240,000 because the demand was greater than the supply.

So how do you calculate the rate of return on home equity in cyclical markets? Is it primarily a function of the geographic area your home is located in? Absolutely not! It doesn't matter whether your home is located in Newport Beach, California; Salt Lake City, Utah; Houston, Texas; or Honolulu, Hawaii. *The return on equity is always the same: zero!* When our home equity increases, we have the misconception that home equity has a rate of return. Equity grows as a function of the home appreciating in value or the debt being reduced, but equity itself has no rate of return.

Let's explore further why home equity does not pass the liquidity, safety, or rate of return tests for prudent investing. When the unexpected happens, such as unemployment, disability, or a financial setback, it is difficult if not impossible to free up trapped equity in your home. People try in desperation to borrow to no avail. They explain to the mortgage lender or bank that they have been paying extra principal on their mortgage for years and ask, "Couldn't you just let me coast for a few months? I should be way ahead on my payment schedule." The fact is, *no matter how much extra you pay against your principal, the next regular payment is still due.* If you had a $100,000 mortgage balance and just paid a lump sum of $50,000 against the principal, the next month you would still have the regular payment due. And if you miss three payments in a row, the trust deed securing the note allows the mortgage lender to foreclose on the property.

If we pay 20 percent as a down payment for a $200,000 home, we have $40,000 of equity. The remaining $160,000 mortgage is secured by the property worth $200,000. What happens when we begin to pay off the home and send extra principal to the mortgage lender? More and more equity gets trapped in the house. Is that good or bad? *Equity is good, but maybe it shouldn't be all trapped inside the home.*

Assume your home appreciates an average of about 5 percent a year. It will be worth double, or $400,000, in fifteen years. In the meantime, let's assume you didn't pay extra principal against your thirty-year mortgage and your balance is now $120,000 (paid down from $160,000). At that point, who is safer: you or the mortgage company? The mortgage company has increased its position of safety because it still has first lien on an asset that is now worth $400,000, and only $120,000 is owed. So if the mortgage company is dramatically safer, who is proportionately less safe? You!

HOW SAFE IS YOUR EQUITY?

Safety is the second reason why home equity should be separated from the property. If you were in a neighborhood that was devastated by an earthquake, flood, tornado, or hurricane and your home was destroyed, would you rather have had your home mortgaged to the hilt with all of your equity in a safe side fund, or would you rather have had your home totally paid for—free and clear. I assure you that those people who have their equity in a liquid environment have greater safety under those circumstances. They have far more options to get into another home than the homeowner who keeps all the equity tied up in the property. (It is wise for a homeowner with a clear and free home to have adequate and very comprehensive hazard insurance—that's why lenders require it.)

Another concept that most homeowners don't understand is that in a soft market, a home will likely sell more quickly and for a higher price when it has a high mortgage with the equity separated in a liquid side fund. Let's say two identical homes valued at $200,000 are for sale in the same neighborhood, but homeowner A has a $180,000 mortgage on it, with only $20,000 of equity trapped in the property. Also assume that this homeowner has $160,000 of otherwise trapped equity sitting in a liquid side fund. So this homeowner has a total of

$180,000 of equity ($20,000 in the house and $160,000 outside the house).

Let's say homeowner B has only a $20,000 mortgage balance remaining and the remaining $180,000 of equity trapped in the house. If I am an interested buyer who just moved into the area, but for some reason it isn't convenient to obtain financing yet (because I haven't sold my previous home yet or I have changed employment), I may be willing to pay top dollar, maybe even a premium price, for your home if you are willing to carry a temporary contract or lease the home to me with an option to buy. If I give you $20,000 down and you are homeowner A, you now have all your equity and can be on your way. If I default (don't make the payments), you simply foreclose, keep the $20,000, and sell the home again (you are almost glad if I default). On the other hand, if homeowner B turns down your offer, because he doesn't have liquidity or safety—his equity is still trapped in the property until someone comes along and cashes him out. So homeowner B keeps the home on the market and gradually lowers the price to eventually get the home sold.

In chapter 7, I will share an example of how I purchased a home for $300,000, in a soft market, which previously had a fair market value of $505,000, with no money down. If the sellers had maintained a high mortgage balance on the home, I'm convinced they could have sold it quicker and for at least $100,000 more. I have counseled people who have been unable to sell their home in a soft market, to refinance it with a new 80 to 90 percent loan-to-value mortgage, and then put it back on the market. By selling the home on contract or leasing it with an option to buy (in the event of a "due on sale" clause in the mortgage contract), they were often able to sell their home more quickly and for a higher price.

THE DOWNSIDE OF DOWN PAYMENTS

With this understanding, let me ask you, "How much interest does the mortgage company pay you on your down payment?" The fact is, you don't earn interest on your down payment. For this reason, I have never made a down payment for any personal residence that I have purchased. (My original work, *Missed Fortune*, contains strategies on how to purchase a home with little or no cash down.)

First, let's understand why. As explained in chapter 2, for deductibility purposes, it is important to establish the highest amount of acquisition indebtedness when purchasing a home. It would be best to secure an interest-only mortgage so the acquisition indebtedness never reduces. Then you can borrow up to $100,000 over and above acquisition indebtedness and deduct the interest expense on your tax return. We will explore why this will make you more money in the next two chapters.

If you pay cash for your home, it would be like paying the largest down payment you possibly could. Again, how much interest are you going to earn on that huge down payment? Let me approach it from another angle. If you were buying a home and took out a thirty-year mortgage, which dollars would you rather use to pay it off: today's dollars or the dollars you will have twenty-five or thirty years from now? Why is it that as years go by, a house payment that once seemed so large, comprising 30 percent of our monthly paycheck, gets easier to handle? Because of the impact of inflation and the increase in income we usually experience as time goes by, the dollars we use down the road are much cheaper than the dollars we use today. If this is true, when would be the least expensive time to pay off your home, now or later? You shouldn't prepay your mortgage with inflated dollars.

WHAT IS THE RATE OF RETURN ON YOUR EQUITY?

One Christmas when I was a young boy, I received a bank bag with tie strings just like bankers used for money they stored in their safes. I would stash my savings in the bag in a secret hiding place between the studs of the wall of my bedroom, behind the intercom. I kept hundreds of dollars hidden there until I learned better. Were the dollar bills in the wall of my home liquid if I needed them? Yes. Were they safe? Yes (as long as my brother and sisters didn't know where the money was). But were my dollars hidden in the wall of my home earning a rate of return? No. In fact, they were losing money, or "purchasing power," because of inflation. What is the difference between the dollar bills I had hidden in my home and the dollar bills that any homeowner keeps trapped in the bricks, mortar, wood, and foundation of his home? None. (Except, I submit, the physical dollars that I had hidden in the wall of my home were *more* liquid and safe; they simply were not earning a rate of return.)

Let's say that the home in figure 6.3 represents your home, it has a fair market value of $100,000, and you have not put your first dollar of equity into it. If you were filling out a financial statement for your bank, what would you list your home as—an asset or a liability? Your home is an asset. So under your assets, you would list your home at $100,000. Now let's say that you have $100,000 of liquid cash sitting in a side fund. What would you list that as on your balance sheet? It would also be an asset. So how much would you have in total assets? Two hundred thousand dollars. It's true, if you had a $100,000 mortgage owing on the house, you would list the amount owed under the liability section of your balance sheet. Thus, $200,000 of assets minus a $100,000 liability would equal a net worth on those assets of $100,000. But let's look at the assets a little more closely.

If your home goes up in value 5 percent during the year, what is it worth at the end of the year? That's right: $105,000. What if your $100,000 side fund grew by 10 percent during the year, what would it be worth? Right again: $110,000. So in this example, you made $5,000 in home appreciation and $10,000 on the equity that was separated from the home, for a total of $15,000. What if the $100,000 of cash had been deposited in the home—what would have been the value of the house at the end of one year? Still $105,000. How come the answer is the same as before? Because equity has no rate of return when it is trapped in the house. Whether the house is mortgaged to the hilt or free and clear, the house appreciates regardless—the amount of equity in the home has nothing to do with it. However, with the equity freed up

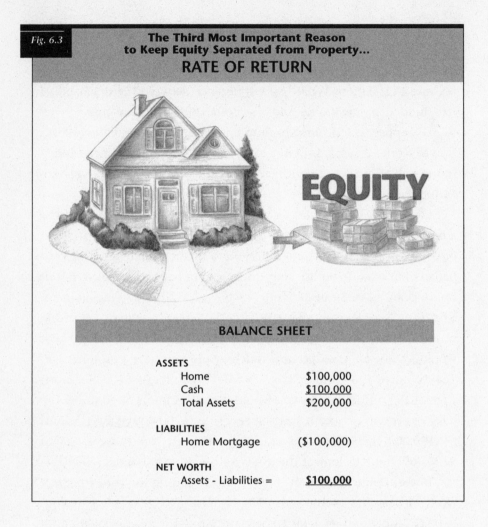

**The Third Most Important Reason
to Keep Equity Separated from Property...**

RATE OF RETURN

Fig. 6.3

EQUITY

BALANCE SHEET

ASSETS

Home	$100,000
Cash	$100,000
Total Assets	$200,000

LIABILITIES

Home Mortgage	($100,000)

NET WORTH

Assets - Liabilities =	**$100,000**

from the property, it has the potential to earn a rate of return. In this example, the results were a gross of three times as much, or $15,000, rather than $5,000. The third reason you should separate equity from your property is to allow lazy, idle dollars to earn a rate of return.

THE VALUE OF YOUR MORTGAGE

Now, you may be sitting there thinking, "But wait a minute, I would have a mortgage, and there is a cost to that mortgage, so would

I really come out ahead?" A good question. Let's address it head-on. But first, let me make perfectly clear that *when you separate equity from your house, you increase your assets.* If I borrow $100,000 from a house worth $100,000 that is free and clear of a mortgage (all the equity is trapped in it), I double my assets. On the other hand, if I pay 20 percent down, 50 percent down, or totally pay cash for a home, I decrease my assets. In the example given, I would be taking one $100,000 asset (liquid cash) and another $100,000 asset (the house) and combining them into one $100,000 asset. I would be cutting my assets in half!

Please study figure 6.4. I recommend that people keep as much equity as feasible separated from their home to increase liquidity, safety, and rate of return. If you separate equity from a home, there are generally only two ways: sell the property or mortgage it. Assuming the objective is to stay in the home, it makes far more sense to use a conduit we refer to as a mortgage to separate our equity. If we incur a mortgage, we are going to have an expense associated with it. The expense is the mortgage interest. But is that expense such a bad thing?

ARBITRAGE AND MORTGAGE—YOUR NEW BEST FRIENDS

If you were a bank, credit union, or business, why would you be willing to incur the expense of paying interest? When we borrow at a lower rate in order to earn a higher rate of interest, we earn the difference, or spread, between the two rates. This strategy is called *arbitrage.*

Arbitrage is the lifeblood strategy of nearly all financial institutions, and most self-made millionaires have mastered it. By using money in a loaned position from other people, it can be invested to earn even higher rates of return. A bank borrows money from us when we deposit it in CDs, money markets, or savings accounts. They gladly pay us 2, 3, 4 percent or more because they know they can invest it or loan it back out again and earn 5, 6, 7 percent or more. After covering their overhead expenses, a financial institution may end up netting only a 1 to 2 percent spread, but they make millions of dollars using this strategy.

Does it do the bank any good to borrow money from depositors

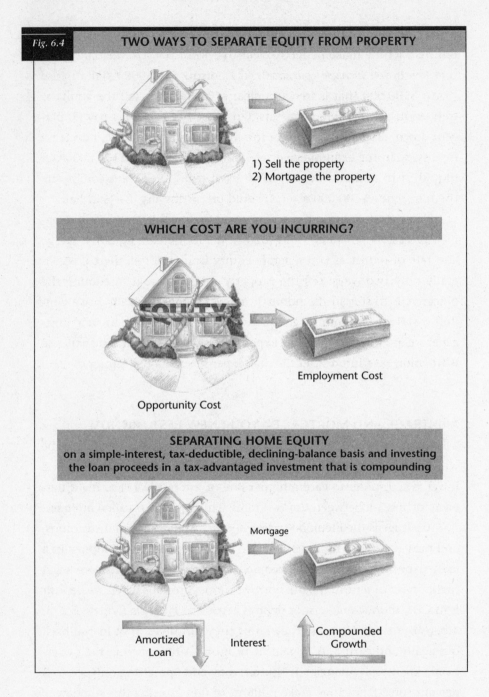

Fig. 6.4

TWO WAYS TO SEPARATE EQUITY FROM PROPERTY

1) Sell the property
2) Mortgage the property

WHICH COST ARE YOU INCURRING?

Opportunity Cost

Employment Cost

SEPARATING HOME EQUITY
on a simple-interest, tax-deductible, declining-balance basis and investing
the loan proceeds in a tax-advantaged investment that is compounding

Mortgage

Amortized
Loan   Interest

Compounded
Growth

and keep it locked up in their vault? No. But that's what they tell *you* to do—keep your money in the bank. Banks turn around and put your money immediately to work; they can't afford not to. So how can you?

When you put money to work, you are going to incur an *employment cost*—the cost of borrowing the money, which is the interest expense. Any sound business is willing to incur a certain amount of employment costs in order to earn a return greater than those costs. (If you are not making your employer more than you are costing, you're probably headed for trouble!) So it is with employing home equity.

OPPORTUNITY COST—DON'T MISS OUT

What most people don't realize is that if we choose to leave our equity in the house, as shown in figure 6.4, we will incur the same identical cost—only we don't refer to this as employment cost; it is opportunity cost. *Opportunity cost* is the actual cost incurred from lost opportunity to invest those lazy, idle dollars trapped in the house. If I have $100,000 of equity that I could separate from my house to earn 6 percent interest, and I don't do it, I have given up the opportunity to earn $6,000. That's a real cost. On the other hand, if I separate $100,000 of equity from my home and incur an employment cost of 6 percent interest, or $6,000, that is also a real cost. So one way or the other, it costs me $6,000. However, if I have no choice to incur one cost or the other, but the employment cost is deductible and the opportunity cost is not deductible, which would I prefer? I would choose to incur deductible employment costs. Why? Because in a 33.3 percent tax bracket, borrowing at 6 percent deductible (preferred) interest is really costing me only 4 percent, or $4,000. That's because I will realize $2,000 in actual tax savings by having $6,000 of preferred interest. So all I have to do is earn 4 percent or better on my borrowed loan proceeds to make a profit. Can I do that? Sure.

Suppose I separate $100,000 of equity from my home at 6 percent deductible interest on an interest-only loan. At a 6 percent interest rate, my annual interest cost would be $6,000. Therefore, my monthly payment would be $500. Because the $6,000 would be deductible, in a 33.3 percent tax bracket I would receive a tax refund of $2,000. But rather than wait until the end of the year to realize the tax savings, as explained in chapter 2, I could change my exemptions to adjust my withholding tax on my paycheck to realize the money now. So receiving $2,000 now, spread out over twelve months, increases my monthly take-home income by $166.66. Therefore, my true cost will be only $4,000 per year, or $333.33 per month. So if my employment cost from separating the equity is $4,000, let's see what happens to my equity as it grows.

If I invest the $100,000 of separated equity into a conservative side fund earning 6 percent, at the end of the first year I will have $106,000. Now, if I wisely choose the right investments that pass the liquidity, safety, and rate of return tests, I will be able to accomplish this. However, if I can also find an investment that will accumulate my money tax-deferred or even tax-free, the results will be dramatically better, as explained in chapter 2. Simple math tells us that if we earn $6,000 and our cost was $4,000, we had a 50 percent increase. But if we earn $6,000 in a taxable environment, we net only $4,000 after tax, and we don't get anywhere. So if we earn only the same rate that we are borrowing at, it is important to invest under tax-favorable circumstances. (I explain which investments are best for doing this in chapters 9 to 11.) Assuming I do this, during year 2, I would earn 6 percent on the new balance of $106,000, which equals $6,360 of interest earnings that year because of the compounding effect.

Let's take a snapshot in time after the fifth year. At the end of five years, my $100,000 of equity accumulating at 6 percent interest, tax-deferred, would have compounded and grown to $133,822. I made $33,822. My cost or investment was a net of $4,000 per year for five years, or a total of $20,000. Therefore, my profit was $13,822 on lazy, idle dollars that used to be trapped in my house earning a zero rate of return. As I enter year 6, I would earn 6 percent interest on $133,822—that equals $8,029 by year-end. So in year 6, I earn $8,029, and my employment cost was $4,000 (because I'm still paying a net after-tax interest cost of only 4 percent on the original loan balance of

$100,000). In year 6, I incurred costs of $4,000 to earn $8,029, result-ing in a net profit of $4,029, or 100 percent (figure 6.5).

Let me put this in perspective. Assume you are a bank president who reported that during the previous year the bank paid out $4 bil-lion in interest to customers on their savings accounts (because the bank "borrowed" their money), yet the bank had been investing that money and made $8 billion, resulting in a $4-billion profit. You would be a hero! By doing exactly what banks and credit unions do, you can earn a tremendous amount of money over time.

In ten years, $100,000 grows to $179,084 at 6 percent—a $79,084 increase achieved with an investment of $40,000 (ten years times $4,000). An investor would have to earn 12.1 percent interest com-pounded annually on an annual investment of $4,000 to arrive at $79,084 in ten years! Suppose I could earn 8 percent interest on my $100,000 of separated equity. My investment side fund would grow to a total of $215,982, or an increase of $115,982 over the mortgage bal-ance owed. An investor would have to earn 18.77 percent interest com-pounded annually on an annual investment of $4,000 to arrive at $115,982 in ten years. Over a thirty-year period, $100,000 grows to $1,006,266 at 8 percent interest. If I can accumulate over $1 million in thirty years by just borrowing $100,000 from my home one time, how much more could I accumulate if I borrowed more equity at first, or every few years as my home goes up in value? You dream with me.

The secret to wealth accumulation, using this strategy, is disci-plined investing—doing what banks and credit unions do. Borrow at a lower net rate and invest conservatively at a little higher rate to realize a net gain, preferably under tax-favored circumstances. Arbitrage is best achieved when you borrow on a tax-deductible, simple interest basis and invest the loan proceeds in investments that compound in a tax-favored environment. Always remember that you should separate equity only to conserve, not to consume. Learning to control and man-age home equity successfully will truly be the key to dramatically en-hancing your net worth over time.

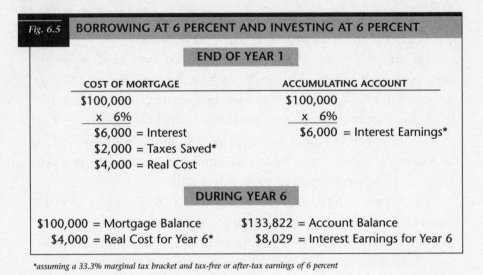

Fig. 6.5   BORROWING AT 6 PERCENT AND INVESTING AT 6 PERCENT

END OF YEAR 1

COST OF MORTGAGE	ACCUMULATING ACCOUNT
$100,000	$100,000
x 6%	x 6%
$6,000 = Interest	$6,000 = Interest Earnings*
$2,000 = Taxes Saved*	
$4,000 = Real Cost	

DURING YEAR 6

$100,000 = Mortgage Balance	$133,822 = Account Balance
$4,000 = Real Cost for Year 6*	$8,029 = Interest Earnings for Year 6

*assuming a 33.3% marginal tax bracket and tax-free or after-tax earnings of 6 percent

CONCEPTS COVERED IN CHAPTER 6

- Most people go about buying their home the wrong way—unnecessarily costing themselves thousands of dollars.
- *Mortgage interest is your friend, not your foe.*
- *It is better to incur preferred (deductible) interest expense* than non-preferred (non-deductible) interest expense.
- *Wise investors do what banks and credit unions do: borrow money at low rates and invest it to earn higher rates.*
- The liability of using OPM is a bank's greatest asset.
- You do not need to pay off your house to be considered "out of debt." *Debt, managed wisely, can be good.*
- Home equity, trapped in the house, does not contain the three elements of a prudent investment: liquidity, safety, and rate of return.
- *Learn to separate and manage your equity to better increase liquidity, safety, and rate of return.*
- The rate of return on home equity is always zero.
- Separate equity to conserve it, not consume it.

- You shouldn't prepay your mortgage with inflated dollars.
- No matter how much extra you pay against your principal, the next regular payment is still due.
- *As a home appreciates, and the loan-to-value ratio goes down, the mortgage company's position becomes safer, but you become proportionately less safe.*
- Real properties with high equity and low mortgages get foreclosed on the soonest.
- In soft real estate markets, your home will likely sell more quickly and for a higher price with a high mortgage balance than with a low mortgage balance.
- *You don't earn interest on your down payment.* Paying cash for your home would be paying the largest down payment possible.
- *When you separate equity from your home, you increase your assets.* When you pay down your mortgage, you decrease your assets.
- *It's better to have access to home equity in a liquid side fund and not need it than to have it trapped in the house and be unable to get it.*
- Since you have no choice, it's better to incur deductible employment costs on home equity than non-deductible opportunity costs.
- *Arbitrage* is the lifeblood strategy of nearly all financial institutions, and most self-made millionaires have mastered it.
- A homeowner can safely make thousands of dollars' profit by borrowing money at one rate, such as 6 percent, and investing the loan proceeds at the same 6 percent, especially when two conditions exist: the borrowing interest rate is deductible and the investing interest rate compounds under tax-favorable circumstances.
- *Learning to control and manage equity successfully is the key to enhancing your financial net worth.*

CHAPTER 7

Manage Your Mortgage to Create Wealth

Unleash the power of your mortgage

I AM FAMILIAR WITH A MARRIED COUPLE who purchased a home—paying no cash down—the year they were married. The husband was 22 years old at the time, and his wife was 21. Nine months later they sold the house and built a new one—again without paying anything down. Two years after that, they were able to build their third home for $150,000—a 6,400-square-foot house—with no money down. They understood a down payment would not earn a rate of return sitting lazily and idly in their house. The market was strong where they lived when they built their third home. They thought they had the world by the tail as they bought and sold other investment properties in a similar manner. They resided in their third home for four years, during which time it appraised, at one point, for $300,000. They felt secure with $150,000 of equity realized through the appreciation of the home. Then something happened, and they had little to no monthly income for nearly a year.

They tried in desperation to borrow on their home, but without the immediate ability to make payments, they couldn't find a lender who would loan them the needed money. They sold as many liquid assets as they could to keep their mortgage current. They finally put their home on the market, seeking relief from the house payment and access to the equity trapped in the house. Due to the region's shift to a soft market (where there is a greater supply of homes for sale than demand to buy), they were forced to continually lower the selling price of their home, from $295,000 to $199,000. Finally, after nine months, they were forced to surrender their house to the mortgage lender (the highest bidder) at a sheriff's auction on the county courthouse steps. Their home was foreclosed on, and they lost $150,000 of equity, and their credit was blemished for seven years. The mortgage lender finally sold their home several months later for $30,000 less. This deficiency balance was also reflected on their credit report for the following seven years.

Through this experience, the couple learned some unforgettable lessons:

- They learned the importance of keeping their assets in investments that were liquid in the event of an emergency.
- They learned the importance of maintaining flexibility in order to ride out market lows and take advantage of market highs.
- They learned it was a lot better to have access to their home equity and not need it than to need it and not be able to get it.
- Most important, they learned that a house was a place to house families, but not to store cash safely.

I know they learned to never allow a significant amount of equity to accumulate in their property without maintaining liquidity, *because my wife and I were that couple!*

THE VALUE OF LESSONS LEARNED

Remember in chapter 1 when I explained the value of intellectual assets? Wisdom is a product of knowledge times experience. People often learn more from their bad experiences than their good ones. Fortunately, my wife and I were able to immediately purchase another home with no money down, even with a poor credit rating. Even though losing a home to foreclosure early in my life was not a pleasant experience, I am grateful for the valuable lessons I learned. However, if I don't capitalize that asset (the wisdom I gained) by sharing the lessons learned with others, it will benefit no one but me. We lost that home in 1982, and since that time, we have helped numerous people understand how to manage the equity in their home successfully to increase liquidity, safety, and rate of return. By capitalizing on that single bad experience, I have enhanced far more human, intellectual, and financial assets than I lost on our home's foreclosure.

So many times in life we find ourselves trapped into a certain way of thinking. Albert Szent-Györgyi, a brilliant scientist who won the Nobel Prize twice in his lifetime, stated, "Discovery consists of seeing what everybody has seen, but thinking what nobody has thought." People often make the mistake of asking people who are trapped inside the same box (or way of thinking) how to get out of the box. What they don't realize is, the instructions on how to escape that box are written on the outside. In other words, if you want to know how to become a self-made millionaire, you should study self-made millionaires.

When briefly introduced to the strategies in this book, people often retort, "I would never borrow on my house to manage the equity in an attempt to increase my net worth!" (Chances are, if you asked such people how they invest their money, they would probably say, "Well, I don't have any money!" There are a lot of people who wear big cowboy hats but don't have any cattle.)

For the purest drink of water, it is best to go to the head of the spring, not the trough after it has run through the corral and become polluted. I'm always wary of marriage counselors who have never been married, child therapists who have never had children, and financial

Money Myth-Conceptions

advisors who don't understand how to capitalize assets to give them a new life (figure 7.1). Likewise, our time is better served learning from those who have actually succeeded in the creation of true wealth. The principles contained in this book are based on the experiences of hundreds of self-made millionaires. Read on to learn from their lessons.

THE DANGER OF IDLE EQUITY

Throughout the United States, different regions will experience periods of strong real estate values with appreciation and periods of soft

values with no appreciation—even depreciation. Because of these cycles, I advise that the highest amount of equity as feasible be kept separated from the property. This is critical to maintain liquidity and
safety of principal and to allow otherwise trapped equity to earn a rate
of return. A major cause of home foreclosure is physical disability. But
the chance of becoming temporarily financially disabled is even
greater. When external forces beyond our control take their toll, it is
imperative to stay in control of your home's equity.

And here's a seldom understood truth: Those properties that have
the most equity will be the ones that generally get foreclosed on the
soonest. If the real estate market in a particular area has gone temporarily soft and you lose your ability to make your house payment,
you are in real jeopardy. Loss of employment, disability, illness, or economic downturns may create such a situation. If you go to your lender
and say, "Hey, I need a loan; I have plenty of equity in my home as collateral," the lender won't do it. *Most banks are not collateral lenders*
(even though they love using it as extra security). They loan on your
ability to repay. If you lack that ability, they won't lend you the money.

I have seen instances where large employers, for one reason or another, have announced impending layoffs. Some of those employees
who felt they might be affected went out and secured equity lines of
credit while they were still employed. Others waited to apply for an equity line of credit until after they were laid off, only to find the lender
turned them down. As explained in chapter 6, it doesn't matter if you
paid $10,000 the previous month against the principal of your mort-
gage, the next regular payment is still due in thirty days. If you miss
three consecutive payments and the loan is secured with a trust deed
note, you agreed that the lender has the right to foreclose on your
property to protect its investors.

If you were a mortgage lender with a portfolio of delinquent loans
(people behind on their payments) in a soft market, which homes
would you foreclose on first? Let's say the average value of homes in
the area was $200,000 a few years earlier in a strong market, but now
home values have temporarily dropped to $150,000. Mortgage bankers

are out to protect their investors with all the contractual rights they possess. They will foreclose on the properties that have the most equity. For example, a home that used to be worth $200,000—now valued at only $150,000 with only $40,000, $60,000, or $80,000 owing on a mortgage—will be foreclosed on soonest. In contrast, a home under the same circumstances that has more owing than what it is worth will get favorable treatment from the mortgage lender. They will sometimes bend over backward to work with the borrower. Why? They really don't want to foreclose on a house that is worth only $150,000 when you owe $160,000 or more.

PREPARE TO ACT INSTEAD OF REACT

You should always position yourself to be able to act instead of react to circumstances over which you may have no control. By maintaining liquidity and safety of principal of your home equity, you are in much better control. When you separate equity for these reasons, you are doing so to conserve equity, not consume it.

On the other hand, when homeowners borrow equity out of their homes to buy depreciating assets such as automobiles, boats, and snowmobiles, they often end up consuming their home equity. When undisciplined borrowers use home equity to consolidate credit card debt, only to run up their credit card balances again, they enter a cycle of debt proliferation that often ends up consuming their equity, which may lead to bankruptcy.

Let's further clarify why and how a homeowner should borrow to conserve rather than consume.

WHEN TO REFINANCE

Often, homeowners will determine whether they should refinance their home using a simple analysis. First, they total all of the costs associated with refinancing, such as appraisal fees, title insurance, credit reports, and other closing costs. They then take the difference in monthly payments they will achieve by refinancing and divide that into the total cost of refinancing. This tells them the break-even point when they will recoup their refinance costs. For example, if closing costs to refinance total $2,400 and by doing so you will save $100 per month, in twenty-four months you will have recouped the cost of re-financing. If you are going to reside in that home for at least two years, you may determine it's wise to refinance. Another rule of thumb dictates you should refinance only if you could lower your interest rate by two percentage points.

I recommend you consider refinancing your home every time the interest rate is even 0.5 percent less than your current mortgage. By doing so, you can possibly shave eight to ten years off the time needed to "pay off" your mortgage. I also recommend you consider refinancing your home every time you have excess, dormant, borrowable equity residing in your home. I can prove why you can be financially ahead to refinance your home to separate equity even if the interest rate on the new mortgage is two percentage points higher than the old mortgage. Every time I personally refinance my home to successfully manage equity, I accelerate the schedule to have a "clear and free" home on my personal balance sheet, sooner than I was on schedule to pay off my older, lower mortgage. This is true regardless of the interest rate environment, because interest rates are relative.

When interest rates for borrowing are low, they are likewise low for saving and investing. Proportionately, when interest rates for borrowing are high, I can achieve higher rates of interest on my savings and investments. When I can borrow home equity at 6 percent, I can usually earn 6 percent or better on my conservative long-term investments. When I borrowed home equity in the 1980s at 12 percent, I was able to earn 12 percent or better on fixed-rate investments. The power in managing equity successfully to enhance net worth is the ability to earn a return on otherwise lazy, idle dollars that reside in the house. *Remember, the primary reasons for separating equity are to increase liquidity and safety.* However, due to the tax-favored treatment we can get on home equity interest, when we borrow at 6 percent that is deductible in a 33.3 percent tax bracket, all we have to earn is 4 percent to make money. If we borrow at 12 percent interest tax-deductible, all we have to earn is 8 percent to make money. Since interest rates are relative, I have always been able to establish a profitable spread between my net after-tax borrowing rate and the net earning rate because of the investment vehicles that I have chosen.

CONTROL YOUR NET WORTH BY CONTROLLING YOUR EQUITY

The key to dramatically enhancing your net worth is learning to control your equity effectively. You will reach your "freedom point" much more quickly by using some of Uncle Sam's money instead of your own in the process. Your freedom point is when you have enough money in a safe, liquid environment that can wash away or cover the liability of your mortgage. If I have enough money available to pay off my home mortgage by placing a phone call or making an electronic transfer of funds anytime I desire, I have arrived at the freedom point; I consider myself "out of debt." This is true even though I may have a million-dollar liability on my balance sheet.

The same principle applies in business. Many large corporations may claim they are debt-free even though they have millions of dollars of liabilities on their financial statements. Why? Because by managing their assets and liabilities wisely, they are able to maintain greater liquidity and safety, as well as earn greater returns. They earmark certain assets or assign them to specific liabilities to maintain their positive net worth—a net worth that is growing faster through wise debt management.

As explained in chapter 6, it costs the same to live in your house whether you borrow by taking out a mortgage or you pay cash for it. If you pay cash, you have all your equity tied up in the property and have given up the opportunity to earn a rate of return. Again, this is because equity has no rate of return when it's in the property—it will go up or down in value regardless of how much equity you have in it. In chapter 6, we learned that if our equity is tied up in the property, we incur opportunity cost; if we separate our equity by borrowing, we incur employment cost—the interest we pay on the mortgage.

THE MYTH-CONCEPTION OF MORTGAGES

Let's look at costly misperceptions held by millions of Americans:

- Most people believe that home equity is a prudent investment, yet I have proved that it does not adequately pass the liquidity, safety, and rate of return tests of prudent investing.
- Most people believe making extra principal payments on their mortgage saves them money.
- Most believe mortgage interest is an expense that should be eliminated as soon as possible.
- Most believe home equity has a rate of return and enhances their net worth.

By the end of chapter 8, I will have dispelled all of these myths.

Most people who want to develop home equity have the misconception that the best method is to accelerate the payoff of their home by making extra principal payments on their mortgage. Some homeowners are lured into thinking that biweekly payment plans are the answer. Others rely on fifteen-year rather than thirty-year mortgage amortizations. In actuality, such methods are not the wisest ways to accomplish a "free and clear" home.

Through another strategy, you can accumulate sufficient cash in a conservative, tax-deferred mortgage acceleration plan to cover the liability of the mortgage on your home just as soon as or sooner than you can with the traditionally accepted methods. Additionally, you will have the following advantages:

- You will maintain flexibility, liquidity, and safety of principal by allowing home equity to grow in a separate side fund where it is accessible in case of emergency, temporary disability, or unemployment.

- You will maximize tax-deductible interest by keeping the loan balance as high as possible until you have accumulated sufficient cash to cover your mortgage. In a 33.3 percent tax bracket, you can actually accumulate enough to pay off a $150,000 thirty-year mortgage in thirteen and a half years by using the same cash outlay required by a fifteen-year mortgage. This is possible partly because of up to $12,000 to $20,000 (depending on your tax bracket) of Uncle Sam's money instead of your own.

- You will maintain control and portability of your home equity to allow an increase in its rate of return. Most homeowners relocate an average of every seven years. As explained, your home may likely sell much more easily and for a higher price with a high mortgage balance than with a low mortgage balance (see chapter 6). Regardless of real estate market conditions, your equity should always be kept highly liquid.

THE DISADVANTAGES OF TRADITIONAL MORTGAGE PAYOFFS

Most homeowners approach the goal of outright home ownership—part of the American dream—in a traditional fashion. They feel that saving mortgage interest and paying off the loan early is the best solution and is accomplished best by applying extra principal to the mortgage, usually with one of four methods (for an in-depth examination of each method, see my more comprehensive book, *Missed Fortune*):

1. Biweekly payments—paying one-half the normal monthly amount every two weeks, which would result in twenty-six half mortgage payments, or a total of thirteen full mortgage payments in each calendar year
2. Doubling the principal—using an amortization schedule to

calculate the amount of principal being paid, then paying double that principal amount with each payment

3. Target year—determining a year by which to pay off the mortgage, then calculating how much extra to pay toward the principal each month to have it paid for by that target year

4. Mortgage-term reduction—reducing the terms of the mortgage, from a thirty-year mortgage to a fifteen-year mortgage,
for example

I contend that all four traditional approaches contain major disadvantages most homeowners don't consider. These disadvantages include:

- Losing control of your home equity
- Increasing the after-tax cost of owning your home
- Increasing your risk of foreclosure and, therefore, the risk of
losing your equity
- Dramatically reducing the return on your equity dollars
- Decreasing your ability to sell your home quickly, at the best
price, if needed
- Unnecessarily extending the time required to become debt-
free, thereby increasing your costs

*Please understand this book is not meant to advocate that people go fur-
ther into debt.* For more than thirty years, I have advised people to get
out of debt as soon as possible. However, I advise they do so by using
the wisest method to maintain flexibility—a method not embodied in
any of the four traditional methods just described.

THE SATISFACTION OF SMART PLANNING

As explained earlier, I consider a home "paid for"—even though it
may be mortgaged to the hilt—if I have sufficient liquid assets in a safe
environment that could wash out the liability of my mortgage. I sleep

better at night with my home fully mortgaged when the equity is re-moved from my property and repositioned in a safer, more liquid environment. Contrary to popular belief, any conceivable financial setback can likely be best resolved if your home equity is separated from your property rather than trapped in it.

If homeowners would deposit any extra principal payments in a separate, liquid, and safe side fund, instead of giving them to their mortgage company, they would accumulate enough money to pay off the mortgage in as short a time frame—or shorter. Let me illustrate.

If I were to take out a new $150,000 fifteen-year mortgage as shown in figure 7.2, my mortgage payment would be $1,433.48. I would pay this amount monthly for fifteen years—equivalent to fif-teen annual payments of $17,202 (column 4). This mortgage payment would be my gross outlay. However, because of the tax benefit I receive (by deducting the interest on my mortgage payment) on Schedule A of my tax return, I am really not shelling out that much from my pocket. Uncle Sam is in essence paying part of my annual mortgage payment with money I would have paid in taxes. Column 3 shows that an in-terest expense of $11,805 the first year, deducted on Schedule A of my tax return as mortgage interest expense, saves me $3,935 in taxes. This results in a net after-tax mortgage payment of $13,267, as shown in column 6.

Over the life of a $150,000 mortgage, a homeowner consistently pays more mortgage interest each year with a thirty-year mortgage than with a fifteen-year mortgage (see circled totals in figure 7.3). Most people view this as a negative. That's why they are motivated to take out a fifteen-year mortgage—in order to pay as little interest as possi-ble. However, by taking out a thirty-year amortized mortgage, the po-tential for tax deductions is greater. Therefore, the net after-tax monthly mortgage payment is substantially less for a thirty-year mort-gage than for a fifteen-year mortgage.

If we take the annual difference between the net after-tax pay-ment on a fifteen-year mortgage and a thirty-year mortgage each year (figure 7.4) and deposit that money in a tax-deferred, interest-bearing

Fig. 7.2		15-YEAR MORTGAGE ANALYSIS				
	Principal $150,000			Type Amortized		
	Payment $1,433.48			Years 15		
	Rate 8.00%			Tax Bracket 33.33%		
END OF YEAR	[1] LOAN BALANCE	[2] PRINCIPAL PAYMENT	[3] INTEREST PAYMENT	[4] TOTAL PAYMENT	[5] TAX SAVINGS	[6] NET PAYMENT AFTER TAX
1	$144,603	$5,397	$11,805	$17,202	$3,935	$13,267
2	138,758	5,845	11,357	17,202	3,785	13,416
3	132,429	6,330	10,872	17,202	3,624	13,578
4	125,573	6,855	10,347	17,202	3,449	13,753
5	118,149	7,424	9,778	17,202	3,259	13,943
6	110,109	8,040	9,161	17,202	3,053	14,148
7	101,401	8,708	8,494	17,202	2,831	14,371
8	91,971	9,430	7,771	17,202	2,590	14,612
9	81,757	10,213	6,989	17,202	2,329	14,872
10	70,697	11,061	6,141	17,202	2,047	15,155
11	58,718	11,979	5,223	17,202	1,741	15,461
12	45,744	12,973	4,229	17,202	1,409	15,792
13	31,694	14,050	3,152	17,202	1,050	16,151
14	16,478	15,216	1,986	17,202	662	16,540
15	0	16,478	723	17,201	241	16,960
	TOTAL $150,000	$108,026	$258,026		$36,005	$222,021

Notes:
a. Tax Savings [5] assumes a state and federal marginal tax bracket of 33.33% multiplied by the interest payment [3].
b. Mortgage interest is generally tax deductible, however, certain limitations are applicable. Please review with your tax advisor.
c. Net Payment After Tax [6] equals Total Payment [4] less Tax Savings [5].

side fund (let's assume 8 percent), you will notice that by year fifteen, the conservative side fund (column 5) will have accumulated $25,159 more than is needed to pay off the mortgage (column 1)! Do you see why I refer to this as the $25,000 mistake millions of Americans make? It's an even bigger mistake if the mortgage is greater than $150,000.

You might say, "But wait a minute, I have to pay 33.3 percent in taxes on the interest or growth I'm earning on my side fund!" Even if you invested the difference in a tax-deferred side fund that will later be taxed, you would still come out ahead. But it would be far better to use

| Fig. 7.3 | 30-YEAR MORTGAGE ANALYSIS |

Principal $150,000   Type Amortized
Payment $1,100.65   Years 30
Rate 8.00%   Tax Bracket 33.33%

END OF YEAR	[1] LOAN BALANCE	[2] PRINCIPAL PAYMENT	[3] INTEREST PAYMENT	[4] TOTAL PAYMENT	[5] TAX SAVINGS	[6] NET PAYMENT AFTER TAX
1	$148,747	$1,253	$11,955	$13,208	$3,985	$9,223
2	147,390	1,357	11,851	13,208	3,950	9,258
3	145,920	1,470	11,738	13,208	3,912	9,296
4	144,328	1,592	11,616	13,208	3,872	9,336
5	142,605	1,724	11,484	13,208	3,828	9,380
6	140,738	1,867	11,341	13,208	3,780	9,428
7	138,716	2,022	11,186	13,208	3,728	9,480
8	136,526	2,190	11,018	13,208	3,672	9,535
9	134,155	2,371	10,836	13,208	3,612	9,596
10	131,587	2,568	10,640	13,208	3,546	9,662
11	128,805	2,781	10,426	13,208	3,475	9,733
12	125,793	3,012	10,196	13,208	3,398	9,810
13	122,531	3,262	9,946	13,208	3,315	9,893
14	118,998	3,533	9,675	13,208	3,225	9,983
15	115,171	3,826	9,382	13,208	3,127	10,081
15 YR TOTAL		**$34,828**	**$163,290**	**$198,120**	**$54,425**	**$143,694**
16	111,028	4,144	9,064	13,208	3,021	10,187
17	106,540	4,488	8,720	13,208	2,906	10,301
18	101,680	4,860	8,348	13,208	2,782	10,426
19	96,416	5,264	7,944	13,208	2,648	10,560
20	90,715	5,701	7,507	13,208	2,502	10,706
21	84,542	6,174	7,034	13,208	2,344	10,863
22	77,856	6,686	6,522	13,208	2,174	11,034
23	70,614	7,241	5,967	13,208	1,989	11,219
24	62,772	7,842	5,366	13,208	1,788	11,419
25	54,280	8,493	4,715	13,208	1,571	11,636
26	45,082	9,198	4,010	13,208	1,337	11,871
27	35,120	9,961	3,247	13,208	1,082	12,126
28	24,332	10,788	2,420	13,208	807	12,401
29	12,649	11,683	1,524	13,208	508	12,700
30	0	12,649	555	13,204	185	13,019
30 YR TOTAL		**$150,000**	**$246,230**	**$396,230**	**$82,068**	**$314,161**

Notes:

a. Tax Savings [5] assumes a state and federal marginal tax bracket of 33.33% multiplied by the interest payment [3].

b. Mortgage interest is generally tax deductible, however, certain limitations are applicable. Please review with your tax advisor.

c. Net Payment After Tax [6] equals Total Payment [4] less Tax Savings [5].

Fig. 7.4	PAY OFF A 30-YEAR MORTGAGE IN 15 YEARS USING $18,420* OF UNCLE SAM'S MONEY**				
PRINCIPAL $150,000			**RATE 8.00%**	**TAX BRACKET 33.33%**	
	[1]	[2]	[3]	[4]	[5]
END OF YEAR	30-YEAR MORTGAGE LOAN BALANCE	15-YEAR MORTGAGE NET PAYMENT AFTER TAX	30-YEAR MORTGAGE NET PAYMENT AFTER TAX	DIFFERENCE BETWEEN NET PAYMENT AFTER TAX	DIFFERENCE EARNING 8% COMPOUNDING
1	$148,747	$13,267	$9,223	$4,044	$4,224
2	147,390	13,416	9,258	4,158	8,911
3	145,920	13,578	9,296	4,282	14,098
4	144,328	13,753	9,336	4,417	19,838
5	142,605	13,943	9,380	4,563	26,188
6	140,738	14,148	9,428	4,720	33,208
7	138,716	14,371	9,480	4,891	40,978
8	136,526	14,612	9,535	5,077	49,557
9	134,155	14,872	9,596	5,276	59,036
10	131,587	15,155	9,662	5,493	69,499
11	128,805	15,461	9,733	5,728	81,037
12	125,793	15,792	9,810	5,982	93,774
13	122,531	16,151	9,893	6,258	107,818
14	118,998	16,540	9,983	6,557	124,286
15	<u>$115,171</u>	16,960	10,081	6,879	<u>$140,330</u>
				$78,325	

$25,159

↑ EXCESS CASH BEYOND MORTGAGE BALANCE ↑

* $18,420 is the difference in additional tax savings using a 30-year mortgage versus a 15-year mortgage for the first 15 years.

** The numbers in this figure were taken from figures 7.2 and 7.3.

a non-taxable side fund such as one of those described in chapters 9 and 10.

What if you didn't have enough to pay off the thirty-year mortgage until the end of the fifteenth year? What if it took six months longer? I still believe it would be better to use a side fund instead of paying extra principal on the mortgage. Why? Because the liquidity, safety, rate of return, and tax benefits I achieve from having my money available in the side account far outweigh any hypothetical disadvantages—especially in the event of a financial emergency. The fact is, I can have all of those benefits and actually have sufficient money accumulated that could wash out my mortgage in a shorter time frame by using a conservative side fund.

The best strategy is to establish a liquid side fund to accumulate the funds required to pay off your mortgage, maintain flexibility, achieve substantial tax savings, and accumulate excess cash. The key is to understand how to have interest work for you rather than against you.

UNDERSTANDING YOUR MORTGAGE AND FINANCE OPTIONS

You should now understand that equity in your home does not enhance your net worth, but separated from your home, it has the ability to enhance your net worth over time. I am often asked, "What kind of a mortgage should I use?"

If you own your home free and clear or have a substantial amount of equity, you may consider obtaining a conventional mortgage or home equity loan. An amortized loan provides for repayment of the debt over a specified time period (term) by means of regular payments at specified intervals. A portion of each payment is applied toward principal reduction and the remainder to interest. On the other hand, interest-only loans require that over a certain time period, only the interest that accrues on the loan is payable until the original principal becomes due, which requires either a balloon payment, a refinance, or conversion to an amortized loan. To maximize the results of successfully managing equity to increase liquidity, safety, rate of return, and tax deductions, I recommend using interest-only mortgages and have a plan to follow that can help provide the discipline to set aside the difference in mortgage payments to accumulate the cash required to cover the mortgage liability.

The *mortgage,* or deed of trust, is the written instrument that provides security for payment of a specified debt. A deed of trust transfers title of the property to a third party who holds it until the loan is repaid. The lender has the right to request the property be sold should the borrower default. When the debt is secured by a mortgage, the borrower signs a document that provides the lender a lien against the property. The mortgage note is the borrower's contract with the lender to repay the loan. This promissory note sets the terms and conditions of repayment.

A *senior mortgage* is the first mortgage recorded, providing the holder with a lien against the property. The senior mortgage has priority over all other liens against the property. The liens held by *junior mortgages* are subordinate (of a lesser priority) to those that have been filed ahead of them. The lender's risk is directly related to the priority of the mortgage. With greater risk, the lender will demand a higher interest rate.

Mortgage insurance protects the lender against loss should the borrower default and foreclosure become necessary. With conventional loans, the lender will require private mortgage insurance (PMI) on most loans with a loan-to-value ratio greater than 80 percent. FHA loans require mortgage insurance premiums (MIP) on all loans. The VA charges a funding fee on all VA loans rather than mortgage insurance. The insurance is generally purchased by the homeowner at closing. The premium may be paid at closing, over a scheduled time period, or added into the loan amount.

Mortgage companies (mortgage bankers and brokers) include individual investors, banks, insurance companies, and other institutional sources of capital. The mortgage companies generate mortgages and are paid a fee for their services. Historically, commercial banks have been in the business of making short-term loans. Recently, they have been making more long-term loans such as mortgages. Credit unions, created for the benefit of their members, may also be a good source for a mortgage. Loans from private sources, such as family members, and controlled loans from employers or private pension plans are considered non-conforming loans that provide additional flexibility.

FIXED-RATE MORTGAGES

Fixed-rate mortgages are quite simple. The interest rates are fixed and the payments are fixed. Fixed-rate mortgages are usually amortized over fifteen or thirty years. The monthly principal and interest payment does not vary unless late-payment interest and/or penalties are incurred. If the lender wants to make sure taxes and home insurance are always current, the payment required by the mortgage company will include those in escrow. The tax and insurance portion of the monthly mortgage may vary each year depending upon those rates. However, the sum of the principal and interest (PI) will be constant with a fixed-rate mortgage.

ADJUSTABLE-RATE MORTGAGES

Adjustable-rate mortgages are loans on which the interest rate may vary over the life of the loan. ARMs allow for lower qualifying incomes because of the initially lower interest rates, making housing more affordable. As a trade-off for the lower initial interest rate, the borrower bears the burden of possible increasing rates in the future. In order to determine the amount of adjustments, interest rates in ARMs are tied to one of many interest rate adjustment indexes that represent the general movement in interest rates. Lenders then add percentage points, referred to as the *margin,* to the index to determine the adjustable rate.

Interest rate caps limit the changes in the interest rate. The periodic rate cap limits the adjustments during a stated time period. The *payment cap* limits the changes in the monthly payment amount. Even though the interest rate can increase, the increase in the monthly payment amount may be limited by the loan's payment cap. The *conversion option* allows an ARM to be changed to a fixed-rate mortgage without the normal expenses of refinancing. A flat fee or a certain number of points is usually charged to exercise this option, and it must be exercised during a specified time period.

DETERMINING THE BEST TYPE OF MORTGAGE TO USE

Whether it's to reduce monthly payments, consolidate monthly payments, free up equity to conserve rather than consume, or manage equity as described in this book, homeowners face a huge variety of options for tapping into available equity. Borrowers can choose to refinance their existing mortgage, apply for a second mortgage, or establish a home equity line of credit. Depending on the option selected, you will need to decide whether to opt for a fixed-rate or a variable-rate mortgage.

The best financing plan for a homeowner using the equity management strategies contained in this book will depend on factors such as:

- Ability to make monthly payments
- Amount of equity available
- Interest rate on the current mortgage
- Expected length of residence in the current home

Those with mortgages at below-market interest rates may not want to refinance that debt. A second mortgage or home equity loan might be more appropriate. In addition to preserving an attractive interest rate on the first mortgage, this strategy usually results in lowering or even eliminating closing costs.

Homeowners with above-market rates of interest on their first mortgages may choose to refinance with a new first mortgage at current rates. This reduces the cost on the balance of their existing mortgage and allows them to obtain a lower interest rate on the additional equity they may be accessing.

Fixed-rate mortgages have been more appealing for many homeowners due to the certainty of monthly payment amounts. However, these can prove more expensive for those homeowners who relocate within four or five years. Adjustable-rate mortgages offer lower interest rates than fixed mortgages, and due to their annual and lifetime interest rate caps, they are likely more economical during the first few years, even if interest rates increase dramatically. Interest-only mortgages should be considered by those desiring lower payments, wanting to maximize tax deductions, or planning to relocate or refinance within a few years. Some innovative programs allow the borrower to have four different options every month when they make a payment. They can choose to pay (1) the fifteen-year amortized payment amount, (2) the thirty-year amortized payment amount, (3) the interest-only amount, or (4) a minimum payment based on a negative amortization formula.

Here I have given only some general items to consider when choosing a particular type of mortgage. The financing option most appropriate for a specific homeowner will vary depending on these and other factors. Consultations with competent professional financial services representatives and mortgage loan officers can assist you with the mortgage selection process.

PAY NO MONEY DOWN

Another common myth with home buyers is that you must always pay cash down when you purchase real property. The fact is, there are many ways to purchase real property without paying cash down. If your budget allows when acquiring a home or other properties, pay little or no cash down, to leverage your dollars and establish the highest amount of acquisition indebtedness for tax-deductibility purposes.

During the first thirty years of our marriage, my wife and I purchased and lived in several different homes to accommodate our family of six children. In every case, we were able to acquire the property without a cash down payment, although we incurred some costs associated with closing or title work. I have also been able to avoid a down payment or using my own cash when purchasing investment (residential and commercial) real estate, as well as recreational property. Don't misunderstand me—paying a cash down payment when purchasing property is not an irreversible mistake. *But I believe that by paying no more money down than necessary, I can keep the equity in a liquid side fund that will maintain safety of principal and can earn a rate of return greater than the cost of those funds.* I never want to tie up equity unnecessarily.

There are many publications, books, videos, and audio programs that explain different methods by which successful real estate investors have purchased property with no money down. In chapter 13 of *Missed Fortune,* I provide details on several strategies I have used.

When you purchase a home in a soft market, there are more opportunities to arrange for the purchase with no cash down payment. Many good deals in the real estate market are found by methodically searching for homes worth more than their selling prices. Patience is required as you search for homes that will appraise for more than the price you can negotiate.

Many opportunities exist where real estate can be purchased with the seller carrying the contract or leasing the property with an option to buy under terms as favorable as an immediate purchase. Often, it takes spending only a few minutes with the seller to determine if he really needs cash out of his property. On several occasions, I have negotiated the purchase of properties with no cash down. By educating sellers about the concepts in this book, they suddenly realize they really don't want to take equity from the sale of their old property and unnecessarily put it into a new property. One of the safest investments for their money would be a trust deed note on property they are very familiar with (the home they are selling), where they can earn above-market interest rates. They can then leverage the purchase of their new property to establish the highest acquisition indebtedness possible for tax-deductibility purposes.

THE INFINITE POSSIBILITIES

My wife and I purchased a beautiful home in 1990 with no cash down. The home was just four years old. The sellers were anxious to sell it because it had been listed for eighteen months in a soft market. They had incurred costs totaling $450,000 in building and landscaping the home. It had been appraised for $505,000 two years earlier. Because they owed only $105,000 and the majority of their equity was tied up in the property, they were forced to continually reduce the price to find a buyer. They turned down several offers to buy their home on contract because their equity was trapped in the house. They felt they needed their equity in the form of cash to build their next home.

We walked into the title company, signed documents with an attorney, and walked out twenty minutes later, having purchased the home for $300,000 without any personal cash outlay (the details of this episode are fully explained in *Missed Fortune*).

We allowed the sellers to stay and rent the home from us while they built their new home so they wouldn't have to move twice. Their rent covered the entire mortgage payment. We moved into the home (after they had completed their new one) nine months later. Shortly after we had settled in, the market became strong again. We received an offer in the mail from a couple relocating from Newport Beach, California, who wanted to purchase the home for $600,000! They had sold their California home for that price. To avoid realizing a taxable capital gain, they were willing to pay $600,000 for our home. We turned down their offer because the home had the perfect amenities for our family of six children. However, had we sold it for $600,000, what would have been the rate of return? It would have been infinite because, technically speaking, none of our money was invested beyond the house payments, which were covered by the rental income (OPM). This is not a 100 percent return because no cash was actually invested for a down payment!

CONCEPTS COVERED IN CHAPTER 7

- *Keep assets in investments that are liquid* so they can be easily accessed in the event of an emergency.
- Maintain flexibility in order to ride out market lows and take advantage of market highs.
- *It's a lot better to have and not need than to need and not have.*
- Houses were made to house families, not to store cash.

- If you want to know how to become a self-made millionaire, study self-made millionaires.
- *Separate the maximum amount of equity as often as possible* to increase liquidity, safety, and rate of return.
- *Always position yourself to act instead of react to circumstances over which you may have no control.*
- Undisciplined borrowers who use home equity to consolidate credit card debt often end up consuming their equity. They may enter a cycle of debt proliferation, which can lead to bankruptcy.
- Every time you refinance your home, it's possible to accelerate the time to have a "clear and free" home on your balance sheet—sooner than you would with the previous mortgage.
- *Interest rates are relative.* When interest rates for borrowing are low, they are likewise low for saving and investing. Proportionately, when interest rates for borrowing are high, you can achieve higher rates of interest on savings and investments.
- *Use some of Uncle Sam's money instead of your own* (through tax savings) to reach your "freedom point" quicker.
- Earmark specific assets and assign them to a specific liability.
- *No method of paying extra principal payments to your mortgage is the wisest or most cost-effective way of paying off your home.*
- You can accumulate sufficient cash in a conservative, tax-deferred, mortgage acceleration plan to cover the liability of the mortgage on your home just as soon as or sooner than with traditional methods.
- The traditional methods most often used to accelerate the payoff of a mortgage result in losing control of your home equity; increasing the after-tax cost; increasing your risk of foreclosure; reducing the return on your equity dollars; decreasing your ability to sell your home quickly; and extending the time required to become debt-free.
- A home can be considered "paid for"—even though it may be mortgaged to the hilt—if you have sufficient liquid assets in a

safe environment that could wash out the liability of the mortgage.

- Any conceivable financial setback can likely be best resolved if your home equity is separated from your property rather than trapped in it.

- The best financing plan for a homeowner using the equity management strategies contained in this book will depend on factors such as the ability to make monthly payments, the amount of equity available, the interest rate on the current mortgage, and the expected length of residence in the current home. *Interest-only mortgages can provide some of the best leverage.*

- When acquiring a home or other properties, pay little or no cash down (if your budget allows), to leverage your dollars and establish the highest amount of acquisition indebtedness for tax deductibility.

CHAPTER 8

Homemade Wealth

The formula to convert your home equity into a million-dollar net worth

THE TALE OF THREE HOMEOWNERS

There once were two friends who lived next door to each other for twenty-five years. They purchased their first homes at the same time for $100,000. They paid 20 percent down ($20,000) and financed the balance of $80,000 at 7.5 percent interest with thirty-year amortized mortgages. They lived in these homes for fifteen years before deciding to relocate to a new development. During this fifteen-year period, they experienced about 5 percent average annual appreciation on their properties. When they decided to move, their homes had a fair market value of $200,000.

During that fifteen-year period, they had paid only regular monthly payments (no extra principal), so their mortgage balances owing at the end of fifteen years were $60,000. They each received $140,000 of equity in cash upon the sale of their homes. They were excited to purchase new homes again next door to each other. The cost of the new homes was $200,000 each. During their second home purchase, they each did things a little differently. We'll refer to one homeowner as Mr. X.S. Down and the other homeowner as Mr. O.K. Leverage.

144

Fig. 8.1	FINANCING OPTIONS	
X.S. DOWN		**O.K. LEVERAGE**
$ 200,000	Home Value	$ 200,000
– 140,000	Down Payment	– 40,000
$ 60,000	Mortgage	$ 160,000
	10 YEARS LATER	
$ 300,000	Home Value	$ 300,000
– 52,000	Mortgage Balance	– 139,000
– 8,000	Principal Reduction	– 21,000
– 140,000	Less Down Payment	– 40,000
$ 100,000	Gain	$ 100,000

Mr. X.S. Down put excess money down when purchasing his new home because he thought that lower mortgages meant lower costs. (No one had taught X.S. Down about opportunity cost.) He took the entire $140,000 of equity from the sale of his previous home and paid it down on the purchase of his new home. Therefore, X.S. Down took out only a $60,000 mortgage on his new home.

On the other hand, O.K. Leverage felt okay about leveraging his money on the purchase of his new home. He paid only 20 percent down ($40,000) and kept the remaining $100,000 of equity from his former home in a liquid side fund. So O.K. Leverage took out a $160,000 mortgage on his new home.

The homes appreciated in value a little more than 4 percent a year, to a fair market value of $300,000 after ten years. Let's take a financial snapshot at that point to see the difference between the two situations (figure 8.1).

X.S. Down's home, worth $300,000, less the outstanding mortgage balance of $52,000, less an $8,000 reduction in mortgage, less the down payment of $140,000, resulted in a $100,000 gain.

On the other hand, O.K. Leverage's home, worth $300,000, less the mortgage balance of $139,000, less a $21,000 reduction in mortgage, less the down payment or original equity of $40,000, resulted in a $100,000 gain.

We have learned that equity has no rate of return when it sits idly in the house. Therefore, the gain resulted from the home appreciating. The remainder of the equity resulted from the mortgages being paid down. However, who had a better net internal rate of return when compared to the amount of equity tied up in the property? O.K. Leverage did by far. Only $40,000 of his equity was tied up in the property to realize a $100,000 gain, whereas X.S. Down tied up $140,000 of equity to realize the same gain.

O.K. had a brother named Max who also purchased a home in the same development. If O.K. Leverage had done what his smarter brother Max did, he would have realized an even better return. Max Leverage purchased his home with maximum leverage by paying no cash down, financed 100 percent, and took out an interest-only loan. Therefore, no equity was tied up in the property. The Leverages took their equity, enjoyed far more tax savings, and socked that money away into a conservative, liquid, and safe side fund. They ended up with enough money to pay off their higher mortgages sooner, with less cash outlay than X.S. Down. They did this by repositioning their assets and allocating them for greater liquidity, safety, and rate of return. Not only that, they used more of Uncle Sam's money to get there than X.S. Down did.

WHAT'S THE DIFFERENCE?

Let's consider the differences between X.S. Down and O.K. Leverage. What does O.K. Leverage have that X.S. Down doesn't have? A higher mortgage payment. That may seem like a negative, but is it really?

O.K. Leverage has a monthly mortgage payment of nearly $1,120 (assuming a fixed, 7.5 percent, thirty-year amortized mortgage). X.S. Down has a monthly mortgage payment of only about $420 (under the same assumptions). That's a difference of $700 per month. However, what else does O.K. Leverage have? A larger tax deduction! O.K. Leverage has about $12,000 in tax deductions. X.S. Down has only about $4,500. That means O.K. Leverage has $7,500 more in tax deductions; he will save about $2,500 more in tax in the first full year than X.S. Down (33.3 percent of $7,500). O.K. Leverage will receive about $333 per month in tax savings from Uncle Sam, compared to X.S. Down's monthly tax savings of approximately $125. So O.K. Leverage's real after-tax house payment is only about $787 a month, not $1,120. X.S. Down's real after-tax monthly house payment is only about $295, not $420.

The true difference between the net after-tax monthly mortgage payment of O.K. Leverage and X.S. Down is approximately $500 ($787 – $295 = $492). As explained in chapters 6 and 7, why would O.K. Leverage be willing to pay $500 more? *Because the $100,000 that he can employ is working for him and has the ability to compound and grow to a much greater value than the net monthly cost of $500.*

The very first year, assuming 8 percent interest, O.K. Leverage can earn $8,000 on the $100,000 of equity he kept separated from his house, while paying only $500 per month ($6,000 a year) in a higher payment than X.S. Down. The net profit the first year in this example would be $2,000.

On the other hand, Max Leverage took out an interest-only first mortgage of $160,000 and a $40,000 equity line of credit totaling $200,000, representing 100 percent of the purchase price of the new home. He invested all $160,000 of his former home's equity in a side fund and effectively paid no down payment. On the extra $40,000 of equity that he kept separated from the property, Max earned $3,200 in interest (at 8 percent) the first year, while the employment cost was only $2,000 (5 percent net after tax), resulting in an additional net profit of $1,200 over his brother, O.K. Leverage. In actuality, Max Leverage's monthly payment was only $46.60 more a month than O.K. Leverage's monthly payment because Max made interest-only payments on the entire $200,000 of loans.

Max Leverage will actually have enough money accumulated in

his side fund to pay off his $200,000 mortgage in four and a half years (if he wanted)! On the other hand, if X.S. Down set aside the difference of $538 (the additional amount that Max Leverage is paying monthly) in an 8 percent interest-bearing account or against his mortgage, it would take six and a half years to pay off his $60,000 mortgage. By that time, Max Leverage will have $335,825 accumulated in his side fund, or $135,000 more than his mortgage balance of $200,000!

What are some of the other advantages the Leverages have that X.S. Down does not have?

- The Leverages have a liquid side fund to use as an emergency fund, to put in a yard, or to finish their basement (thereby increasing the value of their home without having to qualify for a loan to perform improvements).
- They have greater safety of principal in down markets because a larger portion of equity is separated.
- They have greater property portability, with the potential to sell their houses more quickly and for a higher price in a soft market (see chapter 6).
- They can convert some of their non-preferred debt to preferred debt, thereby increasing the return on their money by using that strategy.

Of all these benefits, however, probably the greatest advantage the Leverages have over X.S. Down is the ability to establish a home equity retirement plan, which can increase their net spendable retirement income by as much as 50 percent over their IRAs and 401(k)s, as explained in chapters 3 through 5.

By now, you should see there are more factors to consider when financing a home than just interest rates and closing costs. Homeowners can effectively reduce the time to achieve a "debt-free" home on their balance sheet and enhance net worth through strategic refinancing and proper management of home equity.

Remember, the purpose of managing equity is to conserve and enhance it—not to consume it. You've probably heard that the three most important factors that determine the fair market value of any real estate property are location, location, and location. Likewise, the most important factor to optimize the asset of home equity is the location of the equity—location that

- Increases its liquidity
- Enhances its safety
- Increases its rate of return
- Keeps the home more portable
- Maximizes tax advantages

SEPARATING EQUITY WITHOUT INCREASING OUTGO

How do you separate more equity without increasing your monthly outlay? The myth-conception is that it will always require a higher house payment. On the surface, that may be true, but let's go deeper. Let's look at four mortgage scenarios, all on homes worth $200,000. Let's also assume each homeowner can afford $1,000 a month for a house payment and has $100,000 of equity from the sale of his former home.

Scenario 1

Homeowner A pays $100,000 down and takes out a $100,000 fifteen-year amortized mortgage at a fixed interest rate of 6 percent, resulting in a monthly payment of $843.86. However, he still sends the mortgage company $1,000 a month to "pay off" his home early (although he gets no rate of return on the extra principal payment). Six percent annual interest on $100,000 equals $6,000, resulting in tax savings of approximately $2,000, or $167 a month. If we subtract the monthly tax savings of $167 from the payment of $843.86, we discover the net after-tax payment is approximately $677. His problem, however, is that he will be quickly killing his partner Uncle Sam by destroying his tax advantage.

Scenario 2

Homeowner B pays less down and takes out a $118,504 fifteen-year amortized mortgage at a fixed interest rate of 6 percent, resulting in a monthly payment of $1,000. His monthly tax saving is $198, so his net payment is $802. However, he has $18,504 that can be invested in a side fund that can provide liquidity and earn a rate of return.

Scenario 3

Homeowner C pays even less down and takes out a $166,791 thirty-year amortized mortgage at a fixed interest rate of 6 percent, resulting in a monthly payment of $1,000. His monthly tax savings is $278, so his net payment is $722, or $45 more than homeowner A. However, he has $66,791 of equity he kept separated from the house. Assuming an 8 percent return, he can earn $445 a month in interest on his equity.

Scenario 4

Homeowner D pays nothing down and takes out interest-only loans (a first mortgage of 80 percent loan-to-value and an equity line for the remaining 20 percent) totaling $200,000 at interest rates of 6 percent, resulting in a total monthly payment of $1,000. His monthly tax savings is $333, so his net payment is $667—less than homeowners A, B, or C! To boot, homeowner D had $100,000 of liquid equity he kept separated from the house. Assuming an 8 percent return, he can earn $667 a month in interest on his equity! In other words, in this example, homeowner D, earning a tax-favored return of 8 percent on $100,000 of equity (which stayed separated from the property), earns the amount needed to cover the after-tax payment on a $200,000 interest-only mortgage at 6 percent the very first year. That's because the net cost of a 6 percent mortgage in a 33.3 percent tax bracket is 4 percent, which equals $8,000 per year on a $200,000 mortgage. At the same time, Homeowner D can earn $8,000 by employing $100,000 of equity at 8 percent under tax-favorable circumstances.

All four homeowners are shelling out $1,000 a month, but who will accumulate a greater net worth sooner? All four homes will appreciate, regardless of how much equity is in the home or how large the mortgage is, because equity has no rate of return in the property. To successfully manage home equity, can you begin to see the advantage of keeping as much equity separated from the property as possible and using long-term amortized mortgages, or better yet, interest-only mortgages?

THE POWER OF TAX-PREFERRED BORROWING AND INVESTING

A common myth-conception is that borrowing funds at a particular interest rate, then investing them at the same or lower rate, holds no potential growth returns. Actually, you *can* create tremendous wealth by borrowing money at a particular interest rate and investing it at the same interest rate—or even less—provided two conditions are met: the interest paid on the borrowed funds is deductible, and the investment in which we invest those funds earns compound interest. And if the investment earns compound interest in a tax-favored environment, the potential for growth is even greater.

In chapter 6, I used an illustration of a homeowner borrowing $100,000 of equity at 6 percent interest tax-deductible and investing it at 6 percent, compounding non-taxed. In ten years, $100,000 grows to $179,084 at 6 percent—a $79,084 increase—achieved with an investment of $40,000 (ten years of after-tax mortgage payments of $4,000). An investor would have to earn 12.1 percent interest compounded annually on an annual investment of $4,000 to arrive at $79,084 in ten years! Suppose I could earn 8 percent interest on my $100,000 of separated equity. My investment side fund would grow to a total of $215,893, or an increase of $115,982 over the mortgage balance owed. An investor would have to earn 18.77 percent interest compounded annually on an annual investment of $4,000 to arrive at $115,982 in ten years. Over a thirty-year period, $100,000 grows to $1,006,266 at 8 percent interest.

What if you took withdrawals each month or each year from your side fund earnings to cover your net after-tax mortgage payment? In other words, let's assume you could not separate equity without increasing your monthly outlay, so your side fund would compound and grow at a slower pace. You would still accumulate a sizable nest egg.

Let's consider borrowing $100,000 at 8 percent deductible interest and investing the loan proceeds at 8 percent compounded interest tax-free, using an interest-only mortgage (figure 8.2). In year 1, you earn 8 percent interest non-taxable on $100,000—which equals $8,000, less the net after-tax cost of borrowing ($8,000 less 33.3 percent)—which equals the net increase in your side fund of $2,667. Even by taking withdrawals to make your house payment, by year 10 you would have $138,633 accumulated in your side fund. By year 20, you would have $222,038 in your side fund. In year 30, you would have $402,103 in your side fund, less the mortgage balance of $100,000, which results in a $302,103 profit.

For the remainder of the examples, let's assume you have some discretionary dollars you are saving for long-term goals, such as retirement or college funding for children. If those discretionary dollars were repositioned to cover the net after-tax mortgage payment, it would allow the invested home equity to compound and grow without having to pay the employment cost from the profit each year. Otherwise, by refinancing to more favorable mortgage terms (such as an interest-only mortgage or better interest) or repositioning non-preferred debt such as auto loans into preferred debt, it's often possible to find the money necessary to meet any increase in house payment.

MANAGING EQUITY SUCCESSFULLY

Please refer to figure 8.3. The first example illustrates a homeowner borrowing $100,000 at 7.5 percent tax-deductible and investing the loan proceeds at 7.5 percent compounding free of tax. So we are investing at the same rate we are borrowing. However, we are borrowing in a tax-deductible environment and investing in a non-taxable environment, so tremendous profit potential exists. In ten years, the side

Fig. 8.2	BORROWING $100,000 AT 8% DEDUCTIBLE INTEREST AND INVESTING THE LOAN PROCEEDS AT 8% TAX-FREE COMPOUND INTEREST USING A $100,000 INTEREST-ONLY MORTGAGE				
YEAR	GROSS INTEREST PAID [1]	NET INTEREST PAID (after tax benefit*) [2]	GROSS INTEREST EARNED [3]	NET PROFIT [3] - [2] [4]	NEW BALANCE [5]
1	$8,000	$5,333	$8,000	$2,667	$102,668
2	8,000	5,333	8,213	2,880	105,548
3	8,000	5,333	8,444	3,110	108,658
4	8,000	5,333	8,693	3,359	112,018
5	8,000	5,333	8,961	3,628	115,646
6	8,000	5,333	9,252	3,918	119,564
7	8,000	5,333	9,565	4,232	123,796
8	8,000	5,333	9,904	4,570	128,366
9	8,000	5,333	10,269	4,936	133,302
10	8,000	5,333	10,664	5,331	138,633
10 YR. TOTALS	$80,000	$53,333	$91,965	$38,633	$138,633
11	8,000	5,333	11,091	5,757	144,391
12	8,000	5,333	11,551	6,218	150,609
13	8,000	5,333	12,049	6,715	157,325
14	8,000	5,333	12,586	7,253	164,577
15	8,000	5,333	13,166	7,833	172,410
15 YR. TOTALS	$120,000	$80,000	$152,410	$72,410	$172,410
16	8,000	5,333	13,793	8,459	180,869
17	8,000	5,333	14,470	9,136	190,006
18	8,000	5,333	15,200	9,867	199,873
19	8,000	5,333	15,990	10,656	210,529
20	8,000	5,333	16,842	11,509	222,038
20 YR. TOTALS	$160,000	$106,660	$228,705	$122,038	$222,038
21	8,000	5,333	17,763	12,430	234,468
22	8,000	5,333	18,757	13,424	247,892
23	8,000	5,333	19,831	14,498	262,390
24	8,000	5,333	20,991	15,658	278,048
25	8,000	5,333	22,244	16,911	294,959
25 YR. TOTALS	$200,000	$133,333	$328,293	$194,960	$294,959
26	8,000	5,333	23,597	18,263	313,222
27	8,000	5,333	25,058	19,724	332,946
28	8,000	5,333	26,636	21,302	354,249
29	8,000	5,333	28,340	23,007	377,255
30	8,000	5,333	30,180	24,847	402,103
30 YR. TOTALS	$240,000	$160,000	$462,103	$302,103	$402,103

*assuming a 33.33% marginal tax bracket

fund has grown to $206,103, which results in a net profit of $106,103 after deducting the mortgage balance of $100,000. In year 20, the net profit is $324,785, and in year 30, the net profit is $775,496. If the annual employment cost of $5,000 were invested in an alternative investment earning 7.5 percent, it would grow to only $555,772. To match the profit of $775,496, the $5,000 annual investment would have to earn a non-taxable interest rate of 9.25 percent, or a taxable rate of 13.87 percent.

What if a homeowner borrows at a rate two percentage points higher than the earning rate? The second example illustrates a homeowner borrowing $100,000 at 8 percent tax-deductible and investing the loan proceeds at 6 percent compounding free of tax. Again, because of tax-favorable circumstances, a profit can be realized. In ten years, the side fund has grown to $179,085, which results in a net profit of $79,085 after deducting the mortgage balance of $100,000. In year 20, the net profit is $220,714, and in year 30, the net profit is $474,349. If the annual employment cost of $5,333 ($8,000 – 33.3%) were invested in an alternative investment earning as the same 6 percent, it would grow to $446,914. In this case, equity management produced only $27,435 ($474,349 – $446,914) more profit. Is it worth it? You bet. Don't forget, the primary reasons for keeping equity separated from the property are liquidity and safety of principal. Enhancing the rate of return is the third priority.

HOW TO SYSTEMATICALLY STACK UP $1 MILLION

We've taken a look at some pretty conservative examples. How about more optimistic projections? What if a homeowner earns a rate two and a half percentage points higher than the borrowing rate? Please refer to figure 8.4. The first example illustrates a homeowner borrowing $100,000 at 6 percent tax-deductible and investing the loan proceeds at 8.5 percent compounding free of tax. In ten years, the side fund has grown to $226,098, which results in a net profit of $126,098 after deducting the mortgage balance of $100,000. In year 20, the net

Fig. 8.3	MANAGING EQUITY SUCCESSFULLY		
BORROWING AT 7.5% (Tax Deductible)	**EQUITY REPOSITIONED** $100,000		**INVESTING AT 7.5%** (Compounding Tax Free)
[1] NET CUMULATIVE ANNUAL COST at 7.5% ($7,500-33.33%)		**[2]** Difference [3 - 1]	**[3]** NET CUMULATIVE GROWTH at 7.5% (Less Mortgage of $100,000)
Year			
1	$5,000	$2,500	$7,500
5	$25,000	$18,563	$43,563
10	$50,000	$56,103	$106,103
15	$75,000	$120,888	$195,888
20	$100,000	$224,785	$324,785
25	$125,000	$384,834	$509,834
30	$150,000	$625,496	$775,496

MANAGING EQUITY SUCCESSFULLY		
BORROWING AT 8% (Tax Deductible)	**EQUITY REPOSITIONED** $100,000	**INVESTING AT 6%** (Compounding Tax Free)
[1] NET CUMULATIVE ANNUAL COST at 8% ($8,000-33.33%)	**[2]** Difference [3 - 1]	**[3]** NET CUMULATIVE GROWTH at 6% (Less Mortgage of $100,000)
Year		
1	$5,333	$667	$6,000
5	$26,665	$7,158	$33,823
10	$53,333	$25,752	$79,085
15	$80,000	$59,656	$139,656
20	$106,667	$114,047	$220,714
25	$133,333	$195,854	$329,187
30	$160,000	$314,349	$474,349

profit is $411,205, and in year 30, the net profit is $1,055,825. If the annual employment cost of $4,000 were invested in an alternative investment earning 8.5 percent, it would grow to only $539,092 by year 30. To match the profit of $1,055,825, the $4,000 annual investment

Fig. 8.4	TWO WAYS TO STACK UP $1 MILLION	

#1 SEPARATE $100,000 OF EQUITY		
BORROWING AT 6% (Tax Deductible)	EQUITY REPOSITIONED $100,000	INVESTING AT 8.5% (Compounding Tax Free)
[1] NET CUMULATIVE ANNUAL COST at 6% ($6,000-33.33%)	[2] Difference [3 - 1]	[3] NET CUMULATIVE GROWTH at 8.5% (Less Mortgage of $100,000)
Year		
1 $4,000	$4,500	$8,500
5 $20,000	$30,366	$50,366
10 $40,000	$86,098	$126,098
15 $60,000	$179,974	$239,974
20 $80,000	$331,205	$411,205
25 $100,000	$568,676	$668,676
30 $120,000	$935,825	$1,055,825

#2 SEPARATE $160,000 OF EQUITY		
BORROWING AT 7.5% (Tax Deductible)	EQUITY REPOSITIONED $160,000	INVESTING AT 7.5% (Compounding Tax Free)
[1] NET CUMULATIVE ANNUAL COST at 7.5% ($12,000-33.33%)	[2] Difference [3 - 1]	[3] NET CUMULATIVE GROWTH at 7.5% (Less Mortgage of $160,000)
Year		
1 $8,000	$4,000	$12,000
5 $40,000	$29,701	$69,701
10 $80,000	$89,765	$169,765
15 $120,000	$193,420	$313,420
20 $160,000	$359,656	$519,656
25 $200,000	$615,734	$815,734
30 $240,000	$1,000,793	$1,240,793

would have to earn a non-taxable interest rate of 11.9 percent or a taxable rate of 17.85 percent.

What if a homeowner has $160,000 of available equity? The second illustration employs $160,000 of home equity by separating it at 7.5 percent and investing the loan proceeds at the same rate of 7.5 percent for thirty years. The liquid equity management account balance would be $1,400,793 at the end of thirty years. After deducting the

$160,000 mortgage balance, the net profit would be $1,240,793. In this example, the monthly mortgage payment was $1,000, which equals $12,000 per year. In a 33.3 percent tax bracket, the net after-tax cost of the mortgage would be $8,000. If $8,000 were invested in an alternative investment earning 7.5 percent, it would grow to only $889,235. That's $351,558 less than what was realized by managing equity successfully. If the investment that grew to $889,235 were taxable, the homeowner would net only $592,853 after tax.

THE ADVANTAGE OF REFINANCING EVERY FIVE YEARS

What's wrong with the above illustrations? Nothing! Except if $1 million can be accumulated by employing lazy, idle dollars that would otherwise be trapped in the home, why not separate *more* equity every time it's feasible while the house is appreciating?

Figure 8.5 illustrates a home with a beginning fair market value of $200,000 appreciating at 5 percent a year for thirty years. Based on the Rule of 72, the home will double in value about every 14.4 years (72 ÷ 5). Assuming the homeowner has $100,000 of available equity the first year, it will grow to $875,496 in 30 years if invested at 7.5 percent. The Employed Equity column illustrates 100 percent of the amount of additional equity that would be available every five years for the remaining years to year 30. The last column illustrates the result of separating the equity from the house and investing it at 7.5 percent for the remainder of the thirty-year period at each five-year increment. As shown, by refinancing, or selling the house and buying a new one, thus separating the new equity that is created every five years by virtue of appreciation, the side fund accumulates to $2,225,594 by the end of thirty years. When we subtract the final mortgage balance of $577,270 from the side fund, we net $1,648,324! You may say, "But I couldn't afford a house payment on a $577,270 mortgage!" You will find that if homes were to appreciate an average of 5 percent a year, your income would likely increase at a similar rate as well. However, at any time,

TURBO CHARGE YOUR WEALTH GROWTH RATE

Fig. 8.5

Example of separating $100,000 of equity initially and continuing to separate 100 percent of the equity every five years thereafter, on a home with a beginning fair market value of $200,000 appreciating at 5 percent annually for thirty years, borrowing at 7.5 percent tax deductible and investing the loan proceeds at 7.5 percent compounding with no tax.

YEAR	HOME VALUE AT 5%	EMPLOYED EQUITY	FUTURE VALUE AT 7.5%
0	$ 200,000	$ 100,000	$ 875,496
5	$ 255,256	$ 55,256	$ 336,970
10	$ 325,779	$ 70,523	$ 299,571
15	$ 415,786	$ 90,007	$ 266,320
20	$ 530,660	$ 114,874	$ 236,759
25	$ 677,270	$ 146,610	$ 210,478
TOTALS:			
30	$ 864,388	$ 577,270	$ 2,225,594

you may dip into your side fund and peel off dollars to meet a house payment, because you are maintaining liquidity.

THE POSITIVES OF NEGATIVE AMORTIZATION LOANS

If you can turbo charge your wealth by refinancing every five years, borrowing at 7.5 percent tax-deductible interest and investing at 7.5 percent compounding with no tax, what could you achieve by borrowing at 6 percent and earning 8 percent or better? The net profit would be more than double the ending value shown in figure 8.5. What if you refinanced every three years instead of every five years? The results would be even greater. If this is true, perhaps a negative amortization loan might make sense.

Most people view negative amortization loans as just what the name implies—negative! A negative amortization means your monthly mortgage payment is not even enough to cover the interest on the loan, so each month your loan balance increases. Who would ever want to have that arrangement? Well, now that you have a better understanding of why you do not want equity trapped in your house, you can see how a negative amortization loan can be used to keep equity from accruing and getting trapped in the house. However, I'll issue a warning here: *You must be extremely disciplined to use a negative amortization or you may end up consuming your equity. It's imperative that you set aside the money you are saving (by not paying even the interest owed each month) to make more money. Otherwise, I would suggest that an interest-only mortgage is the most aggressive approach that typical homeowners should undertake.*

UNDERSTANDING THE BIG PICTURE

By borrowing to conserve rather than to consume your equity, and by keeping the money liquid, you are protecting yourself against down markets when it may be critical to meet the liabilities created by separating the equity. The primary reason people get into trouble from leveraging property is they have either consumed the capital they borrowed or not kept the money in a liquid environment to access in case of financial hardship. It is also important to earn a rate of return on leveraged capital that is greater than the net cost of those funds. I remind you, *the strategies in this book are not for financial jellyfish.*

Through managing and controlling home equity, many homeowners not only substantially increase their net worth but also get out of debt in the quickest, smartest way possible. By refinancing as often as feasible and properly managing the excess equity accruing within the home during that time, you, as a homeowner, could achieve the enviable position of having substantial assets that far exceed your liabilities. You should consider refinancing your home every time the interest rate is even slightly better than your current rate, or whenever your current mortgage balance is lower than the fair market value of your home, allowing the separated equity to be effectively employed. Anytime you can separate a substantial sum of equity at a feasible interest rate and recover any closing costs in a short time frame, careful consideration should be given.

OVERCOMING THE "BUT I'M JUST SMALL POTATOES" SYNDROME

When people learn the concepts contained in this book and see the examples given, they often have a hard time understanding how to apply or adapt the strategies to their circumstances. This happens especially with people who feel they are just "small potatoes" or their finances are not worthy of a financial planner's time to help them implement the concepts. Don't forget: It's not what you begin with, but what you end up with, that counts!

Even though you may feel like a small frog in a big pond, if you have decent credit, sometimes only a small amount of collateral or equity is needed to get started. Why, I heard that even Kermit the Frog walked into his credit union one day and asked the loan officer, Patty Black, for a loan, when all he had to offer as collateral was a personal treasure he had kept nurtured on his lily pad. Unsure, the loan officer conferred with the manager about it. Immediately recognizing the value of the collateral, the manager replied, "That's a knickknack, Patty Black, give the frog a loan!"

In all seriousness, if you learn how to borrow to conserve and compound your equity rather than consume it, you can approach retirement, look yourself in the mirror, and sing, "this old man came rolling home—in the dough!" The point is, there are times when the money supply is so great that institutions have "loan sales" with terms liberal enough that many opportunities can be seized and cultivated.

Let's go through a simple example of how the strategies I have explained thus far in the book can be applied by just about anyone. It doesn't matter if it's Thayer/Mighty Young, a 25-year-old couple, or Kotcha/Justin Nickotime, a 60-year-old couple, or Justa Bachelor, aged 35; you can enhance your financial net worth by successfully managing equity. To illustrate, let's use an example of a 40-year-old couple and name them John and Susie Prudent.

When I, or one of my financial planning team members, sit down with prospective clients, we first determine where they are with regard to all categories of assets. Then through a series of questions, we find out where they want to go. Finally, we create illustrations and spreadsheets that show them several ways to get there by repositioning their assets without increasing their monthly outlay one dime. They are often astonished at how much better off they can be down the road toward retirement from simply repositioning and optimizing their assets.

The Prudents are a typical American couple with a combined gross income of $70,000 per year. Let's assume all income over $50,000 is marginally taxed at 33.3 percent. The Prudents purchased a home five years ago for $150,000 and took out a $120,000 thirty-year amortized mortgage at 6 percent interest. The house has appreciated and now has a fair market value of $200,000 with an outstanding mortgage balance of $110,000 (figure 8.6).

The Prudents are trying to save 10 percent of their income for long-term objectives, so they have been contributing $500 per month ($6,000 a year) into IRAs and 401(k)s. They are matched by their employers on only the first $250 of their monthly contribution, so they can reposition the remaining $250 per month for equity management retirement planning and get the same tax benefits indirectly. The Prudents also plan on saving $100 a month in non-qualified accounts to help with their children's education.

The Prudents realize they can separate $50,000 of equity from their home through an equity line of credit or by doing a cash-out refinance at 80 percent loan-to-value, thereby increasing the mortgage(s) to $160,000. For the sake of simplicity, let's focus on the net after-tax cost of interest expense on the $50,000 of equity they separate. Assuming a 6 percent interest-only loan, the monthly payment would be $250 ($3,000 per year). Since this is preferred interest (deductible), it receives the same tax advantages the Prudents were receiving on their IRA and 401(k) contributions. In other words, $3,000 of deductible mortgage

Fig. 8.6

PERSONAL FINANCIAL PROFILE
Prepared for: John and Susie Prudent

Date of Birth: 01/02/1965   Age: 40   Current Marginal Tax Bracket: 33.33%

Property Details ————————————————————————————————————

Fair Market Value of Property	$200,000.00
Original Purchase Price	$150,000.00
Verifiable Cost of Property Improvements	$0.00

Current Mortgage Details ————————————————————————————————

Beginning Date:	04/01/2000
Term:	30 Years
Amount Financed:	$120,000.00
Interest Rate:	6.00%
Monthly Payment:	$719.46
Outstanding Balance:	$110,000.00

Annual Cash Flow Allocation ——————————————————————————————

Planned Savings:	$1,200.00
Planned IRA/401(k) Contribution:	$3,000.00

OBJECTIVES: ——

1. Successfully manage equity in their home to increase its liquidity, safety, and rate of return.
2. Utilize available tax strategies to their advantage.
3. Prepare financially for a comfortable retirement.
4. Increase overall yield on their savings and investments.
5. Complete proper estate planning utilizing trusts and wills.

PLAN SUMMARY
Prepared for: John and Susie Prudent
April 21, 2005

PROPOSED ASSET ALLOCATION

Fair Market Value of Property:		$200,000.00
Amount of Proposed Mortgage:		$160,000.00
LESS:		
Current Mortgage Payoffs	$110,000.00	
Balance of Mortgage Proceeds:		$50,000.00
PLUS:		
Repositioned Assets		
Annual Amounts:		
Annual IRA/401(k) Contribution	$3,000.00	
Planned Annual Savings	$1,200.00	
TOTAL	$4,200.00	
Liquid Assets Available:		$54,200.00

Fig. 8.6 cont.	EQUITY MANAGEMENT RETIREMENT PLANNING Prepared for: John and Susie Prudent	

END OF YEAR	TRADITIONAL IRA/401(k) VERSUS SAVING APPROACH ($250/month growing at 8% tax deferred)	HOME EQUITY RETIREMENT PLANNING APPROACH ($50,000 of equity growing at 8% tax free)
1	$ 3,133	$ 54,000
5	$ 18,492	$ 73,466
10	$ 46,041	$ 107,946
15	$ 87,086	$ 158,608
20	$ 148,237	$ 233,048
25	$ 239,342	$ 342,424

RESULTING RETIREMENT INCOME FROM INTEREST EARNINGS

$239,342 earning 8% = $19,147	**Gross Annual Income**	$342,424 earning 8% = $27,394	
Annual tax at 33.3% = $ 6,382	**LESS: Tax**	Tax on distribution	- 0 -
After-tax income = $12,766	**Net Annual Income**	Non-taxable income = $27,394	
Mortgage Payment = - 0 -	**Annual Interest Payment**	After-tax payment = $ 2,000	
NET: $ 12,766	**Annual Spendable Income**	NET: $ 25,394	

NOTE: To calculate what just $10,000 of home equity can grow to, allocating $50 a month for retirement savings, simply take 20 percent (one-fifth) of the numbers illustrated because you are only investing one-fifth as much. Likewise, to calculate what $250,000 of home equity can grow to allocating $1,250 a month for retirement savings, simply compute 500 percent (five times) the numbers illustrated because you are investing five times as much.

For example, if a homeowner were to successfully manage $250,000 of home equity for 25 years earning an average of 8 percent in tax-favored investments, the ending balance would be $1,712,120, which would generate $136,970 of annual income. After paying the net after-tax mortgage interest payment of $10,000 (assuming a 6 percent interest-only mortgage in a 33.3% tax bracket) the net spendable annual income would be five times what is illustrated above, or $126,970 (5 x $25,394).

interest in a 33.3 percent tax bracket really requires only $2,000 out of their pocket ($3,000 – 33.3%).

In essence, the Prudents are simply repositioning $250 of monthly IRA/401(k) contributions and allocating that same amount to making the interest-only payment of $250 on $50,000 of separated home equity. By doing so, the Prudents pre-fund their retirement fund with a onetime lump sum in the amount of $50,000. Their monthly outlay has not changed.

As shown in the figure, if the Prudents were to set aside $250 per month consistently for twenty-five years to age 65, assuming an 8 percent annualized return, they would have $239,342 accumulated in a tax-deferred account. Assuming they continued to earn 8 percent and took out interest-only withdrawals for retirement income, the Prudents could realize $19,147 of annual income from their IRAs/401(k)s. However, this would be taxable and they might be required to pay 33.3 percent tax on that income, thus netting them only $12,766 of spendable income.

On the other hand, if they separated $50,000 of home equity, they could accumulate $342,424 over the same 25-year period, assuming the same 8 percent return with the same cash outlay. If the Prudents reposition their home equity (which is serious cash) to the types of investments explained in chapters 9 to 11, it can grow tax-free *and* generate retirement income that is tax-advantaged. Assuming the Prudents continue to earn 8 percent and took out interest-only withdrawals for retirement, they could realize $27,394 annual income.

If the Prudents wanted, they could withdraw $50,000 at retirement and pay off the mortgage balance, which would leave $292,424 that would generate $23,394 of annual income at 8 percent interest. However, it would behoove them to continue to manage their equity to maximize their retirement income. By keeping $50,000 of equity separated, it could still continue to generate a net annual profit of $2,000 interest over and above the employment cost. If we subtract the $2,000 of employment cost ($3,000 minus 33.3 percent tax savings) from the non-taxable income of $27,394, the Prudents can realize net spendable retirement income of $25,394. That is nearly double the net income that their IRAs and 401(k)s would generate!

To calculate what just $10,000 of home equity can grow to, allocating just $50 per month for retirement savings, simply take 20 percent (one-fifth) of the numbers illustrated, because you are investing only one-fifth as much. Likewise, to calculate what $250,000 of home equity can grow to by allocating $1,250 a month for retirement savings, simply compute 500 percent (five times) the numbers illustrated, because you are investing five times as much.

For example, if a homeowner were to successfully manage $250,000 of home equity for twenty-five years earning an average of 8 percent in tax-favored investments, the ending balance would be $1,712,120, which would generate $136,970 of annual income. After paying the net after-tax mortgage interest payment of $10,000 (assuming a 6 percent interest-only mortgage in a 33.3 percent tax bracket), the net spendable annual income would be five times what is illustrated in figure 8.6, or $126,970 (5 x $25,394).

In this example, the Prudents also wanted to set aside an additional $100 per month for long-term savings. If they simply invested that amount each month in the same side fund that the $50,000 of mortgage proceeds were deposited in, it would grow to $95,737 in twenty-five years at 8 percent interest. This could generate $7,659 of additional income, as opposed to what they would get from depositing the $100 per month in investments that are taxed as earned.

· I have kept this example very simple because, in reality, the Prudents would likely earn more income as the years went by and would likely have the resources to set aside more for retirement. Their home would likely continue to appreciate also. Therefore, it would be wise for them to separate as much equity from their home as often as feasible, to allow idle dollars to earn a rate of return.

ANOTHER LOOK AT LEVERAGING EQUITY

Let's simplify the future value of just $10,000 of separated equity. Assume we are borrowing home equity at 7.5 percent interest in a 33.3 percent marginal tax bracket, so the net cost of borrowing funds is approximately 5 percent. Let's also use interest-only loans rather than amortized loans for the sake of simplicity.

Every year the net after-tax cost of separating $10,000 of equity would be $500 (figure 8.7). In column 1, separating $10,000 of equity for five years would cost us approximately $2,500; for ten years,

Fig. 8.7	NET WORTH ENHANCEMENT POTENTIAL FROM SEPARATING $10,000 OF HOME EQUITY		
	BORROWING $10,000 AT 7.5% (Tax-Deductible in a 33.3% Bracket)		INVESTING $10,000 AT 7.5% (Compounding Tax-Free less the $10,000 Mortgage)
	[1]	[2]	[3]
END OF YEAR	NET COST TO BORROW	YEAR END ACCUMULATION VALUE	NET PROFIT [2] - [1]
1	$ 500	$ 750	$ 250
5	2,500	4,356	1,856
10	5,000	10,610	5,610
15	7,500	19,589	12,089
20	10,000	32,479	22,479
25	12,500	50,983	38,483
30	15,000	77,550	62,550

$5,000; fifteen years, $7,500; and for twenty years, $10,000. Column 2 shows what $10,000 earns at 7.5 percent interest (after deducting the mortgage balance) each period: $750 in one year; $4,356 in five years; $10,610 in ten years; $19,589 in fifteen years; $32,479 in twenty years; $50,983 in twenty-five years; and $77,550 in thirty years. Column 3 shows the net profit we would realize after subtracting employment cost in column 1. The net profit would be $1,856 in five years; $5,610 in ten years; $12,089 in fifteen years; $22,479 in twenty years; $38,483 in twenty-five years; and $62,550 in thirty years.

Using this example, if you were able to borrow dormant equity from your home at 7.5 percent interest in a 33.3 percent marginal tax bracket and invest the loan proceeds to earn 7.5 percent interest free of tax, you can calculate approximately what your growth potential would be. If you separated $100,000 of equity (10 x $10,000), you could realize a profit of $18,560 in five years; $56,100 in ten years; $120,890 in fifteen years; and $224,790 in twenty years (ten times each number shown in column 3, figure 8.7). In fact, as I illustrated previously, if you separated $160,000 of equity for thirty years at 7.5 percent tax-deductible interest and invested the loan proceeds at 7.5 percent interest compounding tax-free, you would realize a gain in excess of $1 million (16 x $62,550).

So, as seen from figure 8.7, every time you separate an additional $10,000 of equity from your home, you could accumulate a liquid fund worth $32,479 twenty years from then, which is more than triple the value of that equity when it was first separated. (Again, this assumes you borrowed at a tax-deductible 7.5 percent rate, invested at a tax-free 7.5 percent rate, and covered the employment cost by reallocating other dollars earmarked for savings or investments.)

In summary, there are two key elements to remember as you apply the principle of arbitrage:

1. Borrow funds at the most attractive rate possible. An interest-only mortgage is by far the most desirable vehicle because you can maximize the deductibility of the interest, fully using Uncle Sam as your partner. Amortized loans also work well, but they slowly trap your equity in the house again, requiring more frequent refinancing.

2. Invest in a safe environment, yet earn the highest rate of interest possible. Invest in a tax-favored—or even tax-free—low-risk vehicle, as will be introduced in chapters 9 to 11. Moderate returns in a safe environment will yield excellent results. It is not worth incurring high risks on serious money like home equity to try to earn higher returns. This is not a get-rich-quick scheme; let common sense and compound interest create your wealth safely and slowly. Patience will pay.

The twofold power of this strategy is the compounding of your investment in a tax-favored environment and the tax benefit achieved through borrowing funds in a deductible environment.

I hope you are excited about these opportunities. Read on for more dynamic concepts that will help you achieve a greater degree of financial independence.

CONCEPTS COVERED IN CHAPTER 8

- By leveraging your property safely, you can:
  1. Have a liquid side fund to use as an emergency fund or to use for home improvements.
  2. Have greater safety of principal in down markets because a larger portion of equity is separated.
  3. Have greater property portability, with the potential to sell your house more quickly and for a higher price in a soft market.
  4. Convert some of your non-preferred debt to preferred debt, thereby increasing the return on your money.
  5. Establish a home equity retirement plan, which can increase your net spendable retirement income by as much as 50 percent over IRAs and 401(k)s, as explained in chapters 3 and 5.
- There are more factors to consider when financing a home than just interest rates and closing costs.
- Through strategic refinancing and proper equity management, homeowners can reduce the time to achieve a "debt-free" home on their balance sheet and substantially enhance their net worth.
- *Separating equity with a higher mortgage can be accomplished, many times, without requiring an increase in monthly outgo.*
- *To manage home equity successfully, it is advantageous to use long-term amortized mortgages or interest-only mortgages.*
- You can create tremendous wealth by borrowing money at a particular interest rate and investing it at the same interest rate—or even less—provided two conditions are met: the interest paid on the borrowed funds is deductible, and the investment in which you invest those funds earns compound interest. If the investment is tax-favored, the potential for growth is even greater.

- You can systematically stack up $1 million or more over a thirty-year period by borrowing $100,000 at 6 percent tax-deductible and investing the loan proceeds at 8.5 percent compounding free of tax.
- Likewise, you can accumulate over $1 million by borrowing $160,000 at 7.5 percent interest and investing the loan proceeds at 7.5 percent interest.
- Likewise, if a $200,000 home appreciates at an average of 5 percent a year, you can accumulate over $2 million if you begin with $100,000 of equity and continue to separate equity every three to five years.
- If home equity is repositioned to a liquid side fund, it will allow you to peel off dollars to meet a house payment if the need arises.
- The primary reasons people get into trouble from leveraging property are they have either consumed the capital they borrowed or not kept the money in a liquid environment.
- Borrow funds with the most attractive terms possible. An interest-only loan is the most desirable to maximize tax deductibility.
- Invest in a safe environment, yet earn the highest rate of interest possible. *Invest in tax-deferred or tax-free low-risk vehicles.*
- The power of successful equity management is in the compounding of your investment in a tax-favored environment, as well as in the tax benefit achieved through borrowing funds in a tax-deductible environment.

CHAPTER 9

Choose the Right Investments

Three simple tests for serious cash

IF YOU WERE PLAYING IN A GOLF TOURNAMENT with thousands of dollars at stake, which would you rather have, Tiger Woods's swing or his clubs? It would be to your advantage to focus first on your swing. Then you could tweak your game by using the best instruments. Up to this point in the book, I have focused primarily on the swing (strategies and methods for wealth enhancement). Now I am going to introduce what I feel are the best clubs (financial instruments) to win the game of safe wealth accumulation.

By now, you should see that possibly repositioning some or all of your qualified plan contributions or distributions to a non-qualified private status can be a wise strategy for achieving the highest net spendable retirement income. You should also be somewhat convinced that separating equity from your property can be a wise strategy for increasing its liquidity, safety, and rate of return. So let's narrow down which investment vehicles are the best choices in which to reposition serious cash.

WHAT DO YOU DO WITH SERIOUS CASH?

What type of investor are you? Which of the following categories of investments would you be more inclined to invest in?

- High-risk, high-potential-yield investments
- Moderate-risk, moderate-yield investments
- Low-risk, safe investments

As shown in figure 9.1, the closer we approach retirement, the greater the percentage of our assets that should be invested in safe and/or guaranteed investments.

Let's analyze a risk-versus-return model to determine which categories of investments are most advantageous for capital accumulation or repositioning serious cash, such as home equity and IRA and 401(k) funds. In figure 9.2, I have listed sixteen general categories of investments, ranging from highest risk at the top of the pyramid to lowest risk at the bottom. When choosing a place to save, invest, or store cash for conservative, stable returns, we want to ask ourselves the same four questions we ask with regard to our home equity:

1. Is it liquid?
2. Is it safe (guaranteed or insured)?
3. What rate of return am I likely to get?
4. Are there any tax benefits associated with this investment?

I regard my home equity and my retirement funds as serious cash. I don't want to hinder their liquidity, safety, and rate of return; I want to enhance these features.

When we apply the liquidity test, we must eliminate several of the investments because we may not be able to obtain cash when needed (within the time frame we would define a liquid investment). Investments such as business ventures, limited partnerships, raw land, investment real estate, and equity in our home do not allow a quick conversion into cash under normal circumstances.

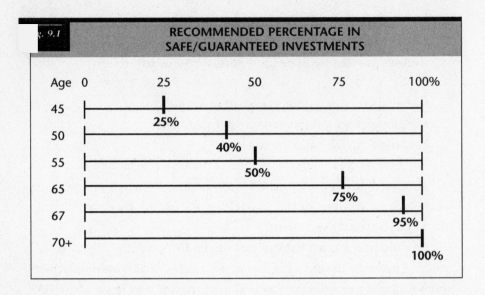

FIG. 9.1

**RECOMMENDED PERCENTAGE IN
SAFE/GUARANTEED INVESTMENTS**

Age	0	25	50	75	100%
45		25%			
50			40%		
55			50%		
65				75%	
67					95%
70+					100%

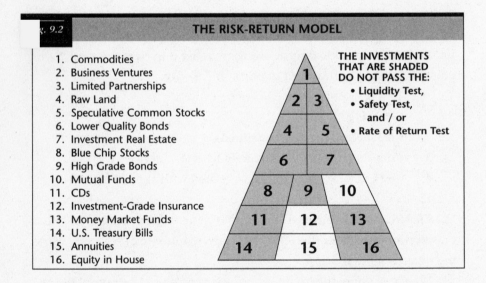

FIG. 9.2

THE RISK-RETURN MODEL

1. Commodities
2. Business Ventures
3. Limited Partnerships
4. Raw Land
5. Speculative Common Stocks
6. Lower Quality Bonds
7. Investment Real Estate
8. Blue Chip Stocks
9. High Grade Bonds
10. Mutual Funds
11. CDs
12. Investment-Grade Insurance
13. Money Market Funds
14. U.S. Treasury Bills
15. Annuities
16. Equity in House

THE INVESTMENTS
THAT ARE SHADED
DO NOT PASS THE:

• Liquidity Test,
• Safety Test,
   and / or
• Rate of Return Test

When we apply the second test—safety—we eliminate five more of the investments. Most financial planners agree that commodities, speculative common stocks, lower-quality bonds, and even blue chip stocks and high-grade bonds are *not* adequately safe investments, because they lack some type of guarantee with regard to money involved (principal or interest).

In applying the third test, we must earn a rate of return—net after tax—that will be in excess of the net cost of the funds used in order to maximize their growth potential. Applying the third test, we eliminate three more investments: certificates of deposits (CDs), money market funds, and U.S. treasury bills. CDs generally do not have a very high rate of return relative to interest rates charged on mortgages, and they are taxed as earned. Money market accounts have the same drawbacks. If the side fund containing your separated home equity were a money market or CD, it would be hard-pressed to earn a net after-tax return that would exceed the net cost of the tax-deductible, simple interest mortgage. U.S. treasury bills fall into the same category; the net return cannot be deemed sufficient to pass the rate of return test.

Thus, after applying all three tests, we are left with three possibilities in which to consider investing our serious cash:

- Annuities
- Some mutual funds
- Investment-grade life insurance contracts

Let's go through a simple analysis of each of these investment alternatives to see which are best suited for our objectives.

UNDERSTANDING ANNUITIES

Today, most annuities are simply savings accounts with insurance companies. When you deposit premium dollars into an annuity, you accumulate your money in a tax-favored environment. Even if it is not a qualified plan, money deposited in an annuity accumulates tax-deferred. But because of the 1984 Deficit Reduction Act, even though any money that accumulates inside an annuity is tax-deferred, when money is withdrawn from the annuity, it is taxed. If funds are accessed from a deferred annuity before age 59½, there is an additional 10 percent penalty on the distributions. This is similar to the early-withdrawal penalty assessed on an IRA, 401(k), or any other qualified plan. In order to avoid a 10 percent penalty when accessing funds from an annuity, it should be done after age 59½. When money is withdrawn from an annuity, it is taxed under LIFO treatment.

LIFO is an acronym for "last in, first out." This means the last money you earn in an annuity is the interest credited most recently on your annuity account. When you begin to withdraw money from your annuity, the IRS regards your distribution as being the last money you earned and treats it as the first money you are withdrawing. Thus, you are taxed on 100 percent of your distributions (assuming interest-only withdrawals) from the first day you start distributions. You can't avoid it. Even if you make principal and interest withdrawals, you must still count the interest earned each year as the first money you withdraw for tax purposes.

A single premium immediate annuity (SPIA) is an annuity in which one lump sum payment is made and the annuitant begins to receive immediate income distributions. Under a SPIA, the taxable portion of the annual distribution is averaged during the period the annuity is calculated to pay out.

For the sake of simplicity, let's assume you deposit $100,000 into an annuity. If that annuity were to pay 10 percent interest, theoretically you ought to be able to pull out $10,000 of interest a year without depleting the corpus of the annuity (which would be the basis, or original principal amount, if you purchased an immediate annuity). The $10,000 of interest you earn is reported on your tax return as an interest withdrawal rather than a withdrawal of any principal. In other words, it is 100 percent taxable income. Only when you begin to deplete the principal will you get a tax break, because the basis was created with after-tax dollars (assuming the annuity is a non-qualified annuity). If you could live off only the interest throughout your entire retirement years, although you would incur tax on that income, you would be able to transfer the principal to your heirs free of income tax.

During the last twenty-five years, fixed annuities have usually credited interest at a rate between 5 and 9 percent, averaging somewhere in the 7 percent range. There are also variable annuities that participate directly in the market and indexed annuities that credit interest at rates linked to an index such as the Standard and Poor's 500 Index. Annuities are deemed a safe and prudent investment under most circumstances because they are obtainable only through insurance companies, which have legal reserve requirements more stringent than banks or credit unions. (Insurance companies usually have higher solvency or higher capital and surplus ratios than many banks or credit unions.) If an annuitant of a deferred annuity should die before withdrawing the funds in the annuity, the remaining balance is paid at face value—the exact amount remaining or accumulated in the annuity— to the surviving beneficiary. Regular annuities do not blossom into a higher death benefit as life insurance does.

You can start receiving an income from your annuity by converting it to an immediate annuity, which means you can choose between several options to create a set income based on your life expectancy. For instance, you can opt to designate a certain number of years for which you and your beneficiary want to receive income, whether you are living or not. Under a period-certain option, the beneficiary would receive income, even in the event of the death of the annuitant, for a set number of years. Under a life-only option, the annuity pays only throughout the annuitant's lifetime. Should the annuitant pass away before the mortality-calculated age (all annuity payouts are calculated based on mortality risk), the insurance company retains the balance of the annuity. But if the annuitant should live beyond life expectancy, the insurance company must still pay benefits up until the eventual death of the annuitant. Annuities also carry several options with regard to survivor benefits.

In the past, many people would choose one of these annuitization formulas. Recently, more people have been using annuities simply as savings accumulation vehicles, similar to saving money at a bank or credit union, except that in the case of an annuity, the money is held by an insurance company. With flexibility in how much can be deposited and the timing and amount of withdrawals, annuities generally pass the liquidity test. They also generally pass the safety test and the rate of return test. However, annuities do not fare as well on the tax test. An annuity will become subject to tax at the distribution phase, and it is taxed under LIFO treatment.

Recently, investors have chosen variable annuities to get tax-deferred growth by using a variety of mutual funds. To protect beneficiaries, the annuity can include insurance that ensures your heirs will get more than the account's current value in the event of death and/or if the investments perform poorly. If you buy stock and bond funds through a variable annuity that includes insurance, you may pay annual expenses of approximately 2.25 percent of assets. The reason for this cost is the mortality and expense charge. The insurance guarantees a minimum death benefit.

Some variable annuities have the provision that your heirs will get back the amount you invested, in the event you lose money on the annuity during your lifetime. Other annuities provide that the heirs will get back at least the amount invested plus 5 or 7 percent in annual interest. Some may even pay heirs the highest value determined on a particular date each year. However, the rising death benefits may have a cap at a certain age, such as age 80. Death benefits will be reduced if you withdraw money from the annuity. (Variable annuities are marketed with such features to provide downside protection.)

Financial advisors should never recommend that home equity be invested in securities or variable products. A homeowner should manage home equity using more stable or fixed investments that contain guarantees.

UNDERSTANDING MUTUAL FUNDS

While a variety of mutual funds meet the liquidity, safety, and rate of return tests, not all mutual funds pass all three tests.

You may have noticed, depending on their most recent experiences in the market, that individual investors will either praise or con-

demn mutual funds. Many investors were apprehensive about investing in mutual funds in the 1980s when the unstable stock market
made fixed money markets and other interest-bearing accounts attractive. During the 1990s, money market accounts, CDs, and bonds hit
their lowest points in years, while stocks soared in an unprecedented
ten-year upward spiral. In 2000, the bullish market experienced a
major correction. Then in 2001, an economic storm erupted, with interest rate adjustments applied to control the money supply, and fall-
out from public fear spurred by the tragedy of September 11, 2001.

Generally, when the stock market is down, bonds, money markets,
and interest rates will go up. Conversely, when the stock market goes
up, bonds, money markets, and fixed instruments tend to gradually go
down. This happens more often when an economy is free from government intervention, such as Federal Reserve manipulation of interest rates and tax rebates.

While the market generally goes up over the long term, there are
also many ups and downs in the short run—much like a person with a
yo-yo walking up a flight of stairs. Americans have never experienced
an extended period in which the stock market went up without some
fluctuations along the way. Likewise, when bond interest rates drop,
they likely won't stay down for long periods of time. In the long run,
interest rates and bond yields will likely be less than the return
achieved during the same ten- or twenty-year period in the stock market. Of course, the deviation (difference in values) between the highs
and lows of bond yields will be narrower than the deviation of stocks.
The question is, what average return are you trying to achieve, taking
into consideration liquidity, safety, and tax consequences?

Even when we deposit money in CDs and money market accounts,
we give up a little safety to earn a little return. We all want the highest
return at the lowest risk, which creates a "risk versus return" paradigm,
as illustrated in figure 9.2. Depending on your risk tolerance, you may
decide what percentage of assets to invest in a growth environment
versus an income environment. An income environment would be investments in bonds, money markets, and other financial instruments

Fig. 9.3	STARTING WITH $100,000 If You Were Approaching Retirement, Which Series Would You Prefer?	
Year	SERIES 1 – Taxable + or -	SERIES 2 – Tax-Free + or -
1	+20%	+8%
2	+21%	+8%
3	+10%	+8%
4	-16%	+8%
5	+12%	+8%
6	-2%	+8%
7	+22%	+8%
8	- 6%	+8%
9	+11%	+8%
10	+15%	+8%

A Taxable SERIES 1 Fund Value at the End of 10 Years = $215,571
A Tax-Free SERIES 2 Fund Value at the End of 10 Years = **$215,892**

that primarily generate needed income or dividends for use in the immediate future. A growth environment would be investments in stocks that are projected to grow in value usually during a long-term period.

Series 1 of figure 9.3 illustrates a typical mutual fund for a ten-year period reflecting seven gain years and three loss years. Only one of the loss years was a substantial reduction in value of the portfolio. The percentage reduction wasn't as significant as many of the gain years. The other two loss years represent relatively small losses when compared to the gain years. This fund started out good and ended good, with the losses tucked in the middle years. However, anytime you experience a 16 percent loss in a portfolio, you are experiencing a 16 percent reduction of the entire portfolio at that time. Thus, a 16 percent loss or even just a 3 percent loss after the account has grown to a sizable amount over time represents a significant dollar loss because of the account's worth when the loss was incurred.

RECOVERING FROM LOSSES

Recovering from market downturns often takes a year, two years, or longer. During a serious downturn in market value, such as a 25 percent loss, the portfolio requires a 33 percent gain to arrive at a net gain of zero percent over that period. For example, a $100,000 investment that suffers a 25 percent loss (down to $75,000) requires a gain of 33 percent on $75,000 ($25,000) to recover to $100,000. A 50 percent loss (down to $50,000) followed by a 50 percent gain (back up to $75,000) is still a 25 percent overall loss. A 50 percent loss would have to be followed by a 100 percent gain in order to break even with a net gain of zero percent over that period.

Often investors look only at the year-by-year history of returns, as shown in series 1 of figure 9.3, and think they are averaging 12 to 15 percent. That can be an illusion. Actually, the $100,000 investment shown in the example would have grown to $215,571 at the end of ten years. If we calculate the true average compounded annual interest rate, we find the rate of return was really only about 8 percent. In fact, if you started out with $100,000 and received a consistent, stable return of 8 percent compounded annually during the same ten-year period, you would end up with slightly more—$215,892.

Which investment would you prefer in figure 9.3—a taxable ten-year gain from $100,000 to $215,000 or a ten-year gain from $100,000 to $215,000 tax-free (not only during the accumulation phase but also during the withdrawal and transfer phases)? Which of the two scenarios would give you more peace of mind, especially during retirement—a consistent, stable return of 8 percent or a range of returns entailing some great gain years along with some unfavorable, uncertain loss years?

One of the problems with a growth mutual fund environment is that when you convert the fund's shares to cash to meet living expenses, you may need to pay close attention to the timing of the portfolio's liquidation. It is always a temptation to hold off in a down market until you can recapture some of your previously attained paper profits. This can create turmoil for people during retirement who are trying to take a stable, consistent income out of their volatile mutual fund portfolios.

TIMING THE MARKET

For most people, timing the market doesn't work, although investors continue to try. Historical results have shown that *investor* returns (the returns that individual investors in the market achieve by constantly trying to time when to buy and when to sell) do not equal *investment* returns (the returns achieved by buying and holding the same investment through the ups and downs). The disparity between investment returns and investor returns has sometimes been dramatic. For example, during a six-year period in a bull market, a group of two hundred growth mutual funds showed an average of approximately 12 percent a year. In contrast, during the same six-year period, investor returns averaged only about 2 percent a year, according to studies conducted by *Morningstar*. Likewise, during the same period, bond funds averaged about 8 percent, compared to investor returns of 1 percent.

Why is there such a significant difference? It is because the holding periods of the individual investors are too short. In other words, *it is not so much which fund you own; it's how long you own it.* According to Dallbar Reports, the average broker-sold equity fund is held for only 3.1 years. The average direct-marketed equity fund is held for only 2.9 years. People try to time the market and often end up buying and selling at the wrong times, instead of just buying and holding. In early spring of 2000, the Dow Jones Industrial Average hit 11,900, and the market experienced $50 billion in net inflows—people buying high. By the summer of 2002, the Dow bottomed out at 7,500, and the market experienced $50 billion in net outflows—people selling low. For this reason—to minimize the impact of volatility and emotions—I usually advocate indexed investments or even fixed-interest investments for serious cash. I'll introduce such investments in more detail in chapter 10.

ADVANTAGES AND DISADVANTAGES OF MUTUAL FUNDS

There are some distinct advantages to mutual funds. Small investors can use a mutual fund because it pools money together with other small investors, thereby allowing small amounts of money to be diversified over perhaps a hundred or more food, machinery, electronics, mining, metals, oil, computer, communications, etc., companies throughout America or the world. By reading a fund manager's prospectus and choosing mutual funds that parallel our particular investment objectives, we can go about our own business, letting professional managers "tend" our money. With diversified mutual funds, if ten or fifteen companies don't do as well as the managers anticipated, you will probably have eighty to ninety other companies in the mutual fund portfolio that will hold you up. Thus, mutual funds can help to reduce the risk of your having a small amount of capital invested in perhaps one or two stocks.

The disadvantage of mutual funds, whether they are qualified for tax-favored retirement funding or not, is that taxes must be paid either on the front end or on the back end. In other words, if it's a non-qualified account, after-tax dollars are invested at the beginning and the dividends and capital gains will be taxed as realized. If it's a qualified account such as an IRA or 401(k), the taxes are deferred and then taxed during the distribution or transfer phase. Tax advantages are not available on the back end except in the case of Roth IRAs or in certain tax-free or tax-exempt bond mutual funds because those are generally funded with after-tax dollars on the front end.

CHOOSE INVESTMENTS THAT GENERATE THE MOST

Throughout thirty years of assisting people with their financial planning, I have discovered that many people have a tendency to choose investments they hope will grow to the highest sum, based on the gross rate of return. Unfortunately, there are many investment vehicles that result in great growth but are inferior to other investments after tax considerations. Some investments may grow to lower sums but generate higher net spendable income. This is generally true with the tax-favored treatment some investments receive during the accumulation and distribution phases of an investment. As explained in chapters 3 to 5, it may be better to pay taxes at today's rates rather than postpone them to tomorrow's higher rates. In addition, accumulating money and postponing the taxes until later may affect the amount of Social Security and Medicare benefits you are entitled to receive.

The biggest mistake I see investors make is choosing short-term investments for long-range goals or choosing long-term investments for short-range goals. When choosing investments suitable for long-range goals such as retirement, you should choose financial instruments that provide the most money at the time in life you will likely need the money most. When considering tax effects, greater growth investment vehicles are often inferior to other investments. Choose investments that generate the highest net spendable income.

INVESTING IN INSURANCE

Many investors in America don't realize that many major life insurance companies are not much different from a conservative mutual fund type of asset management company. Insurance companies are experts in managing risks. As they bank and hold money set aside for future needs, they are responsible for investing that money wisely to achieve a safe rate of return. Many life insurance companies invest their capital in a conservative portfolio primarily consisting of high-grade bonds. They also tend to invest a small percentage of assets in mortgage loans on real estate and sometimes in common stocks and other like investments.

Annual reports and financial statements of many insurance companies reveal they are structured similarly to conservative, income-oriented mutual funds with some growth potential. Because the portfolio of an insurance company is more conservative and is likely less volatile than most mutual funds, it will likely earn a lower rate of return with less deviation. Most insurance company portfolios earn from 7 to 9 percent, whereas most growth mutual funds try to achieve an average return of 10 to 12 percent through periods of gains and losses.

How does achieving an average return of 7 to 9 percent, nontaxable, over a ten- or twenty-year period compare with earning a 10 to 12 percent return and having to pay tax on the gain?

I would prefer to have the more stable, less volatile investment, watch it grow tax-free, and reap the rewards free of tax on the back end, during the harvest period of my life. An investment with these characteristics would help achieve my goals with a higher net spendable income and greater net accumulation value than more volatile investments. For this reason, wise investors are turning more to insurance companies for tax-favored, long-term savings and capital accumulation.

A BRIEF HISTORY OF INSURANCE INVESTING

The insurance industry in America is a trillion-dollar industry and is probably one of the most stable factors in the American economy. In fact, I believe the insurance industry represents the financial backbone of our country.

During the Great Depression of the 1930s, for instance, a large percentage of banks failed and never opened their doors again. Even some real estate dropped as much as 80 percent in value. Many stocks took a long time to recover, if they did at all. However, some of the most stable and safe investments during that time were in life insurance contracts.

Prior to the 1980s, however, life insurance policies were not considered a very attractive investment because the typical whole life insurance policy may have credited only about 2.5 to 3.5 percent return on the cash values that would accumulate. A participating policy with dividends reinvested may have performed two or three percentage points better. During the 1970s and early 1980s, I was a big proponent of buying term insurance and investing the difference in mutual funds.

In fact, for the first eight years of my financial planning career, I recommended that my clients purchase a special product that consisted of a term-to-65 life insurance policy with an annuity rider. A conservative investor could choose to leave two-thirds of the premium dollars in an annuity that earned approximately 7 to 8 percent interest at the time. (This product was actually a precursor to variable life insurance.) Most of my clients opted to assign their annuity cash values each quarter to mutual funds of their choice. However, as explained, traditional, non-qualified mutual fund accounts are subject to taxation during the accumulation phase on dividends and capital gains, as well as on the capital gains that may be realized during the distribution phase.

Well-managed and highly rated life insurance companies, as a general rule, are some of the best money managers in the world. Their track record over the past hundred years would be the envy of some of the wealthiest, most profitable individuals and business entities in the world.

WHY WOULD YOU WANT HIGHER PREMIUMS?

If you study the portfolio of an insurance company and feel that its philosophy and management history are in harmony with your objectives, you might choose that company to manage your money. By doing so, you would be putting your faith in their manager's ability to earn future rates of return similar to those they achieved in the past. You would be, in effect, investing your money into the life insurance company just as you would invest in a mutual fund. To qualify for maximum tax-favored treatment, your accumulation account should include a death benefit. However, instead of trying to get the greatest death benefit for the lowest premium possible, you would purchase the lowest death benefit required by tax law and pay the highest premiums you could afford. This enables you to invest the greatest amount of excess cash in the policy beyond the true cost of the insurance. In other words, you are reversing the approach taken by most purchasers of life insurance in order to use your life insurance policy primarily as a living benefit rather than a death benefit.

This approach is contrary to that of most buyers of life insurance. If your life insurance insures your life, but only benefits those you leave behind at death, it might more appropriately be called *death* insurance. Focusing on the tax-favored living benefits afforded by life insurance better deserves the term "life insurance."

UNDERSTANDING TERM VS. CASH-VALUE INSURANCE

Term insurance premiums generally increase with age. That's because mortality rates increase each year as people get older. Because of this, when purchasing insurance, you would have to pay a higher premium each year (or in actuality, every month) because your chances of dying increase as you age. Since some people do not want to pay a higher premium each month, they pay a level premium based upon the average premium required to cover mortality and expense charges over a five-, ten-, or twenty-year period, or perhaps for an entire lifetime. The company's actuarial department calculates the amount that needs to be collected, then credits the time value of the money invested to arrive at the necessary premium figures. Otherwise, a level premium can also be maintained if the insured elects to purchase decreasing term insurance, in which the death benefit goes down as the person gets older. Term insurance may be a good way to meet specific, short-term needs, but it has no cash accumulation value or living benefits. Coverage will lapse or expire the moment premiums are no longer paid into the policy.

Cash-value life insurance, on the other hand, was designed to accommodate an overpayment of insurance premiums during the early years, thus allowing an underpayment of premiums in later years. This approach creates an average premium paid into the policy over its lifetime. The excess premium paid over and above the mortality and administration expenses creates equity in the policy. The excess money accumulates with interest, then begins to accrue the cash values that can be used for living benefits. If death occurs, cash values are absorbed into the life insurance death benefit, or they can be added on top of the face amount of the insurance policy.

INSIGHT ON INSURANCE

Originally, the principal objective of life insurance was to create an immediate estate in the event of a premature death, helping cover the economic loss suffered by beneficiaries. Cash-value insurance also provides equity buildup inside the policy, which provides a liquid fund that can be used at will—in the event of an emergency, for investment opportunities, or to supplement retirement income. Whole life insurance can be an effective method of purchasing insurance on a long-term basis. The excess premiums are invested by the life insurance company in a long-term portfolio, thus creating additional cash accumulation or dividends that can be reinvested with the insurance company for further growth. New whole life policies, especially those of the last two decades, contain lower costs due to upgraded mortality rates.

Generally speaking, mortality rates continue to improve as modern medicine strives to prolong life. Blood and urine lab tests have been perfected to such a degree that all kinds of life-threatening conditions can be detected, such as harmful drug use or diseases of the heart, kidney, liver, and other vital organs.

Insurance companies try hard to keep their risks at a minimum in order to be more profitable and reward those who live healthy lifestyles. Unfortunately, those who don't live healthy lifestyles are penalized with substandard premium ratings, or they may even be declined altogether. In other words, a rating of "standard" or "substandard" may be assigned to people who lead somewhat "normal" American lifestyles, which may include:

- Using such substances as tobacco, excessive alcohol or caffeine, or drugs

- Suffering from common health problems such as obesity or high blood pressure or having a family history of heart disease
- Working in hazardous occupations
- Participating in hazardous sports

People who do not use tobacco or consume excessive alcohol, whose height and weight are within certain guidelines, and who are fortunate enough to enjoy a fairly active, healthy lifestyle are rewarded by being rated "preferred" or even "ultrapreferred."

TAX-FAVORED TREATMENT OF LIFE INSURANCE

A unique feature of permanent life insurance is that under Sections 72(e) and 7702 of the Internal Revenue Code, the accumulation of cash values inside the insurance contract are tax-advantaged. Not only can the cash values accumulate tax-free, but they can also be accessed without tax under certain provisions of the contract (see chapter 10). Life insurance death benefit proceeds are also free of income tax under most circumstances, as provided under IRC Section 101, no matter how large they are, although they may be included in the total valuation of the deceased's estate. (Upon the death of the second spouse, a large estate comprised partially of life insurance proceeds could be taxable under estate tax unless specifically excluded from the estate through the use of an irrevocable life insurance trust.) Insurance proceeds are not subject to the claims of creditors of the deceased unless they were assigned or pledged as such, or unless the beneficiary was jointly responsible. If the beneficiary of an insurance policy is the estate of the insured rather than the spouse, children, trust, or other party, then the creditors may have a claim.

Hence, *the tremendous and unique advantage of life insurance: It is the only investment that:*

- Allows you to accumulate money tax-free
- Enables you to access your money tax-free

- Blossoms in value and transfers free of income tax when you die

Provided the required premiums are paid, a permanent life insurance policy contract contains guaranteed cash values. These values are supported by company monetary reserves. They also contain maximum guaranteed premium schedules designed to keep the life insurance in force until a certain age under a guaranteed interest rate. Of course, most life insurance contracts credit more than the guaranteed rate stated in the contract.

BUT WHAT ABOUT THE RATE OF RETURN?

As one highly regarded insurance professional, the late John Savage, pointed out, "Contrary to belief, rate of return is generally not the main factor in accumulating wealth." He illustrated this concept by using the following example. Assume a typical American had $10,000 in a bank account earning 5 percent interest, another $10,000 in a different investment vehicle earning 8 percent interest, and a third $10,000 buried in a tin can in the backyard. You might think that ten years down the road, the greatest amount of money would reside in the investment that earned 8 percent interest. However, if the investment earning 8 percent were highly accessible, with the convenience of a drive-up window, many people might dip into that account, regardless of its earning the highest rate of return. On the other hand, if the tin can were soldered shut and inaccessibly buried in the backyard, at the end of ten years, I daresay most Americans would have more money in the tin can, even though it would not have earned a dime of interest.

Life insurance contracts function as an ideal tin can, wherein money can be stored "out of sight, out of mind." Money in a life insurance contract tends to stay put, allowing it to compound and grow, whereas money in banks and mutual funds tend to be accessed more often, becoming depleted.

The real secret to accumulating wealth is not the rate of return, but in-stead, the ability to put money aside, keep it aside, and put it to work for you. We have the best of all worlds when we can stash money away in a "tin can" that grows at a rate of return equal to or greater than the possible net rate of return achieved by higher, more risky, and more volatile taxable investments.

This was the idea behind the creation of universal life in the early 1980s. Structuring a life insurance contract with a minimum death benefit, then filling the policy with cash, results in an overpayment of the premiums normally required to cover mortality and expense charges, and thus a buildup of equity in the policy. This tremendous excess of cash, stored in the insurance company's internal portfolio, will earn interest, continuing to compound through the years. As you continue to overfund the contract, the mortality and expense charges associated with the death benefit usually drain out just a small portion of the overall interest earned on the cash values—often less than 1 percent of the rate of interest earned. So during the life of the contract, if the average gross return was 8.5 percent, after deducting the costs of the insurance, which is necessary for tax-favored treatment of the gain, the net internal rate of return, cash on cash, can be 7.5 percent or better.

But I realize that life insurance may not have been the investment option you thought you were looking for. Prospective clients do not usually come to me wanting or even needing life insurance. They want an investment that passes the liquidity, safety, and rate of return tests. They want tax benefits. They may not object to life insurance benefits, but they often object to paying for them.

In chapter 10, I will show you how to reposition otherwise payable income taxes to pay for your life insurance. I carry a tremendous amount of life insurance on my life. However, I don't really pay for it! Uncle Sam is in effect paying for my life insurance because the mortality and expense charges associated with my investment-grade life insurance contracts are totally covered with otherwise payable income tax. So I'll take as much as Uncle Sam will allow me! Keep reading and I'll teach you how.

CONCEPTS COVERED IN CHAPTER 9

- *Annuities, some mutual funds, and investment-grade life insurance contracts are the three categories of investments that pass the liquidity, safety, and rate of return tests.*
- Most annuities are simply savings accounts with insurance companies that accumulate money on a tax-deferred basis.
- LIFO tax treatment means the last money you earned (the interest) is treated as the first money you are withdrawing.
- Regular annuities do not blossom in value at death.
- Under a life-only option, the annuity pays only throughout the annuitant's lifetime.
- *Home equity should not be invested in securities such as mutual funds, variable annuities, or variable life insurance products.*
- While the market generally goes up over the long term, there are also many ups and downs in the short run—much like a person with a yo-yo walking up a flight of stairs.
- *For most people, timing the market doesn't work;* investor returns do not equal investment returns because investors' holding periods are too short.
- Mutual funds pool money from investors, allowing small amounts of money to be diversified over many companies.
- Unless mutual funds are qualified accounts or tax-free, they are taxed as dividends are paid or capital gains are realized.
- *The biggest mistake investors make is choosing short-term investments for long-range goals or choosing long-term investments for short-range goals.*
- Choose financial instruments that will provide the most money at the time in life you will likely need the money most.
- Many major life insurance companies are not much different

from a conservative mutual fund type of asset management company.

- An insurance company is more conservative and will likely earn a lower rate of return with less deviation than a mutual fund.
- *Wise investors are turning more to insurance companies for tax-favored, long-term savings and capital accumulation.*
- The insurance industry in America is a trillion-dollar industry, a stabilizing economic factor, and the financial backbone of America.
- You can maximum-fund a life insurance policy in order to use it primarily as a living benefit rather than a death benefit.
- Cash-value life insurance was designed to accommodate an overpayment of insurance premiums during the early years, thus allowing an underpayment of premiums in later years.
- Cash-value life insurance provides equity buildup inside the policy, which in turn provides a liquid fund that can be used for emergencies or to supplement retirement income on a tax-favored basis.
- A unique feature of permanent life insurance is that the accumulation of cash values in the contract are tax-advantaged.
- *Life insurance death benefit proceeds are usually free of income tax.*
- *The secret to wealth accumulation is not the rate of return, but the ability to put money aside, keep it aside, and put it to work for you.*
- The cost of insurance may consume only a small portion of the overall interest earned on an overfunded life insurance contract.
- The mortality and expense charges associated with a properly structured life insurance contract can be covered by a portion of the interest that is earned (money that would otherwise be paid in income tax).

CHAPTER 10

Structure Your Life Insurance to Perform as a Superior Investment

Let Uncle Sam pay for your life insurance

ALMOST EVERY FAMILY IN AMERICA uses a wonderful product found in common households—baking soda. When speaking to audiences, I often ask what baking soda can be used for. Responses include, "It removes odors from my refrigerator," "We use it as toothpaste," "It's a laundry freshener," "It's an excellent cleaning agent," "I use it to relax when soaking in the bathtub." The best one I've heard yet is, "It takes the pop out of a pot of beans!" Eventually, someone states the obvious: "Oh, yeah, it can be used when baking!"

Life insurance is the same way. Properly structured life insurance contracts can be used for tax-favored capital accumulation and tax-advantaged retirement income as living benefits, in addition to providing income-tax-free death benefits.

The Internal Revenue Service challenged this concept in 1982 and 1984, through Congress, arguing that life insurance contracts that were overfunded were not really insurance policies but, in fact, investments. They wanted to redefine a life insurance policy. They felt the need to set certain parameters so people would not abuse a life insurance contract that allows for tax-free death benefits, as well as tax-free accumulation of cash values. These parameters were passed as part of the Tax and Fiscal Responsibility Act of 1982 and the Deficit Reduction Act of 1984. In the insurance industry, these two acts are commonly referred to as TEFRA and DEFRA.

HOW TEFRA AND DEFRA AFFECT YOU

The TEFRA and DEFRA citation, or tax "corridor," basically dictates the minimum death benefit required in order to accommodate the ultimate desired aggregate premium basis, based on the insured's age and gender. In other words, if a person wanted to use a cash-value life insurance policy for tax-free capital accumulation purposes, TEFRA and DEFRA guidelines would dictate the amount of the minimum death benefit required.

If you want to purchase a universal life policy with a $100,000 death benefit, the TEFRA/DEFRA corridor will dictate the amount of money you can invest in premiums without exceeding the definition of a life insurance contract. This will make the accumulation of cash values and the death benefit not subject to tax. This is what I call the front-door approach.

As stated in chapter 9, most people who come to me as a financial planner do not want or even need life insurance. What they want is an investment vehicle that has liquidity, safety, and a nice rate of return in a tax-favored environment. They want to create the greatest amount of future net spendable income with investments that are tax-free during the harvest years. I show them several options. Most of my clients do exactly what I do with my own money after they understand the advantages: They choose a properly structured investment-grade life insurance contract designed to accommodate the amount of capital they wish to transfer or reposition from other, inferior investments.

They might choose an investment-grade insurance contract to reposition some of their IRA and 401(k) contributions or distributions under a strategic conversion (roll-out). They may choose to reposition some or all of their home equity into a life insurance contract. The long-term performance of a properly funded life insurance contract, from the standpoint of a cash-on-cash, after-tax, internal rate of return, is usually much better than many IRA and 401(k) investments, mutual funds, annuities, CDs, and money market accounts. In addition, a death benefit comes along for the ride! So, instead of using a front-door approach, I use the TEFRA/DEFRA corridor to calculate the minimum death benefit required by using what I refer to as a back-door approach.

THE BACK-DOOR APPROACH

First, I determine how much the client wants to invest (how much he is going to reposition over a given time period) and enter that data into a computer program. The software then tells me how much life insurance the client gets in accordance with TEFRA/DEFRA guidelines. For example, if your planned ultimate investment were to total $100,000, you would create a policy that could potentially hold up to $100,000 of new cash contributions or premium payments. Let's compare a life insurance policy structured this way to a bucket (figure 10.1).

In this example, $100,000 is the maximum basis (the total of money invested) allowed during the first eleven to twelve years of the policy. If you wanted to fill your bucket in one fell swoop or in one lump sum, you would be allowed to do that and still benefit from tax-free accumulation and tax-free death benefits. However, tax-free access of the cash values, including the interest earned, could be jeopardized unless certain other guidelines are met (I will explain these later). Alternatively, you could choose to spread out your premium contributions over a longer time frame and fill up your bucket over an eleven- or twelve-year period.

It may not be necessary to fill the bucket to the brim with cash contributions (premium payments) if your objective is only life insur-

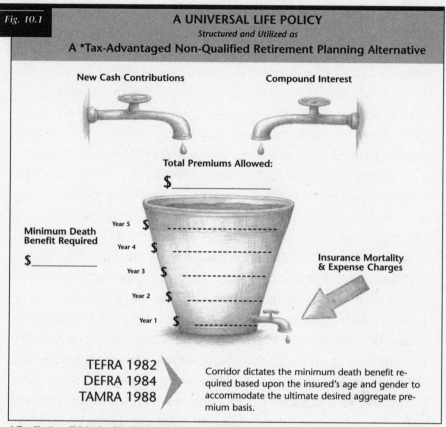

Fig. 10.1

A UNIVERSAL LIFE POLICY
Structured and Utilized as
A *Tax-Advantaged Non-Qualified Retirement Planning Alternative

New Cash Contributions   Compound Interest

Total Premiums Allowed:
$_____

Minimum Death Benefit Required
$_____

Year 5 $ ------------------
Year 4 $ ------------------
Year 3 $ ------------------
Year 2 $ ------------------
Year 1 $ ------------------

Insurance Mortality & Expense Charges

TEFRA 1982
DEFRA 1984
TAMRA 1988

Corridor dictates the minimum death benefit required based upon the insured's age and gender to accommodate the ultimate desired aggregate premium basis.

* Tax Citations: IRC Section 101, IRC Section 72(e), Rev. Rule 66-322, 1966-2 CB 123, TEFRA Section 266, DEFRA Section 221

ance protection. However, death benefits are usually the secondary objective, the primary objective being to accumulate cash with the highest net rate of return on premiums paid. Therefore, it would behoove you to create a bucket (structure a life insurance policy) just big enough, under TEFRA and DEFRA rules, to accommodate the amount of money you will likely put in. By doing so, you are not obligated to fill the bucket to the brim with premiums. You are simply establishing the maximum allowable amount of total contributions you can make to the bucket within a given time frame. This amount is referred to as the *guideline single premium.*

If the premiums paid into a policy reach that limit before the end of the eleventh year, the policyholder must stop putting money into the policy to avoid exceeding the definition of life insurance under TEFRA and DEFRA. In such a situation, you could simply open another bucket (take out a new policy, assuming you pass the physical exam and are approved by the insurance company). The second policy would have the same advantages as the first, provided the tax laws were the same as they were at the time you started your first bucket.

A maximum-funded life insurance policy is not free of costs. The costs associated with a universal life policy most closely resemble those for term insurance, but with a significant difference: If premiums are paid that are far greater than the actual pure term insurance premiums, the policy accumulates an excess cash value. Over time, the interest and compounding of that cash can more than compensate for the continuing costs of owning that policy. The costs can be compared to a spigot draining cash out of your policy from the bottom of the bucket (figure 10.1). These costs, which allow the investment to qualify under the definition of life insurance and, therefore, remain tax-free, are an absolutely critical component for achieving the most attractive results. In the long run, the spigot potentially may consume only approximately 0.5 to 1 percent of the interest percentage credited during the life of the policy.

Over a twenty- or thirty-year period, an investor could very well achieve a net rate of return, cash on cash, of 7 to 8 percent on a life insurance policy crediting an average of 8 to 9 percent interest. Personally, I would rather have a tax-free return averaging 7 to 8 percent over a taxable return of 10 or even 12 percent. The small portion of my accumulated cash that is paying for my life insurance is money that would have otherwise gone to Uncle Sam in taxes on a taxable investment. I think of it as Uncle Sam indirectly paying for my life insurance.

To me, the insurance is more or less "free" if it achieves a net rate of return on a tax-free basis and performs as well as or better than an investment in a taxable alternative (and don't forget it also offers insurance benefits). Yes, I know the reality is, there's no such thing as free life insurance. However, if the insurance costs can be paid for out of a portion of the interest earned on the cash values during the life of the policy, and that small portion of interest is equivalent to or less than the money I would have otherwise shelled out in taxes in traditional investments, then wouldn't I be justified in thinking of it as free?

The nice thing about the TEFRA/DEFRA guidelines is that it doesn't matter how old you are, the spigot on the bucket can be designed to drain out about the same percentage of your interest, regardless. In other words, a 65-year-old qualifying for an insurance policy can structure it to achieve close to the same net rate of return on premium dollars paid into the bucket as a 20-year-old. The difference is, the 20-year-old simply gets more life insurance. But 65-year-olds usually have more money to invest, so the insurance is commensurate.

DEALING WITH MARKET FLUCTUATIONS

Since the early 1980s, when universal life first emerged, interest rates credited on traditional fixed universal life insurance policies with some companies have been as high as 13 percent and as low as 5 percent. I believe an investor need not be concerned about the interest rate fluctuations, because they are all relative. During the 1980s when insurance contracts were crediting as much as 11 to 13 percent interest, a person would be rowing upstream, so to speak, at thirteen miles per hour, but the current of inflation at that time was coming downstream, sometimes at ten miles per hour (10 percent inflation). The actual margin in that case would be only three percentage points. In recent years, interest rates have been lower. Even so, if you row upstream at six miles per hour and the current of inflation is going against you at only two miles per hour, you have a margin of four percentage points.

REMEMBER YOUR OBJECTIVES

An investor should determine the primary purpose for establishing an insurance contract. When done correctly, those who establish a policy for investment purposes are thrilled when they can potentially achieve a safe rate of return that is as good as or better than an annuity. Not only can they access funds on a tax-free basis, which they can't do with an annuity, but should they die, their investment will actually blossom by as much as double or triple—and still transfer to their heirs on an income-tax-free basis! Generally, through structuring a universal life insurance policy correctly to accommodate the full capital invested, a universal life policy will outperform an annuity, especially as it passes through the distribution and transfer phases.

Universal life has become a flexible insurance product. It is not considered term insurance because it accumulates cash values. It is not considered whole life insurance because premium payments can be varied, fluctuated, and adjusted according to circumstances (universal life is also referred to as flexible-premium life insurance). The policyholder is not forced into non-forfeiture options when premium payments need to be adjusted or halted for a while, provided there is already sufficient cash in the policy to cover insurance costs. Thus, the term "universal life" is used because it is applicable to so many situations.

In terms of strategy, if your goal is to accumulate the greatest amount of capital at the highest net rate of return possible, you should only take the minimum death benefit required to fund it, then fill the bucket to the maximum level as soon as possible. During the funding process, your circumstances may change. If you discover you may never be able to fill that bucket to the brim, you may want to maximize the return and minimize the costs. So rather than maintain the original life insurance death benefit, you can easily reduce its size by reducing the face amount of the insurance with the stroke of a pen. If you cut the insurance in half, in essence, you would be cutting your bucket in half. Some care must be taken in doing this because you could violate IRS guidelines regulating how quickly you may fund your bucket, causing your policy to become taxable when you withdraw money. There may also be some surrender charges incurred when reducing the death benefit. A reduction is a permanent change. The only way to increase it again would be to requalify, with a physical exam, for new coverage.

The introduction of universal life has led to a remarkable chain of events. Insurance companies offering whole life have since created more interest-sensitive products yielding higher dividends based on the earnings. For example, if a whole life policy is overfunded, it can perform in a similar fashion to universal life. The insurance industry has continued to introduce new offerings, such as variable and indexed products in the universal life and whole life arenas.

GRANDFATHERING TAX LAWS

In the past, whenever Congress has made far-reaching changes to the tax code, especially regarding life insurance, it has grandfathered policyholders who already had a policy in force. It may behoove you to establish a life insurance policy now that will accommodate the amount of capital you will eventually sock away, in case Congress decides to change the rules again. (The hope is that the existing policies will be grandfathered.) No guarantee can be made by an insurance company or life insurance agent that the client will, in fact, be grandfathered. But because of this precedent, and because of the ex post facto provision in the Constitution wherein new laws are not supposed to adversely affect features that were established under old laws, grandfathering is likely.

As an example, between 1982 and 1988, maximum-funded life policies were attractive when compared to other investment alternatives—especially conservative investments such as CDs, money markets, or even mutual funds. Due to tax benefits, a massive exodus of funds left banks and stock brokerage firms in favor of insurance contracts. Many of my clients filled up their buckets in one single premium payment. Some transferred money in lump sums from CDs, money market accounts, and mutual funds in amounts as high as $500,000, all in accordance with TEFRA/DEFRA guidelines.

Why were the insurance options so popular? Suppose you create a bucket that accommodates a $100,000 guideline single premium when crediting rates are averaging 8 percent. As you begin filling the bucket, immediately after the first premium payment, your beneficiaries would be entitled to a death benefit anywhere from $200,000 to $1,500,000 (remember, this varies depending on age and gender). In the long run, the policy would use approximately 1 percentage point of that 8 percentage points for mortality and expense charges, thus resulting in a 7 percent net rate of return. Assuming interest rates remain stable over several years, you could theoretically pull out about $7,000 a year nontaxable, thereby enjoying an income far greater than having the same amount of money in a taxable CD, money market, or even a mutual fund.

Let's say you had the choice of two certificates of deposit in which to deposit $100,000. One offered you 6 percent, which was taxable. If you happened to die, that CD would transfer to your heirs in the amount of the money that you had accumulated in it. The other CD also offered you 6 percent interest, but this time tax-free. If you happened to die, the second CD would blossom into a tax-free transfer of $200,000 or more. Which of the two CDs would you choose, all other factors (such as safety and liquidity) being equal? The choice is obvious. (Actually, the safety of most insurance companies is considered greater than the safety of many commercial banks.)

One of the best features of a life insurance policy is it can be structured to accommodate the amount of capital you will eventually put into the bucket. In the meantime, you can nurse it along with minimum premiums that barely cover the spigot until impending capital comes in that can fill the bucket—perhaps from the planned sale of a property or an inheritance.

Now back to our story. In 1988, it became apparent that banks and stock brokerage firms were suffering because of this massive transfer of capital out of their institutions into life insurance companies. The public was selecting greater safety, better return, more favorable tax treatment, and better transferability of their conservative investments. The banks and brokerage firms lobbied Congress to make the transfer of money to tax-favored insurance contracts less damaging to them.

THE INTRODUCTION OF TAMRA

On June 21, 1988, the Technical and Miscellaneous Revenue Act (TAMRA) was passed by one body of Congress. In September, the other body of Congress passed it and made the law effective retroactive to June 21. Provisions in the act were directed at the tax treatment of life insurance policies if they were maximum-funded (the bucket was filled to the brim) in less than seven years. However, those who already had policies in existence were grandfathered under the old rules.

TAMRA still allows for a policyholder to pay one large single premium. Such a policy is classified as a Modified Endowment Contract under Section 7702A of the Internal Revenue Code, referred to in the industry as a MEC. If this is done, the cash values still accumulate inside the policy tax-deferred and the death benefit is tax-free. However, if any money is withdrawn out of the policy before age 59½, it will be subject to a 10 percent penalty, much like an IRA or 401(k). In addition, when money is withdrawn, the gain is taxable under LIFO (last in, first out) treatment, just like an annuity.

If a policyholder instead decides to fill the bucket in increments of a certain amount, it still falls under the old rules by which money can be accessed before age 59½ on a tax-free basis. It can provide tax-free distributions for retirement income or other purposes. To comply with TAMRA, the policy needs to pass what is known as the Seven-Pay Test.

THE SEVEN-PAY TEST

The Seven-Pay Test means that a whole-life insurance policy cannot be funded any faster than seven years of equal installments. Under the existing provisions, if the policy is maximum-funded no faster than seven relatively equal installments, then it complies with the TAMRA Seven-Pay Test, and cash values can be accessed tax-free at any time. However, there has been a tremendous misunderstanding, even among insurance agents, because the Seven-Pay Test is a misnomer with regard to universal life. Because of the TEFRA and DEFRA limits that dictate the amount of life insurance required to meet the definition of a life insurance policy, a universal policy can be maximum-funded in as little as three years and one day (four annual installments) by an individual under the approximate age of 50, and four years and one day (five annual installments) for someone over the approximate age of 50. If a universal life policy is funded and filled to the maximum level in essentially five annual installments, it will likely outperform a policy that requires seven annual installments in order to fill it to the brim.

The idea was that by having to spread out the premium payments with four to seven annual installments, the public would be more prone to liquidate their bank accounts or stock portfolios over an equivalent period than to transfer the whole amount of capital in one fell swoop. This would result in a more gentle blow to those financial institutions.

The insurance industry responded immediately to the TAMRA law by offering temporary side buckets, such as a single premium immediate annuity (SPIA), with a term certain of four or five years, or advance premium deposit funds. These temporary side buckets park the excess funds that would violate TAMRA had they been paid into the main policy. The insurance companies usually credit these accounts with interest equal to or greater than what a bank is paying. The interest is taxable, but the side buckets can pour one-quarter or one-fifth of the total money over into the universal life bucket automatically each year until the side bucket is empty at the end of five years and the universal life policy is full and in total compliance with TAMRA. For example, if you wanted to put $100,000 into your bucket and comply with TAMRA, about $20,000 to $25,000 (depending on your age) can be paid into your policy the first year. The remaining $75,000 to $80,000 can be deposited into a SPIA that will transfer the TAMRA-allowed premium into the policy each subsequent year until it is fully funded and compliant.

Even though temporary alternative side buckets were provided by the insurance industry, the law was not repealed, because the law made it just complicated enough to prompt some people to keep their money in banks and stock brokerage firms while filling up their buckets over the allotted period.

The Internal Revenue Code allows a policyholder to overfund an insurance contract in excess of the TAMRA premium and then "perfect" the contract within sixty days of the end of the policy anniversary. A policy owner could violate the TAMRA premium limit, request a refund of the overage that was paid into the contract, and then redeposit it during the first sixty days of the next year. My clients have used this strategy numerous times in order to perfect a contract and avoid a MEC. This preserves the tax-free accessibility of cash values. When someone overfunds a contract in violation of TAMRA, the insurance company still credits interest during the time they have the funds. However, when a refund is made during the sixty-day window after the policy anniversary, the excess interest earned over and above the TAMRA premium will be subject to tax.

MATCH YOUR INVESTMENT WITH YOUR OBJECTIVE

To structure a cash-value life insurance policy as an investment to be used primarily for living benefits, it should be thoroughly understood. Know that if only 20 percent of the bucket size (the total you will eventually pay into the bucket) is filled after one year, the spigot will drain out a much higher percent of the bucket than when it is full. You must be patient as you fill your bucket, adhering to TEFRA/DEFRA and TAMRA guidelines. Do not become discouraged when the net rate of return is not within 1 percent of the gross rate of return after only a few years into the contract. You must let the compounding of interest do its job over time.

Policyholders who understand these concepts do not worry about the net rate of return achieved in the early years of an insurance contract. They know the tremendous benefits they will enjoy that will generate a handsome net rate of return (retroactively to the first day of the contract) that can far outperform alternative investments. The success or failure of an investment can be measured only against its intended time frame. As stated in chapter 9, you should choose investments based on which ones will provide the most when you will need the most. Again, you will enjoy advantages on the back end that far outweigh any disadvantages on the front end.

Unfortunately, many life insurance agents do not totally understand the TEFRA/DEFRA and TAMRA guidelines. Consequently, they are not competent in how to structure a life insurance policy to perform at its optimum level for living benefits rather than just death benefits. That is why I use the phrase "properly structured, investment-grade, cash-value life insurance."

DEFINING "INVESTMENT-GRADE"

In review, if an investor wants to use a life insurance contract to accumulate capital that is tax-advantaged under Sections 72(e) and 7702 of the Internal Revenue Code, it must meet several criteria before I would regard it as investment-grade. The first criterion is that the policy must be structured properly to allow it to perform as an investment rather than just a death benefit policy. This is done by taking the minimum death benefit we can get within TEFRA/DEFRA parameters for the total premiums that are planned to be paid into the policy. (This can be easily calculated through the use of various computer programs.) It also needs to be structured so it can be filled to the brim (maximum-funded) as soon as possible under TAMRA guidelines—and yet maintain flexibility in case circumstances change.

The second criterion that allows an insurance contract to be deemed a prudent investment is the due diligence that must be exerted in researching the insurance companies selected. Insurance companies can be considered investment-grade by several different rating agencies. I generally use three broad guidelines when selecting a life insurance company.

The first of the guidelines is the insurance company's actual track record and philosophy. Personally, I study interest rate histories and performance. I want to make certain I choose an insurance company that is well managed and generous in its rate of return. I have found some life insurance companies credit the least interest they can while staying somewhat competitive. They are more concerned about building up company coffers than policyholders' coffers. Other insurance companies are quite generous and credit the maximum amounts to their insurance policies after covering their overhead and retaining a modest profit. The latter type can perform much like a conservative mutual fund.

The second guideline is to choose insurance companies based upon their industry ratings. Among the most used rating agencies are Standard & Poor's, AM Best, Fitch, Moody's, and Weiss. These rating agencies use different methods and scales for rating companies, often confusing the public, Congress, and the General Accounting Office. For instance, the highest rating that can be assigned by Standard & Poor's is AAA. On the other hand, the highest rating assigned by AM Best is A++. Fitch, Moody's, and Martin Weiss likewise have their own rating systems (figure 10.2).

To make comparisons between the ratings, I use organizations such as LifeLink to help understand which companies are best. LifeLink assigns each company a "Comdex score" from 1 to 100 based upon combined data from various rating agencies and the insurance company. For the establishment of investment-grade contracts, I generally recommend companies that have a Comdex score of at least 70 or higher, and I prefer those that score 90 or higher.

The third guideline I use to select an insurance company is its solvency. I feel it is necessary for an insurance company to maintain liquidity, just as I feel it is necessary for an individual to maintain liquidity. In other words, in order to minimize risk, there needs to be

Fig. 10.2		**THE U.S. GENERAL ACCOUNTING OFFICE'S (GAO) SCALE OF INSURANCE RATINGS***				
RATINGS	**BANDS**	**A.M. BEST**	**STANDARD & POOR'S**	**MOODY'S**	**FITCH**	**WEISS**
Secure	1	A++, A+	AAA	Aaa	AAA	A+, A, A-
	2	A, A-	AA+, AA, AA-	Aa1, Aa2, Aa3	AA+, AA, AA-	B+, B, B-
Vulnerable	3	B++, B+, B, B-	A+, A, A-, BBB+, BBB, BBB-	A1, A2, A3 Baa1,Baa2,Baa3	A+, A, A- BBB+, BBB, BBB-	C+, C, C-
	4	C++, C+, C, C-	BB+, BB, BB- B+, B, B-	Ba1, Ba2, Ba3 B1, B2, B3	BB+, BB, BB- B+, B, B-	D+, D, D-
	5	D, E, F	CCC, (CC,C) , (D) , R	Caa, Ca, C	CCC+, CCC, CCC- DDD, DD, D	E+, E, E-, F

according to the GAO's 1994 study

sufficient cash or cash equivalent on hand. Generally speaking, an insurance company will have a much greater surplus or solvency ratio than other financial institutions, such as banks and credit unions. If times really got tough in the economy, I would prefer my money be easily accessible in case I choose to liquidate my funds. Remember, the size of an insurance company does not determine its strength. An insurance company can be very large and yet have excessive liabilities.

PARTIES TO AN INSURANCE CONTRACT

It's essential to understand the different roles involved in any insurance policy:

- Insurer—insurance company
- Insured(s)—an individual or individuals under joint-life contracts
- Beneficiary—usually a spouse or children of the insured (sometimes an entity such as the insured's business or a charitable organization) to whom the death benefit is paid. It must be determined that the beneficiary named at the time of application

would suffer an economic loss if the insured died, termed an "insurable interest" between the insured and beneficiary.

- Owner—the only one who has power to make changes to the contract, such as renaming a beneficiary, lowering the insurance amount, changing premium schedules, changing death benefit options, or taking out withdrawals and loans on the contract. The owner also owns all the cash values in a policy and the interest earned on those cash values, assuming all tax liability and enjoying all the tax benefits of a properly structured investment-grade policy.
- Premium payor—the one who actually pays for the premiums

A single person or entity often plays multiple roles; however, they can be played by as many as four different parties.

USING LIFE INSURANCE AS AN ESTATE MULTIPLIER

When people die, they usually leave behind some assets that were earmarked to sustain them had they lived longer. Those assets may include bank accounts, CDs, money markets, stocks, bonds, real estate, or cash values of life insurance. Life insurance is the only asset that instantaneously blossoms from the cash values previously used for living benefits into tax-advantaged death benefits. So, if possible, it is usually best to try to insure the individual in a relationship who will likely pass away first, so that the money (cash values) left in the insurance contract can blossom and transfer to the survivor. Insurance proceeds have the effect of replenishing some of the money that was used for retirement income so surviving spouses may have a rejuvenated retirement resource to use for the remainder of their lives.

I have had many client couples who have established life insurance contracts for the purpose of enhancing their retirement income. The procedure I use is to strategically reposition their IRA and 401(k) contributions or distributions and manage the equity in their current home (or former home if the couple sold or downsized) to maintain liquidity and safety and earn a rate of return. When possible, I establish two buckets (insurance policies), one for each, to accommodate the repositioned assets. As a result, I minimize their tax and maximize their net spendable retirement income. They enjoy retirement with a simple, low-maintenance investment portfolio comprised primarily of two life insurance contracts.

Typically, the husband dies first. There might be $200,000 left in his bucket at the time of his death, but it may blossom into $500,000 by virtue of the life insurance death benefit. Thus, his widow gets $500,000 tax-free instead of taxable IRAs containing $200,000 or less! I would then advise her to take the $500,000 of tax-free insurance proceeds and keep it tax-free. She could open a new bucket (take out a new life policy) and, in full compliance with TAMRA, use a side bucket. She can begin accessing tax-free income from the new bucket when she needs it. Then, when she dies, the remaining cash in her bucket may blossom to as much as $1 million and transfer to her children or family trust as a legacy for future generations. This can be far more beneficial than "stretch IRAs" that simply continue to postpone tax.

What if the owner who wants to take advantage of tax-free accumulation and tax-free income cannot qualify for insurance? In that case, it may become necessary to use the spouse as the insured. You can use a surrogate or substitute insured as long as there is an insurable interest between the insured and the beneficiary. For example, when I have a client who wants to establish a life insurance contract for investment purposes but is not insurable due to health history or age, we "borrow" someone else's life to insure. (However, I have successfully insured many clients up to age 90, even with medical histories that included maladies such as cancer that was successfully treated, heart problems, and diabetes.) If someone has been determined to be uninsurable, my recommendation is to use a spouse, children, or grandchildren as insureds, in that order. You do not need to be insurable to be the owner of a universal life policy that provides tax-advantaged growth and access for your own money.

LEVEL DEATH BENEFITS VS. INCREASING DEATH BENEFITS

Universal life has tremendous flexibility, not only with premium payments but also with regard to adjusting the death benefit for meeting the objectives of the policy owner—even if those objectives change. The insured can choose to have either a level death benefit or an increasing death benefit. (Sometimes these two choices are referred to as options A and B.) Let's use the bucket analogy again to visualize the difference between these two options.

I recommend the *level death benefit option* if (1) the primary objective of establishing an investment-grade insurance contract is to achieve the highest internal rate of return as soon as possible (accumulating the most cash values in the shortest time period to use for living benefits); and (2) the secondary objective is to obtain life insurance coverage that is paid for with a small portion of the earned interest that would otherwise go out the window in income tax.

On the other hand, I usually recommend the *increasing death benefit option* if the primary objective is to maximize what you leave behind when you die and the secondary objective is to accumulate cash to access.

What if your objectives change midway into the life of the policy? No problem! You can switch from one option to another with the stroke of a pen!

Under the level death benefit option, the owner elects to have the death benefit stay level as the bucket grows. The bucket grows as a function of the new premium dollars paid into the bucket and the interest credited to the bucket. This represents the cash value of the policy. As the bucket grows with cash value, the cash value can actually qualify as part of the original death benefit required under TEFRA/DEFRA guidelines. The actual amount of insurance the insurance company is at risk to pay is the difference between your cash value and the original required death benefit. Ultimately, the differential between the cash value and the original level death benefit at the issuance of the policy can become so nominal that the net rate of return is within 1 percent of the gross rate of return, retroactive to the first day of the policy!

For example, if an insurance contract for a 65-year-old male designed to accommodate a total of $200,000 of premiums ($40,000 a year for five years to comply with TAMRA) carried a minimum death benefit (required under TEFRA/DEFRA) of $425,000, and in its tenth year had $300,000 in cash value, then the true insurance risk paid by the company is the difference between $425,000 and the $300,000 cash value, or $125,000.

Even though the cost per $1,000 of life insurance goes up each month a person gets older, the amount of actual insurance the insured is paying for goes down! This unique feature results in an enhanced rate of return—your money grows more effectively as the insurance cost gets smaller. In the fifteenth year, the cash value might be $424,000, which, if subtracted from the original death benefit of $425,000, would leave only $1,000 of insurance for which you are paying at that attained age. However, IRS guidelines require that the death benefit stay ahead of the cash values by a certain percentage (such as 5 percent up to age 90, then it can reduce 1 percent a year to age 95, at which point the death benefit may equal the cash value). So in actuality, the life insurance death benefit in the fifteenth year might increase from $424,000 to $446,250 (5 percent more). In the twentieth year, the cash value might grow to $600,000, at which point the death benefit will have increased to $630,000 to stay in compliance. This would continue until age 100, when the cash value might be $1,800,000, which would equal the death benefit.

Therefore, when choosing the level death benefit option at the onset of the policy, it may end up actually having an increasing death benefit, just to stay ahead of the cash values that are growing within the contract. Thus, the terminology—level death benefit or increasing death benefit—can be confusing.

If the increasing death benefit option is selected at the onset of the policy, the spigot on the bucket will get bigger as the insured gets older and the cost per $1,000 of insurance goes up. This is because the base insurance benefit stays at the original amount—$425,000 in this example. The advantage to the increasing death benefit option is that if death occurs, the beneficiaries get the cash value plus the death benefit. However, because of the cost associated with paying for the same amount of insurance as the insured gets older, the cash value will not be able to grow as quickly. The living benefits, such as the amount of tax-free retirement income, will not generate as much under the increasing death benefit option unless the death benefit is carved down.

Under the level death benefit option, an insurance contract for a 60-year-old male who pays maximum premiums totaling $200,000 ($40,000 a year) during the first five years could have a cash value of $1,280,000 and a death benefit of $1,344,000 at age 90 (when he may die). In contrast, he may have only $515,000 of cash value and a death benefit of $1,025,000 under the increasing death benefit option. As a general rule of thumb, unless you have some premonition you are going to die sooner than later (within approximately ten years), the level death benefit option will eventually generate greater cash values and death benefit (based upon the same initial face amount of insurance and the same premiums paid into the contract). My advice under most circumstances is to start with the level death benefit option. Then if the owner's objectives change, the death benefit option can be changed later.

When do I recommend the increasing death benefit option? Let's assume you had $1 million of life insurance with $500,000 of cash value that is growing approximately 7 percent per year with interest, after deducting the costs of insurance. You find out that you have multiple myeloma cancer, and the doctor estimates you have three to seven years to live. This may change your original objective from maximizing a return on cash values to trying to maximize the death benefit left behind. If you left the policy alone, under the level death benefit option, the 7 percent per year ($35,000 or more per year) of additional growth would be soaked into the $1-million original death benefit (because the cash values have not grown yet to exceed the original required death benefit). To avoid this, I might advise you to consider switching to the increasing death benefit option. That does not mean the $500,000 cash value would be immediately added on top of the original $1 million. But at the point in time the option is changed, the actual life insurance would be reduced to the difference between the current cash value and the original death benefit—$500,000 in this case. If you died the next day, the death benefit paid would still be a total of $1 million ($500,000 of cash value and $500,000 of life insurance). But if the doctor's prediction was correct, and death finally occurred five years later, the death benefit would have grown by 7 percent per year, compounded annually, to approximately $1,200,000. In other words, your beneficiaries would receive an extra $200,000 of tax-free life insurance proceeds.

Hence, various types of permanent life insurance can contain tremendous flexibility. On one end of the spectrum, if you want to minimum-fund an insurance contract, it may end up being the least expensive way in the long run to insure your life for your entire life. You can always change your objective and maximum-fund it later if you want to take advantage of the tax-favored accumulation afforded to permanent life insurance. At the other end of the spectrum, if you want to use a life insurance contract to accumulate money in a tax-favored environment to use later for supplemental retirement income, you can maximum-fund the contract according to your own schedule. You can also structure a life insurance policy anywhere along the spectrum, depending on dual objectives (tax-favored cash accumulation and death benefits). Keep reading to understand how you as an owner of an investment-grade life insurance contract can access your cash values free of tax for supplemental retirement income or other purposes.

CONCEPTS COVERED IN CHAPTER 10

- *Properly structured life insurance contracts can be used for tax-favored capital accumulation and tax-advantaged retirement income,* in addition to providing income-tax-free death benefits.
- To use a cash-value life policy for tax-free capital accumulation, TEFRA and DEFRA guidelines dictate the minimum death benefit.
- Use the "back-door approach" to design an insurance contract to accommodate the amount of capital you wish to transfer/reposition.
- The guideline single premium is the maximum total allowable premiums you can pay into a universal life insurance contract the first eleven years.
- The cost of insurance, which allows the investment to qualify under the definition of life insurance and remain tax-free, is a critical component for achieving the most attractive results.
- Over a twenty- or thirty-year period, an investor can achieve a net rate of return, cash on cash, of 7 to 8 percent on an over-funded life insurance policy crediting an average of 8 to 9 percent interest.
- It doesn't matter how old you are, the spigot on the bucket (life insurance contract) can be designed to drain out about the same percentage of your interest.
- A fixed universal life policy structured correctly to accommodate the full capital invested will likely outperform a fixed annuity on the back end, provided it is maximum-funded under IRS guidelines.
- To accumulate the greatest amount of capital at the highest rate of return, you should take only the minimum death benefit required, then fill the bucket to the maximum level as soon as possible.
- Establishing a life insurance policy that will accommodate the

amount of capital you will eventually sock away may allow you to be grandfathered, if Congress ever changes the tax laws affecting it.

- You can nurse along an insurance contract with minimum premiums until impending capital comes in, such as an inheritance.

- A life insurance policy funded sooner than TAMRA allows results in the policy becoming a MEC, wherein cash values accumulate and transfer tax-free, but access to cash is taxed under LIFO treatment.

- You can comply with the TAMRA Seven-Pay Test with as few as four or five annual installments to fund the guideline single premium of a universal life contract.

- A policyholder can overfund an insurance contract in excess of TAMRA and then "perfect" the contract within sixty days of the policy anniversary by requesting a refund of the overage paid.

- A life insurance contract may be regarded as *investment-grade* if it is structured to perform as an investment with minimum death benefits under TEFRA/DEFRA parameters.

- Agencies used for rating the strength of insurance companies are Standard & Poor's, AM Best, Fitch, Moody's, and Weiss.

- Besides the insurer, there are four roles involved with an insurance policy: the insured, the owner, the beneficiary, and the premium payor.

- *Life insurance can be used as an estate multiplier,* which can be far more beneficial than stretch IRAs that postpone tax.

- *You do not need to be insurable to be the owner of a life insurance policy* that provides tax-advantaged growth and access to money.

- Generally, the level death benefit option should be selected if the primary objective is to achieve the highest rate of return possible and the insured is expected to die later rather than sooner.

- Under most circumstances, *it is advisable to start with the level death benefit option*. If desired, it can be changed later.
- *Life insurance contains tremendous flexibility*. At one end of the spectrum, you can minimum-fund the contract as an inexpensive way to have insurance for your entire life. At the other end of the spectrum, you can use it to accumulate money in a tax-favored environment to use for supplemental retirement income.

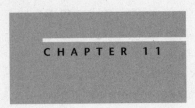

CHAPTER 11

Access Your Money Tax-Free at Retirement

Forget the shortcut—take the "smartcut" to retirement

LET'S ADDRESS HOW a life insurance contract allows the owner to access cash values tax-free. Basically, there are three methods by which owners of insurance contracts can access their money:

1. The sad way
2. The dumb way
3. The smart way

THE SAD WAY

The sad way is by dying. If you establish an insurance contract that will accommodate total premium payments up to $100,000 under TEFRA and DEFRA guidelines, the minimum death benefit may be $1,200,000 if you are age 25; $765,000 if you are age 35; $482,000 if you are age 45; $310,000 if you are age 55; and $210,000 if you are 65. Under TAMRA guidelines, if you paid close to the maximum allowed, approximately one-fifth of the guideline single premium ($20,000 per year), you are still insured for the full death benefits the minute the first minimum premium is paid. So if the insured were to die the day after paying the initial $20,000, it would blossom immediately to whatever the face amount of the policy is. Not only that, but the death proceeds would be transferred to the beneficiary free of income tax as provided under Section 101 of the Internal Revenue Code. That's a phenomenal rate of return, but it comes at a pretty dear price. Of course, I don't recommend accessing your money the sad way, but having that protection provides tremendous peace of mind regarding how beneficiaries would fare in the event of an untimely death.

I have never had a widow turn down an insurance check, whether it was $10,000 or $1 million. If an employer said, "As your employer, we would like to offer you some free life insurance; how much would you like?" my answer would be, "As much as I can get!" So it is when structuring an investment-grade contract. Even when taking the minimum death benefit required under IRS guidelines, you may as well take as much as they give you, if it is not going to end up costing you anything in the final analysis.

Sometimes people can't catch this vision and say, "Well, I really do like the projected investment results of the insurance contract you are proposing; it appears it will outperform the after-tax return on my CDs, money market accounts, and mutual funds. But I really don't need any more life insurance." If I were to reply, "Well, that's okay, it's still the superior investment, so after the policy is issued, you can make me the beneficiary," they may rethink what they would be giving up. In other words, *don't get hung up on what it is; focus on what it does.*

STARTING OUT DUMB AND ENDING SMART

The second and third ways to access your money are the dumb way and the smart way. To understand the difference, I'll explain the options and mechanics using the following assumptions: You're 60 years old, preparing to retire, and you design an insurance policy large enough to accommodate up to $500,000 of total premiums under TEFRA/DEFRA guidelines. You arrive at this size of bucket because you want to reposition $200,000 of net after-tax IRA and 401(k) funds over a five-year period, using a strategic conversion or roll-out from qualified to non-qualified status to alleviate up to 50 percent of ultimate tax. You plan to reposition $200,000 of home equity as you downsize by purchasing a new retirement home to increase its liquidity, safety, and rate of return, and enjoy the tax benefits that help offset the taxes due on the IRA and 401(k) roll-out. You also reposition $100,000 of CDs that are maturing at 3 percent interest, which is 2 percent after tax. The minimum death benefit under TEFRA/DEFRA guidelines would be $1,274,612 for a bucket that will allow a guideline single premium of $500,000. Let's assume you transfer $100,000 into the life insurance policy each year for five years to comply with TAMRA by strategically repositioning the above-mentioned assets.

If you were to receive the equivalent average gross rate of 7.75 percent interest on your cash value, after deducting the mortality and expense charges (the spigot on the bucket), you might have a cash-value balance of $557,328 at the end of the fifth year. The bucket can overflow and grow far beyond the size of the guideline single premium allowed under TEFRA/DEFRA. After filling it to the brim with $500,000, if it continued untouched for thirty-five years, at age 100 it might be worth $6,680,000, assuming a 7.75 gross interest crediting rate. That's okay with the IRS—the growth on the money inside the bucket can do so tax-free and can far exceed the basis.

Since you did this for tax-favored retirement income, let's say that, at age 65 (after the policy has been fully funded), you just let it sit and grow for five more years until you're 70. Then you decide to start pulling out some income to supplement your pension and Social Security. At that point, the bucket may have grown to $770,000. If the net rate of return (after the spigot drains its portion) is approximately 7 percent, you could theoretically withdraw about $50,000 a year and not deplete the principal. Now, the advantage of investment-grade insurance contracts over annuities is that when you withdraw money from the policy, it is treated with FIFO—first in, first out—taxation, not LIFO taxation. Under FIFO tax treatment, the first money into the investment is considered by the IRS as the first money that you are pulling out of the investment. So if you as the policy owner choose to withdraw money from your insurance contract, it is tax-free up to the basis (in this case $500,000). At a withdrawal rate of $50,000 a year, income tax would be avoided during the first ten years (10 x $50,000). Hence, in this example, for the first ten years, your income would be tax-free.

A term synonymous with withdrawal from an insurance policy is *partial surrender*. If a policy owner wanted to cancel his insurance policy and surrender it to the insurance company, the insured and owner would relinquish all benefits, and the insurance company would liquidate any cash values to the owner, less applicable surrender charges. Surrender charges usually apply during the early years of an insurance contract. If a person chooses to withdraw just some of his cash values rather than all of his cash values, the surrender may be deemed a partial surrender—incurring only limited surrender charges, depending on the contract. In that case, only a portion of the contract and its benefits might be surrendered—the death benefit could be adjusted and reduced in direct proportion to the amount of the partial surrender (which wouldn't be a concern if the death benefit was originally intended as a secondary objective). If withdrawals are made in amounts equal to the net annual interest earned, the cash values would likely stay fairly consistent for several years. However, the death benefit would adjust and reduce because of the withdrawal. See the example in figure 11.1.

A partial surrender permanently reduces the size of the insurance contract. So if the owner later wanted to reinvest more money in the contract, he would not have the same latitude he originally had. Another problem is that once the owner has withdrawn his entire basis (ten years, or $50,000, in this example), future withdrawals become taxable. That is because under FIFO taxation, all the basis comes out tax-free first, and the remainder is deemed by the IRS as your gain. That gain would be subject to income tax as you begin to realize it. So, in this example, beginning the eleventh year, another $50,000 with-

Fig. 11.1   TAX-FREE ACCESS VIA WITHDRAWALS AND LOANS

Age	Yr	Annual Premium Outlay	Annual With-drawal	Annual Loan Amount (a)	Annual Loan Repayment (b)	Interest Charged To Loan (c)	Total Loan Balance	Interest Earned on Loaned CV (d)	Net Loan Cost (c)-(d)	Accumulation Value	Surrender Value	Net Death Benefit
61	1	100,000	0	0	0	0	0	0	0	93,500	60,360	1,274,612
62	2	100,000	0	0	0	0	0	0	0	195,219	134,038	1,274,612
63	3	100,000	0	0	0	0	0	0	0	305,880	244,698	1,274,612
64	4	100,000	0	0	0	0	0	0	0	426,268	365,086	1,274,612
65	5	100,000	0	0	0	0	0	0	0	557,238	496,057	1,274,612
66	6	0	0	0	0	0	0	0	0	593,107	534,985	1,274,612
67	7	0	0	0	0	0	0	0	0	632,128	577,065	1,274,612
68	8	0	0	0	0	0	0	0	0	674,580	622,576	1,274,612
69	9	0	0	0	0	0	0	0	0	720,763	671,818	1,274,612
70	10	0	0	0	0	0	0	0	0	771,006	728,179	1,274,612
71	11	0	50,000	0	0	0	0	0	0	769,428	734,160	1,224,587
72	12	0	50,000	0	0	0	0	0	0	767,768	739,579	1,174,562
73	13	0	50,000	0	0	0	0	0	0	766,113	744,522	1,124,537
74	14	0	50,000	0	0	0	0	0	0	764,690	749,217	1,074,512
75	15	0	50,000	0	0	0	0	0	0	763,344	753,509	1,024,487
76	16	0	50,000	0	0	0	0	0	0	762,975	758,297	974,462
77	17	0	50,000	0	0	0	0	0	0	763,252	763,252	924,437
78	18	0	50,000	0	0	0	0	0	0	764,226	764,226	874,412
79	19	0	50,000	0	0	0	0	0	0	766,286	766,286	824,387
80	20	0	50,000	0	0	0	0	0	0	770,222	769,964	808,475
81	21	0	0	50,000	0	1,508	51,765	1,508	0	825,859	774,094	815,386
82	22	0	0	50,000	0	3,053	104,818	3,053	0	883,006	778,187	822,338
83	23	0	0	50,000	0	4,645	159,463	4,645	0	941,663	782,200	829,283
84	24	0	0	50,000	0	6,284	215,747	6,284	0	1,001,824	786,077	836,169
85	25	0	0	50,000	0	7,972	273,719	7,972	0	1,063,629	789,910	843,092
86	26	0	0	50,000	0	9,712	333,431	9,712	0	1,127,114	793,683	850,039
87	27	0	0	50,000	0	11,503	394,934	11,503	0	1,192,063	797,129	856,732
88	28	0	0	50,000	0	13,348	458,282	13,348	0	1,258,420	800,138	863,059
89	29	0	0	50,000	0	15,248	523,530	15,248	0	1,326,116	802,586	868,892
90	30	0	0	50,000	0	17,206	590,736	17,206	0	1,395,424	804,688	874,459
91	31	0	0	50,000	0	19,222	659,958	19,222	0	1,466,389	806,431	879,751
92	32	0	0	50,000	0	21,299	731,257	21,299	0	1,539,990	808,733	870,332
93	33	0	0	50,000	0	23,438	804,694	23,438	0	1,616,639	811,945	860,444
94	34	0	0	50,000	0	25,641	880,335\	25,641	0	1,696,838	816,503	850,439
95	35	0	0	50,000	0	27,910	958,245	27,910	0	1,781,189	822,944	840,756
96	36	0	0	50,000	0	30,247	1,038,493	30,247	0	1,869,841	831,348	831,348
97	37	0	0	50,000	0	32,655	1,121,147	32,655	0	1,961,436	840,289	840,289
98	38	0	0	50,000	0	35,134	1,206,282	35,134	0	2,056,087	849,805	849,805
99	39	0	0	50,000	0	37,688	1,293,970	37,688	0	2,153,908	859,937	859,937
100	40	0	0	50,000	0	40,319	1,384,289	40,319	0	2,255,019	870,730	870,730

drawn from the bucket would be taxable. This would definitely be the dumb way to continue accessing money.

THE SMART WAY

The smart way to access money is for the owner to change the "withdrawal" to a "loan." It's simply a change in nomenclature. Remember, loan proceeds are not deemed earned, passive, or portfolio income by the IRS—they are tax-free! Let's see how the tax-free loan provision works with a life insurance policy by studying figure 11.1.

The owner in this example still has $770,000 of cash value remaining in the contract at the time he converts his $50,000 of withdrawal income to loan income (year 20, age 80) to preserve tax-favored treatment. In essence, he is no longer making $50,000 annual withdrawals from his basis in an amount equal to his interest earnings, so his cash-value balance will resume growing and compounding at the net rate of return (7 percent in this example). Instead of the cash-value balance staying somewhat constant at $770,000 as it did when he was withdrawing $50,000 each year, the $770,000 increases to over $825,000 the next year.

If you had $770,000 in a certificate of deposit at a bank, wouldn't the bank be willing to loan you the equivalent of your annual interest earnings? You bet they would, because of the collateral they have— your $770,000 deposit. Likewise, the insurance company is willing to loan you the equivalent of the interest you are earning and are no longer withdrawing.

Note what happens in years 20 through 22 (ages 80 to 82) of figure 11.1. On one portion of the ledger, you would have a beginning balance of $770,222, which grew by $55,637 to a year-end balance of $825,859 tax-free. On the other side of the ledger, there is a loan balance of $50,000 from the loan you took out. The nice thing about loans on insurance contracts is that the loan is not due and payable during the owner/insured's lifetime. In other words, it's open until death. When the insured dies, the loan balance is deducted from the death benefit automatically. But the interest credited on the cash-value side of the ledger can replenish some or all of the reduced death benefit.

As far as the insurance company is concerned, the owner still really owns only $774,094 in cash values. This is because the $825,859 year-end balance, less the loan balance of $51,765, plus interest equals almost the same $770,000 he would have had if he pulled the money out the dumb way (withdrawals). The smart way maintained the owner's income but was qualified as tax-free. The next year the cash values may grow to approximately $883,000. If he borrows another $50,000 of tax-free loan proceeds, his loan balance will accrue to $104,818, which still results in a net balance of $778,187. After ten years of using tax-free loans, this person has $1,395,424 in the cash-value portion of the ledger and a loan balance of $590,736 (ten years of $50,000 plus interest). The net balance is now $804,688, and he has enjoyed ten more years of retirement income totally free of tax. He can continue this procedure until death occurs, as long as there is a death benefit sufficient to wash out the loan balance. Thus, a taxable event can permanently be avoided as long as the policy has at least enough cash value remaining in it at death to keep the life insurance in force by covering the mortality costs.

PREFERRED LOANS FOR RETIREMENT INCOME

There are a few features that make tax-free loans used for retirement income very attractive. In order for a loan to be construed as a true loan (and therefore not taxable), a reasonable interest rate needs to be charged to the loan by the insurance company. "Reasonable" interest can be 8 percent, 6 percent, or even 4 percent. Let's say the insurance company charges 6 percent on the loan balance. That interest is not deductible because the owner would be getting tax-free interest on the money that was not withdrawn. The policy owner earns his regular interest on the corpus of $770,000. There is also an amount equal to the total loans taken out that is likewise earning interest. The insurance companies I recommend are contractually obligated to pay 4 percent interest on that money if the interest charged on the loan balance is 6 percent. In other words, there is a 2 percent net differential between the interest charge on the loan balance and the interest credited on the cash-value portion that collateralized the loan—a pretty attractive rate.

The insurance companies I recommend have a special classification of loans they call *preferred loans*. Preferred loans were created specifically for retirement income. The insured, depending on his age, may qualify for preferred loans as early as the first years of the policy. Preferred loans can be totally "zero spread" loans. Usually when the insured is qualified to use the preferred loan provision, he is restricted to preferred loans of no more than 10 percent of the corpus annually for a certain time period. In the example we've been using, the owner could take zero spread loans of up to $77,000 (10 percent of $770,000) annually for, say, the first ten years of retirement, then it could be unlimited thereafter. With preferred (zero spread) loans, the insurance company credits the same interest on the cash value used as collateral for the loan as the interest charged on the loan. This results in a net cost of zero percent, as shown in figure 11.1.

I have clients who have enjoyed tax-free income from their buckets for years by using withdrawals up to basis, and zero spread loans thereafter. Some of their policy ledgers reflect several million dollars owing on a loan balance. However, with proper management, the cash values they pledged as collateral for the annual loans (growing with interest) have exceeded the loan balance by a very comfortable margin. They absolutely love having cash flow that doesn't show up anywhere on their 1040 tax returns.

There is one other reason why using loans for retirement income is the smart way to access your money from an insurance contract. Assume a couple took tax-free income of $50,000 a year for ten years from an insurance contract. Now let's say they inherited some money or decided to downsize their home and take up to $500,000 of capital gain tax-free on their personal residence. Under any circumstance, if they have $500,000 in cash they don't know what to do with, this couple could have a grandfathered bucket they could still use. As long as they use the loan provision instead of withdrawals, there is room to re-deposit as much as $500,000 back into the life insurance policy. This would be considered a loan repayment. Having replenished the con-tract with new money, they would then have the opportunity to use their insurance contract just as they always have for further tax-favored accumulation and income.

Suppose after filling a bucket, a couple let their cash values sit and grow for ten years to a balance of $1,100,000, and now they want to access as much of the money as possible. They could totally surrender their insurance policy, but that would be the dumb way to do it be-cause they would relinquish their death benefit and trigger a taxable event. At a tax rate of 33.3 percent, they would owe tax of $200,000 on $600,000 of earnings above their $500,000 basis (because it is taxed as ordinary income). So after withdrawing $1,100,000, they would net only $900,000.

Usually, the smart way to access the maximum lump sum is to bor-row 90 to 94 percent of the cash surrender value, without immediately relinquishing the death benefit. This couple could borrow $1 million tax-free. The remaining $100,000 (which they would have lost to in-come tax had they surrendered their policy) may cover the cost of in-surance for several months or years before additional payments would be required to keep the insurance in force and to avoid a taxable event. Accessing money this way would at least postpone the triggering of a taxable event and would be better if death occurred in the interim. The death benefit, after deducting the loan with interest, may still leave be-hind a substantial sum of cash to the beneficiaries—money that would have been lost by accessing their money the dumb way.

WHAT DO TAX REVENUERS THINK ABOUT THIS?

I hope you now understand how money can be accessed tax-free from an insurance contract and why it is deemed tax-free. When peo-ple learn this, they sometimes comment, "Well, as soon as the IRS or

Congress discovers this, they'll close up this loophole!" The fact is, this is not considered a loophole. The IRS and Congress are aware of these tax-favored vehicles and strategies that allow for tax-free accumulation of cash values and tax-free access. In fact, many congressional members themselves own these types of policies. I doubt they would be shortsighted enough to change the law to hurt prospective retirees trying to provide for retirement.

Nonetheless, I can't predict what Congress may do to alter the tax treatment on the inside buildup and access of life insurance cash values. But I would rather board my boat at retirement with a life preserver likely to keep me afloat while tested under current tax laws than board with an inner tube like IRAs and 401(k)s I know will lose air (by the payment of taxes) as soon as the valve stem is opened. My confidence also lies in one of the strongest lobbies in America: the insurance industry. Congress should be smart enough to realize that if it changed the rules regarding the tax-free inside buildup and access of insurance contract cash values, it would be shooting itself in the foot. Probably all the tax revenue it would hope to generate would be shelled out later in additional Social Security and welfare benefits—to the people whom it taxed. I am convinced that properly structured and properly used investment-grade insurance contracts are the best retirement vehicles for providing liquidity, safety, and tax-favored rates of return. Just in case congressional tax revenuers do something stupid down the road, I am getting as many buckets as I can afford to fill up with cash, in hopes they will be grandfathered under the old laws. I believe it would behoove anyone to do likewise.

INSURANCE COMPARED TO OTHER INVESTMENTS

Let's take a look at a 30-year-old couple, Brian and Mindy Smart. They systematically set aside $6,000 a year in an insurance contract on Brian's life for thirty-five years, compared to alternative investments such as mutual funds, IRA/401(k)s, municipal bond funds, or annuities (figure 11.2). The Smarts can afford this because they are repositioning

| Fig. 11.2 | AN INDEXED UNIVERSAL LIFE POLICY VERSUS VARIOUS FINANCIAL ALTERNATIVES | | | | | | | |

			Initial Payment 6,000	A Municipal Bond Fund Yield 5.00%	An Annuity Yield 6.25%	IRAs & 401(k)s Yield 7.75%	Mutual Fund Yield 10.00%	An Indexed Universal Life Policy Interest Rate 7.75%		Tax Bracket 34.00%
Male Age 30										
				AFTER TAX VALUES				AN INDEXED UNIVERSAL LIFE POLICY		
			[1]	[2]	[3]	[4]	[5]	[6]	[7]	[8]
								Year End	Year End	
Client's Age	Year		Net Payment	A Municipal Bond Fund	An Annuity	IRAs & 401(k)s	Mutual Fund	Accumulation Value*	Surrender Value*	Death Benefit
31	1		6,000	5,988	6,033	6,054	6,029	5,331	2,155	635,176
32	2		6,000	12,212	12,242	12,344	12,407	11,064	4,712	635,176
33	3		6,000	18,681	18,636	18,888	19,152	17,230	10,879	635,176
34	4		6,000	25,407	25,225	25,703	26,287	23,859	17,507	635,176
35	5		6,000	32,398	32,018	32,808	33,835	31,012	24,660	635,176
36	6		6,000	39,665	39,028	40,223	41,818	38,731	32,697	635,176
37	7		6,000	47,219	46,263	47,969	50,262	47,062	41,345	635,176
38	8		6,000	55,072	53,738	56,069	59,194	56,051	50,652	635,176
39	9		6,000	63,235	61,462	64,549	68,641	65,751	60,670	635,176
40	10		6,000	71,720	69,451	73,434	78,635	76,219	71,773	635,176
41	11		6,000	80,541	77,717	82,753	89,205	87,977	84,166	635,176
42	12		6,000	89,710	86,276	92,535	100,386	100,611	97,435	635,176
43	13		6,000	99,241	95,141	102,813	112,212	114,182	111,641	635,176
44	14		6,000	109,148	104,329	113,622	124,722	128,764	126,858	635,176
45	15		6,000	119,447	113,856	124,997	137,953	144,440	143,170	635,176
46	16		6,000	130,153	123,741	136,979	151,949	161,284	160,649	635,176
47	17		6,000	141,281	134,002	149,609	166,754	179,375	179,375	635,176
48	18		6,000	152,850	144,658	162,933	182,413	198,819	198,819	635,176
49	19		6,000	164,875	155,730	176,998	198,976	219,718	219,718	635,176
50	20		6,000	177,375	167,240	191,857	216,496	242,183	242,183	635,176
51	21		6,000	190,369	179,209	207,563	235,028	266,336	266,336	635,176
52	22		6,000	203,876	191,662	224,177	254,630	292,330	292,330	635,176
53	23		6,000	217,916	204,625	241,761	275,364	320,316	320,316	635,176
54	24		6,000	232,511	218,123	260,382	297,296	350,457	350,457	635,176
55	25		6,000	247,683	232,184	280,113	320,494	382,943	382,943	635,176
56	26		6,000	263,454	246,838	301,030	345,032	417,972	417,972	635,176
57	27		6,000	279,848	262,115	323,216	370,986	455,771	455,771	665,426
58	28		6,000	296,890	278,047	346,758	398,440	496,454	496,454	704,964
59	29		6,000	314,604	294,669	371,752	427,479	540,207	540,207	745,486
60	30		6,000	333,019	312,017	398,297	458,195	587,275	587,275	786,949
61	31		6,000	352,160	355,864	469,449	490,685	637,924	637,924	829,301
62	32		6,000	372,058	377,083	503,711	525,051	692,351	692,351	886,209
63	33		6,000	392,742	399,296	540,209	561,402	750,842	750,842	946,061
64	34		6,000	414,243	422,556	579,100	599,852	813,709	813,709	1,008,999
65	35		6,000	436,593	446,917	620,548	640,523	881,289	881,289	1,075,173

Sales charge on payments to column [1]:
MB = 4.00%, AN = 4.00%, IRA = 5.00%, MF = 5.00%

Management fee reflected in columns [2], [3], [4], & [5]:
MB = 1.00%, AN = 1.00%, IRA = .75%, MF = .75%

Tax deferred accounts are assessed: Income tax on withdrawals in column [1].
Additional income tax on withdrawals before age 59 1/2: 10.00%.

* This illustration assumes the nonguaranteed values shown continue in all years.
This is not likely, and actual results may be more or less favorable.
Format and design created through the use of InsMark® software.

| Fig. 11.2 continued | AN INDEXED UNIVERSAL LIFE POLICY VERSUS VARIOUS FINANCIAL ALTERNATIVES |

	Male Age 30	Initial Payment 6,000	A Municipal Bond Fund Yield 5.00%	An Annuity Yield 6.25%	IRAs & 401(k)s Yield 7.75%	Mutual Fund Yield 10.00%	An Indexed Universal Life Policy Interest Rate 7.75%		Tax Bracket 34.00%
			AFTER TAX VALUES				AN INDEXED UNIVERSAL LIFE POLICY		
		[1]	[2]	[3]	[4]	[5]	[6] Year End Accumulation Value*	[7] Year End Surrender Value*	[8] Death Benefit
Client's Age	Year	Net Payment	A Municipal Bond Fund	An Annuity	IRAs & 401(k)s	Mutual Fund			
66	36	-64,000	387,310	399,077	590,277	609,817	878,901	878,901	1,054,682
67	37	-64,000	336,081	348,755	557,800	577,338	942,069	876,149	1,055,143
68	38	-64,000	282,828	295,823	523,123	542,983	1,006,691	872,873	1,054,078
69	39	-64,000	227,472	240,145	486,038	506,645	1,072,768	869,016	1,051,387
70	40	-64,000	169,929	182,176	446,379	468,207	1,140,304	864,520	1,046,968
71	41	-64,000	110,114	122,222	403,967	427,550	1,209,302	859,324	1,040,720
72	42	-64,000	47,935	60,215	358,610	384,545	1,279,987	853,590	1,019,988
73	43	-64,000	-16,868	-4,021	310,105	339,057	1,352,454	847,345	996,115
74	44	-64,000	-84,912	-72,272	258,233	290,941	1,426,829	840,646	969,061
75	45	-64,000	-156,357	-144,790	203,132	240,047	1,503,263	833,575	938,804
76	46	-64,000	-231,375	-221,839	145,507	186,214	1,581,990	826,291	905,390
77	47	-64,000	-310,144	-303,704	85,241	129,272	1,662,319	818,029	901,145
78	48	-64,000	-392,851	-390,685	22,214	69,041	1,744,203	808,664	895,875
79	49	-64,000	-479,694	-483,103	-45,024	5,332	1,827,588	798,063	889,443
80	50	-64,000	-570,878	-581,297	-117,474	-62,540	1,912,400	786,069	881,689
81	51	-64,000	-666,622	-685,628	-195,538	-134,891	1,998,532	772,492	872,418
82	52	-64,000	-767,153	-796,480	-279,652	-212,018	2,085,878	757,136	861,430
83	53	-64,000	-872,711	-914,260	-370,285	-294,235	2,174,312	739,788	848,504
84	54	-64,000	-983,547	-1,038,401	-467,942	-381,879	2,263,691	720,212	833,396
85	55	-64,000	-1,099,924	-1,172,364	-573,168	-475,307	2,354,194	698,490	816,199
86	56	-64,000	-1,222,120	-1,313,636	-686,548	-574,901	2,445,742	674,447	796,734
87	57	-64,000	-1,350,426	-1,463,739	-808,716	-681,069	2,537,708	647,354	774,239
88	58	-64,000	-1,485,147	-1,623,222	-940,351	-794,243	2,629,816	616,831	748,322
89	59	-64,000	-1,626,605	-1,792,674	-1,082,188	-914,887	2,721,761	582,466	718,554
90	60	-64,000	-1,775,135	-1,972,716	-1,235,018	-1,043,494	2,813,929	544,536	685,232
91	61	-64,000	-1,931,092	-2,164,011	-1,399,692	-1,180,588	2,906,209	502,814	648,125
92	62	-64,000	-2,094,846	-2,367,261	-1,577,128	-1,326,731	3,000,312	458,896	578,908
93	63	-64,000	-2,266,789	-2,583,215	-1,768,315	-1,482,519	3,096,747	413,168	506,071
94	64	-64,000	-2,447,328	-2,812,666	-1,974,320	-1,648,590	3,196,133	366,126	430,049
95	65	-64,000	-2,636,894	-3,056,458	-2,196,289	-1,825,621	3,299,231	318,404	351,396
96	66	-64,000	-2,835,939	-3,315,486	-2,435,462	-2,014,335	3,405,890	269,719	269,719
97	67	-64,000	-3,044,936	-3,590,704	-2,693,170	-2,215,506	3,513,215	217,039	217,039
98	68	-64,000	-3,264,383	-3,883,123	-2,970,851	-2,429,953	3,621,030	160,049	160,049
99	69	-64,000	-3,494,802	-4,193,818	-3,270,052	-2,658,554	3,729,892	99,161	99,161
100	70	-64,000	-3,736,742	-4,523,932	-3,592,441	-2,902,242	3,844,000	38,426	38,426

Sales charge on payments to column [1]:
MB = 4.00%, AN = 4.00%, IRA = 5.00%, MF = 5.00%

Management fee reflected in columns [2], [3], [4], & [5]:
MB = 1.00%, AN = 1.00%, IRA = .75%, MF = .75%

Tax deferred accounts are assessed: Income tax on withdrawals in column [1].
Additional income tax on withdrawals before age 59¹/2: 10.00%.

* This illustration assumes the nonguaranteed values shown continue in all years.
This is not likely, and actual results may be more or less favorable.
Format and design created through the use of InsMark® software.

money they were contributing into IRAs and 401(k)s for retirement purposes. The Smarts keep their tax deductions high during these contribution years by keeping as high a mortgage balance on their home as possible, so they free up $500 per month by using an interest-only mortgage rather than a fifteen- or thirty-year amortized mortgage. Therefore, we are assuming the Smarts indirectly get the same tax benefits they would get on a qualified plan contribution.

The alternative investments I'm illustrating, even though they may be tax-favored up until age 65, are not as attractive as the potential after-tax value of the insurance contract, as shown in the right-hand columns of figure 11.2. In this example, alternative investments have not performed even as well as the insurance contract by age 65, as illustrated, with their after-tax values, across the line in year 35. There is an even more dramatic difference as the retirement income commences after thirty-five years of accumulation. Notice how quickly a municipal bond fund and an annuity run out of steam (when they turn negative, indicated in bold), compared to the tax-free withdrawal or loan of $64,000 we can take out of the insurance contract to deplete the money gradually to age 100. (We have instructed the computer software to calculate the maximum average withdrawals and/or loans required to gradually deplete the insurance contract of cash value until age 100. Retirement income of $50,000 to $60,000 rather than $64,000 would prevent the depletion of the cash values and could even result in continued growth in spite of the withdrawals and loans taken.) The IRAs and 401(k)s and the mutual funds also run out of money long before an assumed life expectancy of age 85, as shown on the line in year 55. They are respectively $573,168 and $475,307 in the hole at age 85. This happens because it would require a taxable income of approximately $96,000 ($8,000 a month) to equal a tax-free income of $64,000 in a 34 percent tax bracket. In other words, based on the need for a net spendable income of $64,000 a year, the Smarts would have outlived their money using traditional investments, based on these assumptions.

On the other hand, at age 85, the insurance contract is still generating a net spendable income of $64,000, with cash values remaining in the contract worth $698,490. The insurance contract crediting a gross interest rate of 7.75 percent provides $64,000 of retirement income for twenty-one years longer than a mutual fund yielding 10 percent. That equals $1,344,000 ($64,000/yr x 21 yrs) more in retirement resources! If Brian Smart did pass away at age 85, the $698,490 in the insurance contract would immediately blossom into a tax-free transfer of $816,199 to his wife, Mindy, or their heirs.

Another way to look at it is to study the age 100 results (year 70). The mutual fund is negative $2,902,242, and the IRAs and 401(k)s are negative $3,592,441 (based on the same interest crediting rate as the insurance contract) when the insurance contract is finally depleted. So, at age 65 (year 35), the insurance contract is valued at $881,289, versus the mutual fund with an after-tax value of $640,523, resulting in a difference of $240,766. But the significant difference is $2,902,242, which represents how much the insurance contract outperformed the mutual fund over a seventy-year period to age 100, based on a net spendable annual retirement income of $64,000! And don't forget to consider the tax-free transfer of the death benefit in the far right-hand column, should death occur anytime during retirement, compared to the other investment alternatives.

Please note in figure 11.3 that the various investment alternatives illustrated with the normal tax considerations and fee would have to be crediting interest rates from 8.22 percent (if it were a municipal bond fund) up to 13.43 percent (if it were a mutual fund), to match the same values achieved by the insurance contract crediting 7.75 percent. If the mutual fund in this example averaged a 12 percent yield, it would still be $234,428 in the hole at the end of seventy years, when the insurance contract crediting only 7.75 percent was finally depleted down to $38,426.

Some proponents of mutual funds may say, "Well, a good mutual fund may perform an average of 15 percent." (If it did, a good indexed universal life may perform at 10 to 12 percent during the same time period.) Some investments may perform better during the contribution and accumulation phases. But more important, others may generate

Fig. 11.3

Male Age 30	Initial Payment 6,000		An Indexed Universal Life Policy Interest Rate 7.75%	Tax Bracket 34.00%

Gross interest rate needed by various investments over 40 years to match an Indexed Universal Life Policy

Investment	Interest Rate	Indexed Universal Life Policy	
A Municipal Bond Fund	9.08%	Accumulation Value	$3,844,000
A Municipal Bond Fund	8.22%	Surrender Value	$38,426
A Municipal Bond Fund	8.22%	Death Benefit	$38,426
An Annuity	10.19%	Accumulation Value	$3,844,000
An Annuity	9.49%	Surrender Value	$38,426
An Annuity	9.49%	Death Benefit	$38,426
IRA's / 401(k)s	9.94%	Accumulation Value	$3,844,000
IRA's / 401(k)s	9.24%	Surrender Value	$38,426
IRA's / 401(k)s	9.24%	Death Benefit	$38,426
Mutual Fund	13.43%	Accumulation Value	$3,844,000
Mutual Fund	12.13%	Surrender Value	$38,426
Mutual Fund	12.13%	Death Benefit	$38,426

Income Tax Considerations

1. A Certificate of Deposit - Interest is taxed as earned.
2. A Municipal Bond Fund - Interest is tax exempt.
3. An Annuity - Interest is tax deferred. (Values assume tax is assessed in year shown only.)
4. Mutual Fund - Interest is taxed as earned.
5. An Indexed Universal Life Policy:
   a. Death Benefit including cash value component is income tax free.
   b. Loans are income tax free as long as the policy is kept in force.
   c. Withdrawals and other non-loan policy cash flow up to cost basis
      (not in violations of IRC Section 7702) are income tax free as a return of premium.
   d. Cash values shown assume most favorable combination of b and/or c.

Format and design created through the use of InsMark® software.

the most during the distribution phase, as well as the transfer phase, when death finally occurs. Greater growth investment vehicles may be inferior to other investments, when considering tax effects. Remember, choose financial instruments that generate or provide the most money at the time in life you will likely need the money most.

One of the reasons an insurance contract is probably the best alternative in most circumstances is that during the transfer phase, whatever amount is left in the policy blossoms to a larger sum and is transferred free of income tax to the heirs. Other investments do not blossom upon transfer, but transfer at face value and may be subject to taxation—especially qualified accounts upon which the heirs ultimately have to pay income tax and possibly estate tax as well.

You may have studied this example and said to yourself, "But I'm going to need more than $64,000 a year in retirement income due to the cost of living increase!" Don't worry. As long as you discipline yourself to set aside a percentage of your income each year, as your income increases, so will your retirement resources. When you fill up one bucket (insurance contract) to the maximum allowed under IRS guidelines, you can begin a new one. For this reason, I personally have many buckets insuring myself, my wife, and all of my children. Remember, it's not what you begin with that counts, but what you end up with. But start doing something! Now!

As I hope you can see, it can be far more advantageous to have tax-favored treatment on the harvest of our investments than just tax-favored treatment on the seed money. Simply put, if you have $1 million accumulated at retirement and you are earning 10 percent, you can theoretically take out $100,000 a year of income and never run out of money. That's because you wouldn't be depleting the principal. If the $100,000 is not deemed earned, passive, or portfolio income, but instead a return of basis, or a loan proceed, it is tax-free. *But if you need $100,000 a year to live on during retirement and you have your $1 million trapped in IRAs, 401(k)s, or other yet-to-be-taxed investments, in a 33.3 percent tax bracket, you will need to withdraw $150,000 a year and pay tax of $50,000 to net that $100,000.* Withdrawing $150,000 a year will totally deplete a $1-million nest egg earning 10 percent within eleven to twelve years! You probably wouldn't be dead yet, but you may likely be dead broke!

VARIOUS TYPES OF LIFE INSURANCE CONTRACTS

So which type of cash-value life insurance do you select? There are five generally recognized types of cash-value life insurance that have been on the market during the last decade: whole life, variable life, and three kinds of universal life—fixed, variable, and equity-indexed. Understanding them will help you choose.

Whole Life Insurance

Whole life is typically referred to as permanent or traditional cash-value life insurance. It offers guaranteed death benefits, cash values, level premiums, and possibly dividends. The most basic form of this type of policy is "ordinary" or "straight" life. Newer whole life policies have lower costs due to upgraded mortality rates. Of course, there is tax-deferred growth of the cash-value accumulation. A policyholder can access cash values via withdrawals or loans. The dividends of a whole life insurance policy are tax-free. The projected return on a whole life policy is based upon a long-term portfolio of assets.

Variable Life Insurance

Variable life, like universal life, has a death benefit created by term insurance with an equity investment side fund. The insured may choose the investment vehicle to be used for cash accumulation, and the values are dependent upon the return of the chosen investment vehicle. The premium payable is a specified amount based upon the insured's age and the face amount of the policy. Investment options may include:

- Money market fund
- Guaranteed or fixed account
- Government securities fund
- Corporate bond fund
- Total return fund
- Growth fund

As investors' objectives change, they may switch from one investment portfolio to another. Personally, *I don't recommend that homeowners invest home equity in variable life contracts*. Financial planners should never advise that home equity be invested in securities or variable products. To safely manage home equity, you should select more stable or fixed insurance contracts that contain guarantees.

Universal Life Insurance

Universal life insurance was created with flexibility in mind. Both premium payments and insurance death benefits may be varied, within limits, to meet the needs of the client. As a policy owner pays premiums into a universal life contract, a portion is used to pay the pure term insurance rates. The balance is deposited into a side fund on which interest is paid. If the premium paid is not sufficient to cover the cost of the term insurance, the balance is taken from the side fund. The policy owner may elect to pay premiums higher or lower, subject to some limits, and may even elect to skip premium payments without losing coverage if there is adequate cash value in the savings portion of the contract. Universal life generally contains low mortality costs due to updated mortality rates. Of course, the same tax-advantaged growth of cash values is inherent in universal life as it is in whole life. Universal life typically credits a competitive interest rate to the cash values of the policy. Cash values can be accessed tax-free via withdrawal or loan. The entire cash values and accumulated earnings can transfer to heirs free of income tax.

Fixed Universal Life Insurance

Of the three kinds of universal life, fixed universal life is the most conservative approach. It is the least management-intensive and incurs the smallest expense charges. The term "fixed" does not mean the interest that is credited on the policy owner's cash value is fixed at the same rate for the life of the contract. It means the cash values are credited with interest that is earned by the relatively fixed portfolio of the insurance company. For example, a large life insurance company with strong ratings may have approximately 75 percent of its assets invested in high-grade bonds, 15 percent invested in mortgaged-backed securities, and the remaining 10 percent represented by a combination of stocks, real estate, cash, and short-term investments or policy loans. So if you owned fixed universal life, the insurance company would credit you interest based on the amount it could afford as a result of the return it is getting on its invested assets.

Depending on the company, a fixed universal life policy will generally have a guaranteed minimum interest rate, usually around 4 percent. I know of very few companies that have credited only the guaranteed rate. Whenever a universal life policy is purchased, the NAIC (National Association of Insurance Commissioners) requires the policy owner to sign an illustration showing the projection of the policy benefits based upon the intended premium payments that will likely be made into the policy. The illustration can show projections based upon the interest rate credited by the company at the time the policy was taken out.

The illustration must also show the worst-case scenario, which assumes that only the minimum guaranteed interest rate is credited on the policy cash values from the inception of the policy. It also assumes that the maximum mortality charges allowed contractually by the company are assessed throughout the life of the policy. The worst-case scenario would be a highly unlikely event, but serves to show the owner of the life insurance contract what could happen under those circumstances. The actual mortality charges assessed are usually considerably less than the maximum allowable, and policies will usually far outperform the minimum interest guarantee.

Insurance companies can usually afford to pay higher interest rates than banks and credit unions because their portfolio of investment assets doesn't turn over quickly. Fixed universal life tends to be more stable, responding slowly to market swings. Figure 11.4 contains a pie chart of a typical life insurance company with a Comdex score in excess of 90, according to LifeLink. Note the five-year history of this company's returns on invested assets. This is a good indication of the approximate interest rate investors might experience with such a company before subtracting the expenses and the profit margin that companies must maintain to operate successfully.

Variable Universal Life Insurance

Variable universal life insurance combines the premium flexibility of universal life with the investment flexibility of variable life. In ad-

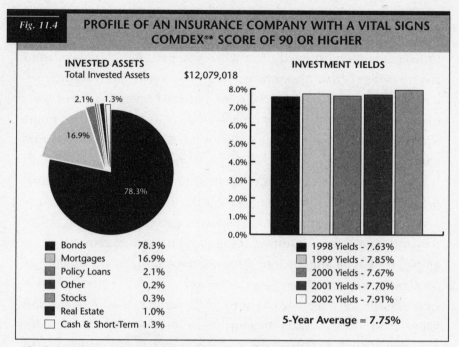

Fig. 11.4 **PROFILE OF AN INSURANCE COMPANY WITH A VITAL SIGNS COMDEX®* SCORE OF 90 OR HIGHER**

INVESTED ASSETS
Total Invested Assets $12,079,018

INVESTMENT YIELDS

■ Bonds	78.3%
▨ Mortgages	16.9%
▨ Policy Loans	2.1%
■ Other	0.2%
▨ Stocks	0.3%
■ Real Estate	1.0%
□ Cash & Short-Term	1.3%

■ 1998 Yields - 7.63%
□ 1999 Yields - 7.85%
▨ 2000 Yields - 7.67%
■ 2001 Yields - 7.70%
□ 2002 Yields - 7.91%

5-Year Average = 7.75%

*Comdex is a proprietary composite of carrier's ratings issued by LifeLink Corporation.
Format and design created through the use of LifeLink Pro® software (www.lifelinkpro.com).*

dition to the ability to select from various investment funds, as is the case with variable life, the policyholder may elect to adjust the premiums higher or lower, with limits determined by the insurance company and federal tax laws. The policyholder may even elect to skip premium payments without losing coverage if there are adequate accumulated values in the investment funds.

Generally, all of the cash values of the policy, except the portion needed to cover the mortality and expense charges, are removed from the umbrella of the insurance company. These cash values are usually invested in equities. Therefore, with variable universal life, there is no guaranteed minimum interest rate. In fact, if a loss is experienced during a certain time period and there is not sufficient value in the portfolio, the policy owner may have to make additional premium payments to keep the mortality and expense charges covered—and continue doing so until the cash values of the policy have recovered. Because variable insurance contracts are vulnerable to market downturns, perhaps occurring at times when you need liquidity the most, *I don't recommend that homeowners invest home equity in a variable environment. I reemphasize: Financial planners should never advise that home equity be invested in securities or variable products.* To safely manage home equity, you should select more stable or fixed insurance contracts that contain guarantees.

When I do a comparison of internal rate of return on the actual premium paid into a life insurance contract, typically a variable universal life policy must perform at about a 3 percent better gross rate of return to match a fixed universal life's internal rate of return. For example, if I pay premiums into a fixed universal life in the amount of $500 per month for fifteen years and earn a gross interest rate of 8 percent (resulting in a net rate of return of 7.5 percent), I would have cash values of $166,590. During the same fifteen-year period with a variable universal life policy, I may have to earn a gross rate of as much as 10.5 percent to realize a net rate of return of 7.5 percent to end up with the same $166,590. This is because the administration fees are much greater on a variable contract than on a fixed contract. If you choose variable universal life, you should do so with the understanding that the gross return expected will be at least 3 percent higher than the return a fixed universal life will likely earn.

Variable universal life can be an attractive option for younger investors who have twenty or thirty years or more to experience possible growth. *I discourage the use of variable universal life for elderly clients who are generally seeking more stability,* which is inherent in fixed universal life products.

Equity-Indexed Universal Life Insurance

Equity-indexed universal life was designed to help investors who want to have a guaranteed floor on the minimum rate credited on their cash values and yet have the potential to participate indirectly in the market when it is experiencing growth. The interest crediting rate is linked to an index such as the S&P 500 Index. The S&P 500 Index is a commonly used broad indicator of performance and is considered a benchmark of U.S. stock market performance. It represents over 70 percent of the total domestic equity market value. Its broad diversification counterbalances the extreme highs and lows of any one stock. It is a price index and therefore does not include dividends.

Over the long term, the S&P 500 Index has outperformed government and corporate bonds, certificates of deposit, and the rate of inflation. Indexed universal life linked to the S&P 500 Index enables you to benefit from increases in the S&P 500 Index through an adjustable index factor. In addition, your money is protected. If the S&P 500 drops or remains flat, your policy values are protected by a guaranteed interest rate—usually between 1 and 3 percent.

The nicest feature of equity-indexed universal life is that the cash values of the insurance contract never leave the protective umbrella of the insurance company. The policy owners are allowed to participate in potential profits realized by virtue of having their interest linked to an index, but it is not deemed an actual equity investment. So, in essence, the policyholder is saying to the insurance company, "Hey, if the market is bullish, let me participate (at a specified percentage) in whatever the S&P 500 Index does. As a trade-off for not participating 100 percent in the market, when the S&P loses money, don't let me lose—give me a floor of at least 1, 2, or 3 percent interest!"

An indexed universal life policy often carries slightly higher expense charges than a fixed universal life policy but lower charges than a variable universal life policy.

Figure 11.5 illustrates an example of a comparison between fixed, variable, and indexed universal life in relation to their guaranteed interest crediting rates, what their typical crediting rates might be over a twenty-year period, and some of their highest crediting rates (based on actual history). Pay particular attention to the rate of return that must be achieved in each of the three types of contracts in order to achieve the same bottom-line results over the long term.

Fig. 11.5	EXAMPLES OF 3 TYPES OF UNIVERSAL LIFE INVESTMENT-GRADE INSURANCE CONTRACTS				

20-Year Historical Crediting Interest Rates

	Guaranteed	Lowest	Average	Highest	Interest Rate Required to Achieve Same Accumulation Values
Fixed	4%	5.75%	7.5%	13.75%	7.44%
Variable	None	<30%>	10%	35%	10.52%
Equity Indexed	3%	3%	8.2%	21%	8.20%
(Linked to S&P 500)				(60%)*	

*participation rate

INTERNAL REVENUE CODE COMPLIANCE

When an insurance contract is structured to accommodate serious capital, such as equity funds coming from a mortgage refinance, it is important to comply with the Internal Revenue Code. As a person changes from one residence to another and a new mortgage is obtained on the new home, we don't have to worry about the deductibility of interest on the new mortgage. As explained in chapter 2, qualified mortgage interest is deductible on the acquisition of a new residence for up to $1 million of indebtedness. We simply need to comply with TEFRA/DEFRA and TAMRA guidelines as we fund the insurance contract using our previous home's equity (to avoid the insurance contract being classified as a MEC). In chapter 2, I quoted from Section 163(h)(3) of the Internal Revenue Code and Temporary Regulation 1.163-8T(m)(3), which states that qualified residence interest is allowable as a deduction *without regard to* the manner in which such interest expense is allocated. This section of the code should put a taxpayer at ease for deducting interest on home equity indebtedness (up to $100,000) when borrowing on a current residence and using the loan proceeds for any purpose, including investing them in an insurance contract.

In contrast, Section 264(a)(2) of the Internal Revenue Code stipulates no deduction shall be allowed for "any amount paid or accrued on indebtedness incurred or continued to purchase or carry a single premium life insurance, endowment, or annuity contract." Section 264(b) states, "For the purposes of subsection (a)(2), a contract shall be treated as a single premium contract—(1) if substantially all the premiums on the contract are paid within a period of four years from the date on which the contract is purchased, or (2) if an amount is deposited with the insurer for payment of a substantial number of future premiums on the contract."

It is unclear how Section 264 relates to a universal life contract versus a single premium life insurance contract. However, to be on the safe side, I recommend a taxpayer who desires to deduct interest expense from a cash-out refinance on an existing home where the loan proceeds are invested in an insurance contract (although Section 163 may allow deductibility) avoid having the life insurance classified or construed as a single premium contract. By filling the bucket (funding the policy) no sooner than the maximum prescribed premium schedule to comply with TAMRA (which is generally five years with universal life and seven years with whole life), we can avoid falling under the definition of a single premium life insurance contract. Because a person's particular set of circumstances can be unique, I always recommend each person seek competent legal and accounting advice.

I believe it is best that a life insurance contract not be funded solely with the equity from a current home. Remember to use fixed or indexed insurance contracts rather than variable contracts when repositioning home equity. I usually recommend that no more than 40 percent of the total premiums paid into an insurance contract should come from home equity obtained from a refinance of a current home. The remaining 60 percent of premiums should come from other sources, such as repositioned IRA and 401(k) contributions or distributions, or perhaps from repositioned CDs, money markets, and mutual funds. This 60 percent differential could also include redirected annual planned savings meant for capital accumulation.

However, to reemphasize, if a home is sold and a new one is purchased, the equity from the former home may be used free of capital gains tax. In that case, the equity could be used solely to fund an insurance contract using a single premium immediate annuity or other side fund to comply with TAMRA. Interest on the new home mortgage would be deductible on up to $1 million of acquisition indebtedness as provided under Section 163. This strategy alone has motivated many couples (who were debating whether to sell their home and relocate) to sell their home, take the tax-free gain, and use the equity to generate tax-free retirement income while using mortgage interest deductions on their new home to offset tax liability on their IRA and 401(k) distributions. So if you are looking for a good excuse to sell your home and purchase a new one, maximizing equity management may be the best reason not to hesitate.

Compliance with Sections 163 and 264 of the Internal Revenue Code can be a somewhat complex arrangement; however, a trained professional who understands these parameters and guidelines can structure and fund a life insurance policy to comply. I cannot overemphasize the importance of seeking advice from a competent tax advisor. With proper planning and counsel, modern cash-value life insurance can be designed to accumulate and store cash safely and provide tax-favored living benefits, as well as income-tax-free death benefits, while maintaining liquidity and safety and achieving an attractive rate of return.

CONCEPTS COVERED IN CHAPTER 11

- When structuring an insurance contract for investment purposes, the death benefit can provide an incredibly high return, at death, on premium dollars—but that is *the sad way to access your money.*
- *The advantage of investment-grade insurance contracts is that when you withdraw your money, it is treated with FIFO taxation* (first in, first out), so your withdrawals are tax-free up to the basis.

- *The dumb way to access money* from an insurance contract would be to continue "withdrawing" your money after you have recovered your basis, because it would trigger unnecessary tax.

- *The smart way to access money* is for the owner to change the "withdrawal" to a "loan"—simply a change in nomenclature.

- Loan proceeds are not deemed earned, passive, or portfolio income.

- Insurance companies can loan you the equivalent of the interest you are earning each year to avoid tax on the distribution of your cash.

- Loans on insurance contracts can be open until death, at which time the loan balance is deducted from the death benefit automatically.

- A taxable event can be permanently avoided if a life insurance policy has enough cash value remaining in it at death to keep the life insurance in force by covering the mortality costs.

- Preferred loans were created specifically for retirement income.

- *Preferred loans can be totally "zero cost" or "zero spread" loans.*

- Insurance companies may credit the same interest on the cash value used as collateral for the loan as the interest charged on the loan.

- *New money can be reinvested into a life insurance contract that has an outstanding loan balance by simply "repaying the loans."*

- *Properly structured and properly used investment-grade insurance contracts can be the best retirement vehicles for providing liquidity, safety, and tax-favored rates of return.*

- Because of the tax-free accessibility of cash values that can be used for retirement income, *maximum-funded insurance contracts can far outperform alternatives like IRAs, 401(k)s, annuities, and mutual funds.*

- A taxable investment would likely need to earn as high as 12 percent average to match the net, tax-free income generated by an insurance contract crediting an average of only 7 to 8 percent.

- In a 33.3 percent tax bracket, you would need to take 50 percent more retirement income to net the same amount as tax-free vehicles.
- Generally, there are five types of cash-value life insurance on the market: whole life, variable life, and three kinds of universal life—fixed, variable, and equity-indexed.
- Variable life has a death benefit created by term insurance with an equity investment side fund.
- Universal life was created with flexibility in mind—both premium payments and insurance death benefits may be varied.
- Fixed universal life tends to be more stable, responding slowly to market swings.
- *Home equity should not be invested in variable contracts* because they are vulnerable to market downturns and loss of principal.
- Equity-indexed universal life was designed to help investors have a guaranteed floor on the minimum rate credited on their cash values and yet have the potential to participate indirectly in the market.
- Indexed universal life often carries slightly higher expense charges than a fixed universal life policy, but lower than a variable policy.
- If you change from one residence to another and obtain a new mortgage on the new home, you don't have to worry about the deductibility of interest on a new mortgage up to $1 million.
- A taxpayer who desires to deduct interest from a cash-out refinance on an existing home (where the loan proceeds are invested in an insurance contract) should avoid having the life insurance classified a "single premium insurance contract" by complying with TAMRA.
- *Use fixed or indexed life insurance contracts when repositioning home equity* rather than variable life insurance contracts.
- Because a person's particular set of circumstances can be

unique, *each person should seek competent legal and accounting advice.*

- Modern cash-value life insurance can be designed to accumulate and store cash safely and provide tax-favored living benefits, as well as income-tax-free death benefits, while maintaining liquidity and safety and achieving an attractive rate of return.

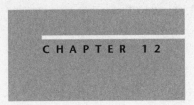

CHAPTER 12

Give New Life to Your Assets— Develop the Proper P.L.A.N.

How to make your "true wealth" live forever

I ONCE SPENT A CONSIDERABLE AMOUNT OF TIME training a major credit union's investment counseling division on some of the strategies contained in this book. They asked me to teach a seminar for about three hundred of their customers. Following the seminar, 83 percent of the attendees wanted to come into the credit union for consultation and analysis regarding their retirement planning. I was dismayed when I found out later that nearly all of the customers were directed by the credit union to use certificates of deposit, IRAs, and annuities in the traditional way. When I asked the president of the Credit Union Service Organization why they enticed their customers to learn more about unconventional wealth-enhancement strategies and then steered them back to traditional savings plans, he remarked, "Well, what the public doesn't know won't hurt them—it's too much trouble to educate them!"

I contend that what Americans don't know *will* hurt them. As I have cautioned, the worst form of ignorance is when we reject something we know little or nothing about. Many people, including professional CPAs, attorneys, and financial advisors, are often guilty of prejudging little-known concepts like those contained in this book. I have discovered that when they take time to learn about the principles herein, they usually do a 180-degree turnaround and become proponents of concepts they now understand better.

The story is told of a woman who had a lifetime dream to go on a luxurious Caribbean cruise. She meticulously scrimped and saved for a long while until the time arrived for her voyage. She felt she had barely enough money for the cruise fare and maybe a little left over. She packed one of her suitcases with cheese and crackers to eat each day so she could afford to splurge the last night of the cruise. Every day when all of her fellow passengers enjoyed wonderful meals in the dining room, she passed time in her cabin eating the cheese and crackers. The cruise was spectacular. Finally, the last evening arrived and she dressed up to attend dinner with the other guests. She received a special invitation to sit at the captain's table. As she was relishing the exquisite cuisine, the captain asked, "Where have you been during our previous dining experiences? I haven't seen you in the dining room the entire week." She confessed that she couldn't afford to attend all the meal functions, so she stayed in her cabin. In dismay, the captain said, "Oh, my dear, fine lady, I'm so sorry you were not aware, but the fare you paid for the cruise included all of the meals. You could have been dining with us every evening!"

All of us who want to prepare for our future ship to come in will pay the fare we select based on the experience we want. The journey can include many amenities that we are already paying for. They are included in the price if we become aware of them. I have assisted hundreds of clients during the past thirty years to reposition their assets and implement the strategies contained in this book, without increasing their monthly outlay one dime. Their financial net worth has been enhanced as a result.

FINANCIAL STEWARDSHIP

On our path to financial independence, it may behoove us to consider the joy of the stewardship that accompanies prosperity. The parable of the talents found in the Bible's Gospel of Matthew, chapter 25, verses 14 to 30, offers a valuable perspective on individual stewardship.

The parable is about a man who entrusted his servants with some of his goods. To one he gave five talents, to another two, and to another one, based on their ability to manage those assets. The one who received five traded and doubled them to ten. Likewise, the one who received two gained another two. But the servant who received one was afraid, and he hid his talent. When the lord of the servants returned to receive an accounting of their stewardship, he said to each of the servants who had doubled their talents, "Well done, thou good and faithful servant: thou hast been faithful over a few things, I will make thee ruler over many things: enter thou into the joy of thy lord." But some of the harshest words spoken in the Bible are used against the servant who hid his talent and did not multiply it: "Thou wicked and slothful servant . . . Thou oughtest . . . to have put my money to the exchangers, and then at my coming I should have received mine own with usury."

In other words, the slothful servant should have at least put the money entrusted to him to the exchangers (banks, credit unions, insurance companies, money management firms, or even stockbrokerage firms) so that when the lord came back, he would have received what he could (even if it only kept up with inflation) with usury (the earning of interest on money in a loaned position).

The lord of the servant continued by saying, "Take therefore the talent from him, and give it unto him which hath ten talents. For unto every one that hath shall be given, and he shall have abundance: but from him that hath not shall be taken away even that which he hath. And cast ye the unprofitable servant into outer darkness. . . ."

As we all know, in life we either progress or retrogress; we increase our talents and abilities or else those we have will wither and die. There truly is enough to spare for every human being to have an abundant life. Abundance breeds more abundance. It is our opportunity to become profitable and teach these principles to others.

THE POWER OF SHARING

I had a life-changing experience a few years ago when I conducted an activity to teach this principle to two hundred teenagers in our church. It was October and the traditional activity had been to invite an inspirational speaker, and following his or her message, the teens would mingle for a while and consume punch and cookies. The budget to spend for the activity was $400. Inspired by a friend, I decided to call this special activity "Project Share."

I invited a guest to our church who had a child that was being treated at Primary Children's Medical Center in Salt Lake City for a respiratory disease. She brought the child, who could breathe only through a tracheotomy tube, and she told her story. None of us will forget her life-affirming message. After she spoke, we discussed the parable of the talents and handed each of the teens $2 in an envelope—money that had been previously allocated for refreshments. The challenge was to see what could be done in six weeks from the $400 that was distributed ($2 to each teenager). Project Share had to be accomplished amid their school activities and job responsibilities. The rule was they could not merely ask for donations; they had to perform acts of service, and the $2 was to be used as seed money.

Well, one young man invested his $2 in flyers to distribute to our neighbors, offering to seal their cement driveways to retard chipping and corrosion. He sealed six driveways within thirty days at $60 each and netted a $240 profit.

Another young man also invested in flyers to advertise his services to the neighbors. He offered to wire a sparkless wrench to their gas meters so they could shut them off safely in the event of an earthquake. He also offered to strap their water heaters to the wall or floor in order to make them earthquake-safe. Several neighbors took him up on the offers, and he netted $180 for his $2 investment.

Our two oldest daughters, aged 15 and 16, formed a partnership, and with their pooled resources of $4, they purchased gasoline and chain oil, borrowed a chain saw, and obtained permission to cut firewood from dead trees around our cabin. My wife and I helped with safety supervision as they worked several hours to fill the orders of firewood from neighbors. They not only made enough money to purchase a chain saw but also netted $160 each from the $4 initial capital—a fortyfold increase! They were proud of what they accomplished and expressed overwhelming gratitude for the experience.

Some young men and young women did such things as making and selling dozens of pizzas. Others did lawn mowing and aerating. One young lady sold suckers where she worked at a fast-food restaurant.

All of the teenagers were excited to report their success at our gathering six weeks later. Many of them told their stories and related the lessons they learned in the process. Remarkably, the average return on $2 was a tenfold increase! Over $4,000 was generated from $400 of seed money in six weeks.

The youth next attended the Primary Children's Medical Center's holiday fund-raising event, where they made the $4,000 contribution by purchasing decorated Christmas trees donated to the event by others. We then delivered the trees to eight rest homes and sang Christmas carols and visited with the residents for a couple of hours. Several friends and priceless memories were made that day.

To this day, I cross paths with some of the youth who still express joy in that experience. They report successes in their life, such as having a thriving landscape business or other enterprise, inspired from the lesson they learned about multiplying their talents and giving back to others.

THE POWER OF SHARING AT HOME

Because my family has gained so much from applying the principles of empowered wealth, I am a proponent of these strategies. Allow me to share another personal story.

To help our six children, their spouses, and our grandchildren gain greater clarity, balance, focus, and confidence in every aspect of their life, my wife and I have begun a tradition of holding two family retreats a year with a specific purpose. As explained in chapter 1, the family balance sheet is comprised of human, intellectual, financial, and civic assets. In order to help our children learn how to capitalize every category of assets on the family balance sheet, we have developed a system that helps accomplish the following:

- Enhance each individual's health, happiness, and well-being
- Encourage family leadership
- Capture family virtues, memories, and wisdom
- Protect, optimize, and empower our family's intellectual and financial assets

We've found the best way to accomplish this is to create an environment where these assets can be shared with one another. In 2003, we held a family-empowered retreat in Maui, Hawaii. Our children knew a year in advance when the retreat was going to be held and what the agenda was. The accommodations were handled by the "family bank," but they were responsible to schedule time off from school and work and get themselves there.

Our family loves to scuba dive, boat, golf, swim, bike, and hike. But if you ask any of our children what they remember most about Hawaii, 2003, it won't be the scuba diving or golfing we did. It was the time we spent gathered under a pavilion for several hours talking about what's really important in life. They were all assigned to give an oral report, as well as submit a written report (a deposit into the family archive), about how they had enhanced each category of assets (human, intellectual, financial, and civic) in their personal life (figure 12.1) during the previous year. They were also asked to make a "withdrawal" from each category. For example, our newlywed children asked for specific advice on how they could buy their first home with no money down while still in college on a low income. That represented a withdrawal from the intellectual portion of our family bank.

Each of our children responded to the question, "If we were sitting here three years from now, looking back over that three-year period,

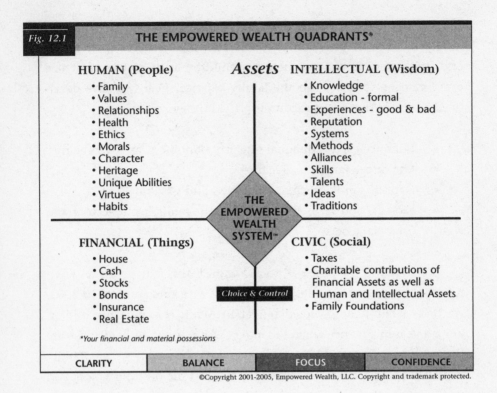

Fig. 12.1 — THE EMPOWERED WEALTH QUADRANTS®

HUMAN (People)
- Family
- Values
- Relationships
- Health
- Ethics
- Morals
- Character
- Heritage
- Unique Abilities
- Virtues
- Habits

Assets **INTELLECTUAL (Wisdom)**
- Knowledge
- Education - formal
- Experiences - good & bad
- Reputation
- Systems
- Methods
- Alliances
- Skills
- Talents
- Ideas
- Traditions

THE EMPOWERED WEALTH SYSTEM™

FINANCIAL (Things)
- House
- Cash
- Stocks
- Bonds
- Insurance
- Real Estate

Choice & Control

CIVIC (Social)
- Taxes
- Charitable contributions of Financial Assets as well as Human and Intellectual Assets
- Family Foundations

Your financial and material possessions

CLARITY   BALANCE   FOCUS   CONFIDENCE

©Copyright 2001-2005, Empowered Wealth, LLC. Copyright and trademark protected.

what has to have happened for you to be happy about the progress you made?" Dan Sullivan, the strategic coach, authored this and calls it the relationship-factor question. They all responded in past tense, as if they had already achieved their goals. Inspired with the idea from Lee Brower, president of Empowered Wealth, we also had them write down and share three "I remember when" stories that happened during their life. We laughed and cried for hours about experiences that heretofore had been told and retold, but no one had ever written them down. We now have them recorded in our family history.

The members of our family were extended the invitation to make a financial withdrawal as a stewardship from the family bank as seed money for any project of their choice to help them multiply their talents. They also identified what charity they would give to from the gain. (Giving at least 10 percent to your favorite charities, causes, or church is among the most empowering principles for the perpetuation of true wealth.)

That night the banana splits melted and wasted away, but no one was interested in eating; they were preoccupied with loving and sharing. Empowered-wealth living is simply a process of teaching children how to love, learn, give, and earn. "Family retreats with a purpose" are a powerful method to teach and enhance true principles.

You may feel overwhelmed after learning some of the concepts and strategies contained in this book. That's okay. I'm more concerned that you understand *why* you should cultivate a Perpetual Life of Asset Nurturance™ (P.L.A.N.) than learning all the details of *how* to accomplish your P.L.A.N. Therefore, I'm going to conduct a retreat by "leading you back" through practical applications of the concepts contained in this book. A retreat is a place for meditation, study, and instruction. So please give place to my words as I identify some of the myths I have dispelled and summarize the financial strategies you have learned. As an aid, I will provide examples of how these strategies have worked for myself and my clients.

SUCCESSFULLY MANAGING EQUITY

Following are ten equity management strategies that I have introduced in this book. I have listed them by identifying the common myth and explaining the reality associated with each.

1. Avoid the $25,000 mistake that ensnares millions of Americans.

    Myth: The best way to pay off a home early is to pay extra principal on your mortgages.

    Reality: No method of applying extra principal payments to your mortgages is the wisest or most cost-effective way of paying off your house.

    Strategy: Establish a liquid side fund to accumulate the funds required to pay off your mortgage, maintain flexibility, achieve substantial tax savings, and accumulate excess cash.

2. Avoid expensive risks. Position yourself to act instead of reacting to market conditions you have no control over.

    Myth: Home equity is liquid.

    Reality: When you need it most, you may not have it. Home equity is usually non-liquid.

    Strategy: Separate as much equity from your property as is feasible, positioning it in financial instruments that will maintain liquidity in the event of emergencies and conservative investment opportunities.

3. Separate home and equity to increase safety. Real properties with high equity and low mortgages get foreclosed on the soonest.

    Myth: Home equity is a safe investment.

    Reality: A home mortgaged to the hilt or totally free and clear provides the greatest safety for the homeowner.

    Strategy: Separate as much equity from your home as feasible to achieve greater safety of principal and reduce the risk of foreclosure.

4. The return on equity is always zero—no matter where your property is located.

    Myth: Home equity has a rate of return.

    Reality: Equity grows as a function of real estate appreciation and a mortgage reduction; however, equity has no rate of return.

    Strategy: Separate as much equity from your home as feasible in order to allow idle dollars to earn a rate of return.

5. Make Uncle Sam your best partner. Mortgage interest is your friend, not your foe.

    Myth: Mortgage interest is an expense that should be eliminated as soon as possible.

    Reality: Eliminating mortgage interest expense through traditional methods eliminates one of your best partners in accumulating wealth and financial security.

Strategy: Use the difference between preferred and nonpreferred interest expense to make interest work for you instead of against you.

6. Use debt for positive leverage.

   Myth: Any and all debt is undesirable.

   Reality: Some debt, when managed wisely, can be desirable.

   Strategy: Use debt wisely as a positive lever for equity management purposes, conserving and compounding equity rather than consuming it.

7. Understand the cost of *not* borrowing—compare deductible versus non-deductible costs.

   Myth: Lower mortgages, resulting in lower payments, mean lower costs.

   Reality: If you take opportunity costs into consideration, low mortgage-to-home-value ratios create tremendous hidden costs that increase the time needed to pay off a mortgage.

   Strategy: Choose to incur deductible employment costs rather than non-deductible opportunity costs, since you have no choice but to incur one or the other.

8. Turbo charge your wealth growth rate by creating homemade wealth.

   Myth: Borrowing funds at a particular interest rate, then investing them at the same or lower interest rate, holds no potential growth returns.

   Reality: You can earn a tremendous profit—regardless of the relative interest rates—by positioning your money in a tax-favored, interest-compounding investment that earns a return greater than the real net cost of obtaining that money.

   Strategy: Learn to apply the fundamental principle that highly profitable financial institutions use to accumulate and create wealth—arbitrage. Employ equity to earn a rate of return higher than the net cost of separating that equity. By doing so, you will create tremendous wealth and substantially enhance your net worth.

9. Strategically refinance your home as often as feasible to increase your net worth and put those idle dollars to work.

   Myth: Equity in your home enhances your net worth.

   Reality: Equity in your home does not enhance your net worth at all. Separated from your home, however, it has the ability to dramatically enhance your net worth over time.

   Strategy: Set the stage to substantially increase your net worth. Refinance your home as often as feasible to separate equity and accelerate the process of accumulating the resources to cover all your debts.

10. Keep your mortgage balance high to sell your home more quickly and for a higher price.

    Myth: The amount of equity you have in your home has no bearing on how marketable it is.

    Reality: Your home may likely sell much more quickly and for a higher price if it has a high mortgage balance (low equity)—rather than a low mortgage or no mortgage balance (high equity)—especially in soft real estate markets.

    Strategy: Always maintain as high a mortgage—with flexibility—on your home as feasible to keep it marketable at the highest possible price should you want to sell the property.

To gain a deeper understanding of these ten concepts, I recommend that you study my more comprehensive original work, *Missed Fortune*. Now let's look a little further at other major concepts covered in this book.

HOME EQUITY RETIREMENT PLANNING

Please don't be intimidated by any of the examples used thus far. You can utilize tax-favored retirement planning as a superior alternative to IRAs and 401(k)s by simply establishing an investment-grade insurance contract for as little as $50 or $100 per month. A properly trained insurance professional can assist you in doing this. Remember, it's not what you begin with that counts, but what you end up with! Be sure to structure it correctly to accommodate the maximum premiums you can afford with the corresponding minimum death benefit. Remember that maximum-funded life insurance contracts are the only investment vehicles that accumulate money tax-free, allow access to the money tax-free, and blossom tax-free upon transfer to heirs. The common myth is that life insurance is a poor investment. The reality is that life insurance is an excellent place to accumulate and store cash. You should strongly consider managing some or all of your equity and repositioning some of your IRA and 401(k) contributions or distributions through properly structured investment-grade life insurance contracts to maximize liquidity, safety, rate of return, and tax benefits.

MY HOUSE PAYMENT IS MY RETIREMENT CONTRIBUTION

Often, people look at my personal house payment and exclaim, "How can you afford that?" They don't realize I do not view my house payment as a regular house payment—it is my retirement and investment-funding mechanism, my method of forced savings. When I put aside the monthly house payment, this is money I would have otherwise been paying into an IRA, 401(k), or other retirement fund. Instead of getting tax deductions using these retirement vehicles, I am able to get a similar tax deduction on the front end by using the mortgage. I have pre-funded my retirement account with several hundred thousand dollars of my home equity every time I refinance or sell my home. My fund is extremely liquid in the event I need to access it for emergencies. Additionally, my retirement fund has the potential to grow to a much larger sum of money (which will generate a greater net spendable income) than if I were plodding along making regular contributions toward a traditional retirement nest egg.

You can do the same by simply reallocating your IRA or unmatched portion of your 401(k) contributions to an insurance contract, or by using the funds to cover the net higher house payment incurred by transferring home equity (when refinancing or selling a home). By enjoying the harvest years under tax-favored circumstances, your retirement income can be 50 percent greater than traditional retirement plans, and can provide that income indefinitely until you pass away, when it can transfer tax-free to your heirs. Position yourself to retire with the highest possible net spendable income stream. Minimize, even eliminate, the payment of unnecessary taxes on assets generating your retirement income.

STRATEGIC ROLL-OUTS

You should periodically evaluate repositioning some or all of your qualified plan contributions or distributions into a non-qualified private retirement fund. This will reduce tax liability and help you achieve the highest net spendable income in your retirement years. If you feel trapped in your IRA or 401(k), you can free yourself and substantially reduce, if not eliminate, otherwise payable taxes. I'll use two examples.

A 62-year-old couple came to me for a consultation after attending a seminar. They were intrigued with equity management concepts but hesitated at the idea of mortgaging their free and clear properties. They both had defined benefit pensions we maximized through bringing life insurance along for the ride, as we strategically repositioned their supplemental IRAs and 401(k)s. They chose no-survivor benefit options, thus creating an additional $500 per month of income they didn't think they would get. They were likely going to pay a minimum of $160,000 in tax on their IRAs and 401(k)s if they took the minimum distributions. But by accelerating the process and doing a strategic roll-out over a five-year period, we reduced their tax liability to $60,000.

Out of curiosity, this ultraconservative couple asked me to prepare a simple illustration of what benefit they might receive if they separated the equity in their home by taking out a mortgage. We found that by doing so they would reduce the tax liability to $20,000. They asked what would happen if they also refinanced their cabin. We reduced the tax liability even further, to just $9,000. They decided to mortgage both properties.

I have another set of clients who used this strategy successfully because they stayed committed to their plan. For the first five years of their strategic conversion from their qualified accounts to a non-qualified status, they endured the tax pain on the front end. Without the strategic roll-out, at a minimum, they were headed toward paying more than $1.2 million in tax by stringing out the distributions from age 70½ for the rest of their life. By completing a roll-out in five years, they paid about $500,000, some of which was at a high 38.2 percent rate. However, now they have enjoyed several years of considerable tax-free earnings and income with no tax liability on their tax return. When they pass away, they will leave behind substantially more (replenishing the $500,000 they paid in tax), free of income tax, than they would have if the money had remained in their qualified accounts.

Remember the example of Ben and Shirley Liberated in chapter 5? If you are in similar circumstances, you, too, can sell your home and realize up to $500,000 of capital gain tax-free. Instead of paying cash for two condos (summer and winter dwellings), Ben and Shirley paid only 20 percent ($100,000 down) and kept the remaining $400,000 of cash to invest (in an insurance contract). Their net after-tax cost of the mortgages at 6 percent interest was only 4 percent, or $16,000 per year. However, they have the potential to earn $24,000 to $32,000 per year at 6 to 8 percent in a tax-free environment, resulting in an $8,000 to $16,000 net annual profit. Not only that, but during the roll-out process for IRAs and 401(k)s, the tax deductions can help to offset some or all of the tax. Then when death finally occurs, the money remaining in the insurance contracts will blossom and transfer tax-free to the beneficiaries.

TAKING ADVANTAGE OF YOUR EQUITY IN RETIREMENT

Today there are more than 20 million Americans over the age of 62 who own their homes totally free and clear. This represents more than $2 trillion in home equity. However, if you were to interview most of those people, I doubt the majority would feel they were financially secure. In fact, at least 5 million of those Americans, or about one-fourth of them, are under the national poverty level for income. They are what I call "house rich, cash poor." You may know someone in this category, or you might be in this category yourself. You are living in an asset that is free and clear but find yourself with too much month at the end of the money!

Unfortunately, many elderly homeowners could not afford to make a mortgage payment if they wanted to. Their Social Security or other retirement income is hardly sufficient to meet their minimum living expenses. Retired seniors with few assets face serious issues, especially when they realize they may have to downgrade their lifestyle just to fill prescriptions.

A 1998 *New York Times* survey indicated that only 11 percent of the population over age 64 lived in retirement communities, while 84 percent of all older Americans would prefer to stay in their own home. Seniors do not want to be a burden on their children.

My advice to people preparing for retirement is that they should always retain the key to unlocking the value of one of their most important assets—home equity. At the least, these people ought to obtain an equity line of credit that will be good for possibly five, ten, or fifteen years. By doing so, they will have the option of simply writing a check in the event of an emergency and using that dormant equity in the home.

During the last decade, there have been more opportunities for retirees to convert the equity from their home into income during this critical time in their life. These strategies allow people to annuitize the equity in their home. The most common way is through a reverse mortgage.

UNDERSTANDING REVERSE MORTGAGES

A reverse mortgage is a safe and easy way for seniors to turn their home's equity into an additional source of income to meet any financial need. A reverse mortgage is a loan available to senior homeowners who are at least 62 years of age. It turns home equity into cash with no out-of-pocket closing costs. So instead of the homeowner making a mortgage payment to the mortgage company, it works in reverse. The mortgage company makes a payment to the senior homeowner based on the retired couple's combined average age or on a single homeowner's age. Loans are offered through federal programs and private lenders and can be arranged as a lump sum, a monthly payment, or a line of credit. The money a couple receives through a reverse mortgage is tax-free, and they never have to make a payment on the loan. In fact, the loan comes due only when the borrower decides to move from the home permanently, decides to sell the home, or dies. *Also, the amount of the loan with accruing interest can never exceed the value of the house.* The reverse mortgage is simply a lien, so the homeowner retains full ownership of the home and can stay in the home for as long as he or she wishes.

If a reverse mortgage is taken out, I feel the best way to pass down your home free and clear to your heirs is to use a portion of the reverse mortgage proceeds to purchase an inexpensive second-to-die life insurance policy. A second-to-die policy is less expensive than a normal life insurance policy because it covers two lives and pays only one death benefit after both individuals have passed away. For example, if an 80-year-old couple had a home worth $200,000, had taken out a reverse mortgage generating a monthly income of $790, and had both passed away after ten years, their mortgage may have accrued to $145,491 (assuming an 8 percent interest rate). If their home appreciated during that time period at 5 percent, it would then be worth $329,400. They could have used a portion of the tax-free cash flow each month to purchase a second-to-die life insurance policy with a $150,000 death benefit for a monthly premium cost of about $232. Thus, they would have realized a net monthly tax-free income of $558.

The heirs would then have the option of taking $150,000 of tax-free insurance proceeds and paying off the mortgage balance.

THE ULTIMATE ARBITRAGE

Elderly retirees (between the ages of 75 and 90) often approach me seeking to reposition assets from unstable, volatile investments into stable, guaranteed investments. Many times I can get them guaranteed returns of 6 to 9 percent or better. I'll illustrate how.

Let's assume a female aged 80 with a life expectancy of ten years has $1 million. Her goal is to achieve a stable, guaranteed, after-tax return of at least 6 percent annually for retirement income. If she were to secure a single premium immediate life-only annuity with a payout rate of 14 percent, she would receive a guaranteed lifetime income of $140,000 annually. Is the 14 percent payout primarily a function of the market? Not really. You see, if I borrowed $1 million from a bank and paid it back over ten years at zero percent interest, my annual payment would be $100,000 per year, or a 10 percent annual payback. Insurance companies historically have credited about 6 to 7 percent on fixed annuities. So if the insurance company "borrows" $1 million from an annuitant and the company is to pay it all back over a ten-year period, let's say at 6.65 percent, it would require an annual principal and interest payment of $140,000. So even though the payout amount of $140,000 represents 14 percent of $1 million, the insurance company is really crediting only 6.65 percent interest. However, with a guaranteed life-only annuity, if the 80-year-old woman (in this example) dies before the tenth year, the annuity payments stop and the balance of the $1 million is kept by the insurance company. But if she lives longer than ten years, the insurance company is contractually obligated to keep paying her $140,000 a year for as long as she lives.

The IRS allows her 78 percent exclusion for the first ten years, because they regard 78 percent of the $140,000 annual income to be a return of her $1-million basis. So she would need to pay taxes on only 22 percent of the annual income (to her life expectancy), which would be $30,800. Assuming a 39 percent tax bracket, her annual tax liability would be $12,000. Her after-tax income the first ten years would be $128,000. The net after-tax rate of return on a life-only annuity can be very attractive.

The unattractive feature of a life-only annuity is the relinquishment of the $1 million if she happens to die sooner than later. She would likely want to replace the $1 million when she passes away to preserve that asset and leave it behind to her heirs or favorite charity. Often the annual premium for a life insurance policy on someone that age is about 5 percent of the death benefit. In an actual case, we insured an 80-year-old female for $1 million with an annual premium of $38,000. So after paying the asset-replacement insurance premium from her $128,000 after-tax annuity income, she would still enjoy a net annual income of $90,000. That is a 9 percent net return (figure 12.2).

Remember, her goal was to achieve a guaranteed annual income of $60,000 on her million. Instead, we were able to get her $90,000, which allowed her to contribute the $30,000 excess annual cash flow to her favorite charity—money she neither was receiving before nor needed.

I have used this strategy with clients who had health histories enabling them to receive higher age-rated payouts on the annuity and yet receive favorable ratings from life insurance issuers. For example, a 77-year-old male with a history of cancer, artery blockage, and diabetes (which were all successfully treated) was able to receive a 17.6 percent payout on his annuity (due to an age rating of 85). Per $1 million deposited into the annuity, he receives a guaranteed annual income of $176,000 for the remainder of his life. After the tax exclusion, his net after-tax annual income is $147,000. We were able to secure insurance on his life for an annual premium of $40,000 per $1 million of death benefit. So his net income is $107,000, or a 10.7 percent return!

You may be sitting there thinking, "Well, I don't have a million to do this." The math is the same, whether you have $100,000 or $1 million. So where can you find the money? The man in this example used

---

Fig. 12.2 RETIREMENT INCOME / CHARITABLE STRATEGY

A Single Premium Immediate Annuity (SPIA)
Combined with a Life Insurance Policy

Female, Age 80 (Normal Life Expectancy is approximately 10 years)

$1 million deposited into a SPIA = Guaranteed payout rate of 14% for life

(A loan amount of $1 million at 6.65 percent interest requires an annual
payment of $140,000 to pay it back over a ten year period.)

This results in a guaranteed lifetime income of:	$140,000	annually
Taxable portion after exclusion = $30,000x40% =	$<12,000>	tax liability
Net after-tax annual income	$128,000	
Asset Replacement Life Insurance ($1 million):	$<38,000>	annual premium
Net consumable annual income:	**$90,000 = 9.0% net return**	

Creating a win/win using a lender:

Is there a way to generate more cash flow without using your own money?

Annual guaranteed income from $1 million annuity:	$140,000
Less: Taxes (if owned by an individual)	$<12,000>
Less: Annual premium for $1 million life insurance	$<38,000>
Results in net annual income by using your own money:	**$90,000 (9.0%)**

A loan can often be obtained from a financial
institution with favorable terms such as:
- $1 million at 5% annual interest
- The loan is open until death
- Repaid by life insurance proceeds
- Serviced from annual SPIA payout   [$50,000] interest

Net annual income to charitable foundation: $40,000 gift

Without Requiring Any Cash Outlay by the Donor

---

his own money first. Then when he saw what could be accomplished,
he decided to use the lazy, idle dollars trapped in his home. He sold his
home (which was free and clear) for $1.25 million and bought a new
one at the same price, using only $250,000 of his former home's eq-

uity. He established $1 million of acquisition indebtedness on his new home with a new mortgage. The interest on the new mortgage was fully deductible. Therefore, at 6 percent interest, the true net after-tax cost of the mortgage was only about 4 percent, or $40,000 per year. By depositing the $1 million of his former home's equity into the annuity described above, he generated an additional $107,000 of net annual income. He could easily make his after-tax mortgage payment of $40,000 from the $107,000, resulting in a net annual profit of $67,000—all from the dormant equity that resided in his former home. (Not only that, but his wife absolutely loved the new home.) In the event he didn't need the cash flow, he could allocate some of the $67,000 for the purchase of a larger death benefit. In this case, more than $2.5 million of life insurance could be purchased by using the net annual cash flow. Then when he dies, the $1-million mortgage could be paid off, and there would be an additional $1.5 million of tax-free insurance proceeds for his heirs or favorite charity.

GIVE MORE WITHOUT GIVING UP ANYTHING!

The ultimate arbitrage strategy has been used to successfully raise millions of dollars for charitable foundations without the donors having to use any of their own cash. I work with colleges and universities throughout the country helping their affluent alumni give more without giving up anything.

In my work with charities, I have discovered that about 92 percent of interested donors express a desire to make a major gift to the charity before they pass away. The reality is, only about 6 percent get it done. Why? There are four primary reasons:

1. They don't know how.
2. They fear their children will feel disinherited.
3. They are hesitant to give up assets they may need for long-term health care.

4. They don't want to feel the charity is anxious for them to die for the gift.

Through the utilization of life-only annuities and/or life insurance coupled with carefully borrowed money (at attractive rates where the loan interest is paid by the annuity payout and will ultimately be paid back from life insurance proceeds), we can narrow the gap of those who want to give more but heretofore haven't.

The principle of arbitrage can be used in these situations, provided that the spread is sufficient to cover the annual loan payment. Care must be taken to ensure that the loan interest will be covered by the spread between the net after-tax annuity payout and the asset-replacement life insurance. Generally, this works only with annuitants in the age bracket of 75 to 90 who are also insurable. Persons younger than 75 do not qualify for the payout ratios needed unless they are extremely unhealthy, in which case they usually can't qualify for insurance. Many life insurance companies will insure individuals up to age 90 who qualify medically. For an investor who wants to achieve an attractive return using this strategy, he could possibly arrange to be the premium payor, recipient of the annuity payout, and beneficiary of the life insurance on an elderly surrogate insured (such as a family member, provided there is an insurable interest) who qualifies with a sufficient arbitrage spread.

When the right situation can be found, three possible charitable income-enhancement strategies can be implemented:

1. Increase the stability, safety, and rate of return of the donors' own portfolio, providing the opportunity to contribute any excess achieved (beyond their need) to a charity
2. Safely use arbitrage (which can be reinsured) to generate a charitable fixed-income stream or provide a large death benefit with no cash outlay required by the donors
3. The charitable foundation can possibly reposition some of its own trust funds using donors as the annuitants/insureds, with

the foundation as the owner/beneficiary of the annuity and life insurance to obtain a handsome, guaranteed return.

Again, for a more comprehensive explanation of reverse mortgages or the Ultimate Arbitrage Plan®, please refer to chapters 14 and 22 of *Missed Fortune.**

ADVANTAGES OF EQUITY MANAGEMENT

Let's now summarize the advantages that can be realized from successfully managing your home equity. With proper equity management a homeowner can effectively:

- Increase liquidity
- Increase safety
- Earn a rate of return by employing dormant equity
- Realize tax savings through higher tax deductions
- Eliminate non-preferred debt
- Create opportunities for other investments
- Create greater property portability (sales options)
- Create an emergency fund
- Establish a private retirement planning strategy perhaps superior to qualified plans

Let's put equity management to one more test. Let's rate it against the six components of sound financial planning (figure 12.3):

1. Cash flow management
2. Credit management
3. Asset management

---

*For more information on the Ultimate Arbitrage Plan®, you may contact Douglas Andrew at Wealth Enhancement Strategies and Creative Opportunities (WESCO) via e-mail (info@pfs-inc.org) or call toll-free at 1-888-987-5665.
Or visit www.missedfortune.com.

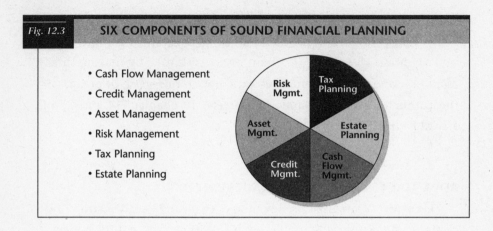

Fig. 12.3   SIX COMPONENTS OF SOUND FINANCIAL PLANNING

- Cash Flow Management
- Credit Management
- Asset Management
- Risk Management
- Tax Planning
- Estate Planning

4. Risk management
5. Tax planning
6. Estate planning

Cash Flow Management

Successfully managing equity allows a homeowner to employ a large sum of cash on an installment basis in a manner that can fit into his or her budget. The additional monthly interest expense, if any, can be offset by repositioning cash flow. Most people take their house payments seriously. By having the house payment become your investment or your retirement fund contribution, you are in effect disciplining yourself for good installment investing. Otherwise, if you had to make the choice to invest in other vehicles each month, you may not be as faithful in setting aside money for future goals. It provides a method of systematic savings that can enhance long-term results without increasing outgo.

Credit Management

Successfully managing equity allows the opportunity for good credit management. By having cash in a position of liquidity, you do not have to worry about getting behind on your mortgage—you can dip into your liquid cushion if the need arises. I would rather have a slightly higher house payment with a liquid side fund than a slightly lower house payment with no liquidity—especially if I get into a temporary bind and need to maintain my credit rating by making timely payments. So you can protect your credit rating and use the equity earning a rate of return as a source of payment if the need arises.

Asset Management

Controlling your home equity is good asset management. In this book, I have outlined the primary reasons for this: increased liquidity, safety, and rate of return. A secondary reason is you gain total control of your cash. You can establish an emergency fund and also use the strategy as a hedge against inflation. It also allows for the establishment of a pre-funded retirement strategy.

Risk Management

Managing your home equity properly is also good risk management. You are maintaining the greatest position of safety for your equity. The initial risk accepted by the mortgage company can remain the same ratio rather than gradually having it transfer to you. You can also transfer the risk to an insurance company (a specialist in managing risks) if you employ your equity in an insurance contract. The insurance contract can enhance your income and your equity asset as a tax-favored living benefit. It can also replace the asset at death while allowing liquid access to funds, and it can be structured to supplement your income should you become disabled.

Tax Planning

Successfully managing equity is great for tax planning by potentially providing an interest deduction. Remember to always consult your tax advisor, because tax planning relates to your personal situation. In doing so, a plan can usually be created that allows tax deductibility in compliance with the Internal Revenue Code, as explained herein. Tax-deferred earnings and tax-free access are other features you can implement through the use of properly structured life insurance contracts as your side fund. You also have tax-advantaged proceeds should you die, because the death benefit will pass to beneficiaries free of income tax. Through the use of mortgage interest offsets, unnecessary tax can be avoided on a strategic roll-out of qualified funds.

Estate Planning

Successfully managing your equity is an excellent estate planning tool because it multiplies the estate while avoiding probate. Very seldom do my clients come to me wanting or even needing life insurance. But when they can receive the insurance benefits with otherwise payable income taxes, they are thrilled. Never underestimate the merits of having adequate life insurance protection.

THE PROTECTION OF ADEQUATE LIFE INSURANCE

I have a client and dear friend who lost her husband due to an unfortunate accident. At the time of his passing, they were enjoying their family of six children, all under the age of nineteen. Their children continue to be a strength to their mother as she likewise helps provide for their needs. At the time of his death, her husband had a 401(k) through his employment with a $63,000 balance. In addition, he carried a $1-million life insurance contract that had $40,000 of cash values. Both plans were designed to accumulate capital for living retirement income benefits. The 401(k) left behind a net value of $40,950 after the income tax liability. On the other hand, the $40,000 of cash values in the insurance contract blossomed into $1 million that transferred to the beneficiary free of income tax and estate tax. If you were to ask her which retirement planning vehicle she appreciated the most—her husband's 401(k) or the life insurance contract—what do you think her answer would be?

I have been richly blessed in my life with a wonderful family heritage. I have four sisters and one brother, and we are all very close. I remember the day I sat in my brother's office when I was completing a life insurance application for him. He wanted to establish a life insurance contract for retirement purposes. I advised him to make the policy large enough not only to accommodate the amount of money he may eventually want to set aside for retirement objectives but also to protect his family in the event of an untimely death. He did so. Little did I know that what was designed to be a living retirement benefit would in a few years turn into a tax-free death benefit. He was killed in an automobile accident. To lose an only brother was emotionally devastating. He was a wonderful brother, husband, father, and grandfather. Some solace came in knowing that my dear sister-in-law could continue to accomplish their family's dreams. What tremendous peace of mind for her during that crucial moment in her life because one of the most important facets of my brother's financial life was in order.

"CONSERVE, DON'T CONSUME"

If you were to take a road trip from New York City to Los Angeles, you would increase your chances of a safe and timely arrival with the use of road signs and maps. Likewise, your journey to arrive at financial independence and a secure retirement should involve the use of a detailed road map so you do not get lost. If you are excited about employing your home equity for all of the advantages I have outlined, let me issue a warning. It is important you proceed with a detailed and organized plan to arrive at your desired destination. Occasionally, I have learned of people who attended one of our seminars, and rather than establishing a conservative, detailed plan to accumulate wealth, they ran out, borrowed their home equity, and either spent it or put it at unnecessary risk in speculative investments.

When weighing risk versus return, I personally use maximum-funded insurance contracts because I want the safest and most stable return while minimizing risks. Tax-favored, conservative returns can create tremendous wealth over time. Don't forget the most important concept regarding managing equity successfully: to conserve rather than to consume it. The goal is to enhance liquidity, safety, and rate of return.

GIVE A NEW LIFE TO YOUR ASSETS—DEVELOP A P.L.A.N.

Through the wise implementation of wealth-enhancement strategies, you can be on the road to the accumulation of tremendous financial wealth. Time will be on your side in accomplishing financial independence. This book has focused primarily on unique strategies for the creation of financial wealth. It is my sincere hope the reader will not experience the misfortune of a missed fortune! Don't be led astray by money myth-conceptions!

Victor Hugo once said, "There is something more powerful than all the armies in the world, and that is an idea whose time has come!" My sincere desire is that a meaningful transformation will take place as you give new life to all of the assets on your family balance sheet by developing a Perpetual Life of Asset Nurturance™ (P.L.A.N.), as explained in chapter 1. I wish you a wonderful life of abundance and rich experiences. May you always strive to enhance your human, intellectual, financial, and civic assets for the empowerment of yourself and your family. In so doing, may you gain tremendous clarity, balance, focus, and confidence for yourself and your family.

CONCEPTS COVERED IN CHAPTER 12

- *What you don't know can hurt you.* The worst form of ignorance is rejecting something we know little or nothing about.
- *We either progress or retrogress.* We must increase our talents and abilities or those we have will wither and die.
- There is enough to spare for everyone to have an abundant life.
- Capitalize every category of assets on the family balance sheet by developing a system that helps to do the following: enhance each individual's health, happiness, and well-being; encourage family leadership; capture family virtues, memories, and wisdom; and protect, optimize, and empower your family's intellectual and financial assets.

- *Empowered living is simply a process of teaching children how to love, learn, give, and earn.* "Family retreats with a purpose" are a powerful method to teach and enhance true principles.

- First understand *why* you should cultivate a Perpetual Life of Asset Nurturance before learning details of *how* to accomplish your P.L.A.N.

- *Establish a liquid side fund* to accumulate the funds required to pay off your mortgage, maintain flexibility, achieve substantial tax savings, and accumulate excess cash.

- Separate as much equity from your home as feasible to increase liquidity, safety, rate of return, and tax deductions.

- Use the difference between preferred and non-preferred interest expense to make interest work *for* you instead of *against* you.

- *Use debt wisely as a positive lever for equity management purposes,* conserving and compounding equity rather than consuming it.

- *Choose to incur deductible employment costs rather than non-deductible opportunity costs.*

- *Use the principle of arbitrage* by employing equity to earn a rate of return higher than the net cost of separating that equity.

- *Refinance your home as often as feasible* to accelerate the process of accumulating the resources to cover all your debts.

- Always maintain as high a mortgage—with flexibility—on your home as feasible to keep it marketable, especially in soft markets.

- A common myth is that life insurance is a poor investment. The reality is, *life insurance is an excellent place to accumulate cash.*

- *Your house payment can become your retirement contribution.*

- You should periodically evaluate repositioning some or all of your qualified plan contributions or distributions into a non-qualified fund.

- *You can minimize, even eliminate, the payment of unnecessary tax.*

- *Avoid being "house rich, cash poor" during your retirement years.*
- A reverse mortgage is a safe and easy way for seniors to turn their home's equity into an additional source of income to meet needs.
- Elderly affluent retirees can often secure guaranteed returns of 6 to 9 percent by using a single premium immediate life-only annuity coupled with an asset-replacement life insurance policy.
- The Ultimate Arbitrage Plan® can be used with affluent seniors to raise millions of dollars for charitable foundations—without the donors having to use any of their own cash.
- Successfully managing equity can substantially enhance cash flow management, credit management, asset management, risk management, tax planning, and estate planning.
- Never underestimate the merits of having adequate life insurance.
- Make a meaningful transformation as you give new life to all the assets on your family balance sheet. Develop a Perpetual Life of Asset Nurturance (P.L.A.N.).

For more information on how to optimize your human, intellectual, financial, and civic assets, visit www.missedfortune.com or www.empoweredwealth.com. You may contact Douglas Andrew via e-mail at info@pfs-inc.org or call toll free, 1-888-987-5665.

Index

accumulation phase, 3–4, 40–41, 69

acquisition indebtedness, 31–32, 33, 34, 91, 110, 240

adjustable-rate mortgages (ARMs), 137, 138

after-tax dollars, 61–62, 63

amortized mortgages, 104, 105, 131, 151

  fifteen-year vs. thirty-year, 131–35

  negative amortization loans, 158–59

annuities, 173–76, 184

  comparison to life insurance contracts, 226–31

  deferred, 64, 66

  fixed, 174–75

  life-only option, 175, 260–61

  liquidity of, 176

  period-certain option, 175

  safety of, 175, 176, 198

  single premium immediate (SPIA), 174, 202–203, 240, 260

  survivor benefits, 175, 176

  tax-deferred, 95, 96

  tax treatment in distribution phase, 174, 176

  variable, 175, 176

appreciation of real estate, 111, 120, 146, 151, 252

  cyclicality of, 123–24

  refinancing every five years, 157–58

arbitrage principal, 62, 91, 97, 103, 113–15, 117, 118, 253–54

  borrowing at one interest rate and investing at a higher rate, 154–57

  borrowing at one interest rate and investing at the same or lower rate, 151–54

  conserving, not consuming capital and, 117, 125, 148–49, 159

  ultimate arbitrage, 260–65

asset management, 267

banks and credit unions:

  arbitrage principal used by, 62, 91, 97, 103, 113–15

  being your own, 97, 103–104

  mortgage loans from, 136

basis, 219

  for principal residence, 33

  stepped up, 49

For more information about these concepts . . .

The wealth-enhancement principles contained in this book are explained in Douglas Andrew's more comprehensive original work, *Missed Fortune*.

If you would like to explore and possibly implement strategies contained in this book, but are not sure how to do so, please seek advice from a financial professional.

If this book was given or recommended to you by a financial professional, you may choose to seek his or her advice, as well as advice from your personal tax advisor.

If you prefer, we can refer you to a professional trained in the strategies contained in this book. This network of financial professionals is referred to as The Equity Alliance Matrix (TEAM). If you would like to contact or be contacted by a TEAM member in your area, please contact Paramount Financial Services, Inc. toll-free at 1-888-987-5665, e-mail us at info@pfs-inc.org, or contact us through our Web site at www.missedfortune.com.

If you are a financial professional and would like information on how to become a certified TEAM member, we invite you to contact us in the same manner.

About the Author

Douglas R. Andrew has extensive experience in business management, economics, accounting, gerontology (as it relates to the economics of aging), financial and estate planning, and advanced business and tax planning. He is currently the owner and president of Paramount Financial Services, Inc., a comprehensive personal and business financial planning firm with several divisions.

As a financial strategist and retirement specialist, Doug shows people how to accumulate money on a tax-favored basis to achieve the highest possible net spendable retirement income. His firm, Paramount Financial, helps people to successfully manage equity to enhance its liquidity, safety, and rate of return, as well as maximize tax benefits. Doug also specializes in helping affluent individuals enhance and perpetuate their wealth. Douglas Andrew is a national advisory board member of Empowered Wealth LLC, a company dedicated to optimizing not only financial assets, but also human, intellectual, and civic assets.

BUSINESS PLUS

Recognized as one of the world's most prestigious business imprints, Business Plus specializes in publishing books that are on the cutting edge. Like you, to be successful we always strive to be ahead of the curve.

Business Plus titles encompass a wide range of books and interests—including important business management works, state-of-the-art personal financial advice, noteworthy narrative accounts, the latest in sales and marketing advice, individualized career guidance, and autobiographies of the key business leaders of our time.

Our philosophy is that business is truly global in every way, and that today's business reader is looking for books that are both entertaining and educational. To find out more about what we're publishing, please check out the Business Plus blog at:

www.businessplusblog.com